Remembering J. Z. Smith

NAASR Working Papers

Series Editor: Brad Stoddard, McDaniel College in Westminster, Maryland.

NAASR Working Papers provides a venue for publishing the latest research carried out by scholars who understand religion to be an historical element of human cognition, practice, and organization. Whether monographs or multi-authored collections, the volumes published in this series all reflect timely, cutting edge work that takes seriously both the need for developing bold theories as well as rigorous testing and debate concerning the scope of our tools and the implications of our studies. NAASR Working Papers therefore assess the current state-of-the-art while charting new ways forward in the academic study of religion.

Published

Constructing "Data" in Religious Studies: Examining the Architecture of the Academy
Edited by Leslie Dorrough Smith

Hijacked: A Critical Treatment of the Public Rhetoric of Good and Bad Religion
Edited by Leslie Dorrough Smith, Steffen Führding, and Adrian Hermann

Jesus and Addiction to Origins: Towards an Anthropocentric Study of Religion
Willi Braun
Edited by Russell T. McCutcheon

Method Today: Redescribing Approaches to the Study of Religion
Edited by Brad Stoddard

"Religion" in Theory and Practice: Demystifying the Field for Burgeoning Academics
Russell T. McCutcheon

Forthcoming

Imagining Smith: Mapping Methods in the Study of Religion
Barbara Krawcowicz

Key Categories in the Study of Religion: Contexts and Critiques
Edited by Rebekka King

Remembering J. Z. Smith

A Career and its Consequence

Edited by
Emily D. Crews and Russell T. McCutcheon

SHEFFIELD UK   BRISTOL CT

Published by Equinox Publishing Ltd.

UK: Office 415, The Workstation, 15 Paternoster Row, Sheffield, South Yorkshire S1 2BX

USA: ISD, 70 Enterprise Drive, Bristol, CT 06010

www.equinoxpub.com

First published 2020

ISBN-13   978 1 78179 968 0   (hardback)
              978 1 78179 969 7   (paperback)
              978 1 78179 970 3   (ePDF)

British Library Cataloguing-in-Publication Data

A catalogue record for this book is available from the British Library.

Library of Congress Cataloging-in-Publication Data

Names: Crews, Emily D., editor. | McCutcheon, Russell T., 1961–, editor.
Title: Remembering J. Z. Smith : a career and its consequence / edited by
   Emily D. Crews and Russell T. McCutcheon.
Description: Sheffield, South Yorkshire ; Bristol, CT : Equinox Publishing
   Ltd, 2020. | Series: NAASR working papers | Includes bibliographical
   references and index. | Summary: "The volume documents the role that the
   late Jonathan Z. Smith's work has played, while providing a basis for
   further considering the future direction of the field"—Provided by
   publisher.
Identifiers: LCCN 2020010102 (print) | LCCN 2020010103 (ebook) | ISBN
   9781781799680 (hardback) | ISBN 9781781799697 (paperback) | ISBN
   9781781799703 (ebook)
Subjects: LCSH: Smith, Jonathan Z. | Religion historians—United States.
Classification: LCC BL43.S645 R46 2020 (print) | LCC BL43.S645 (ebook) |
   DDC 200.92—dc23
LC record available at https://lccn.loc.gov/2020010102
LC ebook record available at https://lccn.loc.gov/2020010103

Typeset by JS Typesetting Ltd, Porthcawl, Mid Glamorgan

For Elaine

Contents

Part V: Appendix

Preface

Emily D. Crews and Russell T. McCutcheon

One of us was involved in co-editing a collection of interviews that Jonathan Z. Smith did, over the years, which was published recently enough that the reviews are only now appearing in print. One in particular caught the attention of both of us, published online at the American Academy of Religions' Reading Religion site. It struck us as somewhat conflicted, inasmuch as what some of us would see as gains in the field that are associated with Smith's work are acknowledged, yes, but then minimized and, as we read the review, contradicted by its end. For despite claiming that "[o]ur field needs more of his influence, not less," the author undermines what at least we see to be the crux of Smith's contributions by claiming that a shortcoming of his work is that he did not "try to enter their world [that of the religious insider] ... That requires more vulnerability—and more epistemic humility—than Smith was willing to grant."

In a field populated by more than a few scholars who are rather confident in what religion *really is* or *really does*—whether their work be theologically, humanistically, or scientifically inflected, understanding religion either as humankind's deepest yearnings and transcendental feelings or as an evolutionary adaptation of questionable modern use—we find Smith's approach a refreshing alternative *precisely because of its humility*; for his work made no attempt to tell us what religion really was; instead, it staked out a position on how place or identity was made, in those inevitably collaborative, social workshops where any item of history or culture is produced, circulated, and negotiated over, and then went on to make claims about how we, as scholars, should be using our tools, such as the comparative method when trying to make sense of them. With both of those in place, he then looked at some of the stories, actions, or locations commonly designated *as* religious—inviting readers to be curious about what we might learn if we approached each in this rather than that way, seeing them all as ordinary, sure, but curious nonetheless. (Why? Because he thought that the world was represented there as being tweaked or exaggerated, just a bit.) Judging the gain of making such a move in the study of religion was then left to the reader. (We use "reader" purposefully, given that most of us came to know Smith through his writings, though, as this volume makes clear, there are plenty of us who met him through his teaching.) That there are many who consider themselves part of this field but don't see this as a gain is obvious—again, we think of that reviewer who wants more of Smith's influence, on the one hand, but who also resists following him in treating religion no differently than any other item that we might study

Although the early stages of organizing this volume were already under way when that book review was posted, we both discussed it and decided that it confirmed for us that we were on the right track in pulling the following pieces together to make this book; for the review came to conclusions about Smith's work that had little in common with how each of us read him and used his writings in our own work. And given that we are each members of different academic generations, studying rather different things, let alone the fact that only one of us studied religion at Chicago (where Smith's influence has long been in the air, despite him, for the most part, not holding at appointment at the Divinity School), our agreement on what we each thought that Smith contributed to the field suggested to us that a volume such as this was very much needed—what with the existence of such divergent opinions and readings.

Of importance to note is that the following chapters do not reflect an image of Smith and his work that we've crafted to suit our tastes (as you might expect had we handpicked the participants ourselves). Instead, we see this little book as an archive that we've worked to make more public, for little that appears here has been specially written for this book. Instead, we invited all of the participants from three separate panels devoted to Smith's career and its consequences for our field (panels at the American Academy of Religion, the Society of Biblical Literature, and the North American Association for the Study of Religion, all held in Denver, in late November 2018). What each organization's criteria were in selecting their panelists was their business, of course, so we also include an introduction from the chairs of each of these panels (one of which was co-written by one of us, though he was unable to attend the meeting that year). We then decided also to invite a variety of bloggers who had each taken their own initiative to post their own remembrance of Smith, shortly after his death at the very end of 2017, asking each of these authors to revise their brief pieces as they saw fit. And finally, given that the Department where we both work regularly produces a podcast, organized and hosted by our colleague, Michael Altman, in which a variety of interviewees remembered Smith in an episode posted in the Spring of 2018, we obtained the permission of each interviewee to include an extended transcript of their conversation with Mike about Smith, thereby adding an even more personal tone to some of the chapters that precede this final section. This is why we see this little book more as an archival item, one that makes available, in one place, things that either exist across the web or existed orally (and thus briefly) at a conference which by now is only part of memory. The volume concludes with an original afterword, by one of us, written for this occasion.

Whether or not this collection amounts to mythmaking, as the reviewer who was mentioned earlier might conclude, we of course leave to its readers to decide—though we certainly hope that our contributors and readers alike are all well acquainted with Smith's own thoughts on the inevitable role that translation and interests play in all acts of re-presentation. (On the problems associated when the common notions of presence and authenticity are used to authorize a reading, please see Part V for a previously unpublished, brief paper of Smith's.) For while we too hope that more work is done on Smith and his role in the field at a particular point in its history, we have each learned enough from him that we don't mind sharing the following pieces by people who, though never having worked with Smith himself, nonetheless worked with the products of his labors—his teaching and his writing—applying them, elaborating on them, and sometimes critiquing them. And if the following pieces prompt newcomers to find Smith's own writings, to read and to consider his essays for themselves, to decide what's to be done with the approach that he advocated, then all the better. For, as already indicated, at the end of the day it's up to readers to decide what to do with all of this.

Before concluding, we would like to thank all of the contributors for agreeing to be included in this book and, in many cases, for revising their pieces for publication here. We're also grateful to Brad Stoddard and the NAASR Working Papers series that he edits, for its interest in this book, as well as Equinox Publishing for agreeing to add it to their list of, in our eyes, some of the more important, and always affordable, books in our field today. And, finally, we appreciate the work on the manuscript that was done by Sierra Lawson, a B.A. and M.A. grad of our department, during the summer before she headed off to pursue a Ph.D. degree of her own at the University of North Carolina at Chapel Hill.

Emily D. Crews is a Ph.D. candidate in History of Religions at the University of Chicago Divinity School. Her work focuses on the formation of gendered and embodied subjects in African and African immigrant religions.

Russell T. McCutcheon is University Research Professor and longtime Chair of the Department of Religious Studies at the University of Alabama; he has published widely on a variety of topics in the history of the field and on the tools that scholars use when going about their work.

Introduction: Remembering J. Z. Smith (1938–2017)

Russell T. McCutcheon

I think religion is a nice subject to teach because nearly everybody has an opinion about it.
　　　　　　　　　　　　　　　　　　　　　　　　　　　　　—J. Z. Smith[1]

On the afternoon and early evening of New Year's Eve 2017/18 many of us were shocked to learn the sad news that Jonathan Z. Smith, arguably the world's most influential scholar of religion over the past fifty years, had died the previous day, in Chicago, from complications due to lung cancer. He was 79 and had been undergoing treatments since his diagnosis in the summer of 2017.

As should be obvious, there is a tremendous (even intimidating) challenge for anyone writing about not just Jonathan's career but also his life.[2] For many of his professional contributions are already so very well known, inasmuch as reading his work—from his early set of essays, *Map Is Not Territory* (Smith 1978), and his still influential work on theory of ritual (Smith 1987, along with his contributions to Hamerton-Kelly 1988) to Christopher Lehrich's edited collection of some of Jonathan's pedagogical pieces, *On Teaching Religion* (Smith 2013)—has come to be seen as *de rigueur* in the field. His writings are therefore read in classes by novice students,[3] as preparation for comprehensive exams by grad students, or simply by scholars worldwide, as part of the current literature. But his personal life was just that, personal, and generally not the topic of public record. He was, after all, not just of a generation that's largely not enthralled with social media disclosures but was famously alien to all things digital, thereby foreclosing one avenue whereby many today come to feel that they know scholars who are removed from them in space and time.[4] What this leaves us with is a curious contradiction: for while he is an utterly *familiar* figure to almost everyone in the field (at least inasmuch as they have regularly met him in his pages, as an author, or because many would occasionally spy his characteristic profile across hotel lobbies or in the hallways of conferences, maybe even hearing him deliver a paper in what, as he aged, became his slow and steady style, leaning over the podium, reading from his typed or, just as likely, handwritten manuscript), he also remained one who was utterly *unfamiliar*; for only those who knew him personally may have also met his gracious wife, Elaine, or known of his daughter, Siobhan, along with his son, Jason and his wife Rachel, or perhaps Hazel, the granddaughter he loved so much and of whom he would happily speak if asked, and even his sister, Pamela, all of whom survive Jonathan. Readers certainly might have known that he grew up in

Manhattan, had an early interest in agrostology (the branch of botany that deals with grasses—hence his lifelong interest in taxonomy),[5] did his first degree in Philosophy at Haverford College, and then developed an interest first in myth, via reading Ernst Cassirer, and then in the demythologizing work of Rudolf Bultmann (and thus we see his entrée to New Testament studies). They could also be aware how this all led to two years of study at Yale Divinity School,[6] before moving to Yale's just-instituted Department of Religion, where he was the first to earn a Ph.D. in the history of religions (in 1969), by writing a 574-page dissertation, "The Glory, Jest, and Riddle: James George Frazer and *The Golden Bough*." But would such readers know it remains unpublished—as with many dissertations of that era—or that, technically, the late Will Oxtoby supervised it?

> The great advantage that I had [in Yale's newly established Department of Religion] was that they had no faculty in the field. So I was able to entirely teach myself ... [B]asically I sat in the library and read, and it was a quite wonderful way to doing it. I chose Frazer and called him a laboratory of comparison ... So that was my topic ... Finally, after I was already out teaching and just finishing the dissertation, they appointed a young guy who was a friend of mine as Yale's first appointment, Willard Oxtoby. He had to give me my exam, which I had not taken yet, because there was no faculty. He called me on Friday and I went on Monday, and sat for a week of exams. I then gave him my dissertation. (Braun and McCutcheon 2018: 45)

Perhaps readers may have heard that, while he was completing that dissertation, Jonathan became the first new faculty member to be hired into the University of California at Santa Barbara's just established Department of Religious Studies (beginning there in 1966—its founding members were transferred in from other units at UCSB), or that, after two years in California, he left for what turned out to be a forty-five year career at the University of Chicago. (All of this can be learned from his informative "bio-bibliographical" essay, "When the Chips Are Down," which opened his essay collection *Relating Religion: Essays in the Study of Religion* [2004].)[7] But those familiar with such public details may not have also known that he was a longtime vegetarianism and a conscientious objector, that, before he stopped drinking in his later years, he preferred Wild Turkey bourbon, that he lived in Hyde Park, a short walk from his office at the University of Chicago, or that his home was a brownstone originally built for the 1893 Chicago World's Fair (near to the lakeshore, back in pre-air conditioning days, originally lacking window panes so as to catch the lake's summer breeze, as he would tell visitors), which has long been filled with art and newspapers and whose upper floors housed his home office as well as rooms that had been converted into library stacks for his books. They would likely also not have known of what he himself described as his inherent shyness or the touching letter that he wrote to Gary Lease's widow, Dorothea, just days after Gary's death from cancer—a letter that she asked to be read publicly during the memorial service (on February 2, 2008)[8]—or of the simple manner in which Jonathan and Elaine lived, his love of his garden, not to mention that his birthday often fell during North America's main annual conference in late November. Unless they were a student attending his office hours they would surely not have known of the "Hutzpah is not hubris" sign that appeared in his office at the university or his habit of having a coffee after class, where students could find him to chat. Unless they were one of his correspondents they would not have experienced the pleasure in receiving one of his neatly printed, handwritten letters (sometimes in pencil and often including lengthy quotations and citations to support a point he was making in reply).[9] Only if they'd read the delightfully meandering and, at times, revealing, interview done with him by the already-cited *Chicago Maroon*, an independent student newspaper, back in June 2008 (and which is still available online)[10] would readers know that the tree-trunk of a cane that he always had with him in later life and on which he would lean, chin-on-hands-on-top-of-it, while seated, staring at the floor, listening intently to papers being read at conferences, was made by his uncle, from wood that was, as Jonathan described it, "liberated" from the Great Smoky Mountains National Park. And while they might know of the rumor that one of our field's most critically minded scholars lived next door to an abandoned church (built in 1917), what may not have been evident was that it still sits empty today not because of an intellectual dispute over the place of the sacred (a scenario some in the field might like to imagine, given the nature of Jonathan's work) but, rather, due to a neighborhood dispute over its re-development as condominiums. Ironically, perhaps, it was the encroachment of secular that proved intolerable.

And so it is this relationship between the *familiar* and the *strange*—things known and things undisclosed—that strikes me as a fitting lens through which to view Jonathan's life and his career; it's an especially apt viewpoint given his own work's recurring focus on how knowledge is produced by the comparative method's navigation of just these two poles. In fact, it would count among what he himself described (in the previously cited essay, "When the Chips Are Down") as his career's persistent preoccupations (Smith 2004: 13 ff.).

So, concerning his professional accomplishments—and, remember, it is with just this lens in mind—a familiar tribute to him would surely report that Jonathan was a longtime member of, and frequent contributor to the International Association for the History of Religions (he was an Honorary Life Member, awarded in 2013).[11] He delivered one of the plenary lectures at the 2000 IAHR Congress, held that year in Durbin, South Africa (via a real-time hook-up with Chicago since, as was widely known at the time, a smoking flight from the US was not easily found for him to travel to deliver it in person) and it was first published in *Numen* in 2001 (also as chapter 16 in Smith 2004). What's more, as President of the Society of Biblical Literature (in 2008; see Smith 2009 for his agenda-setting Presidential Address) he initiated conversations with the IAHR (in Chicago in 2008) that, when continued by others beyond his term, resulted in the SBL being provisionally affiliated with the IAHR.[12] And, as someone who once held the position of Executive Secretary and Treasurer for the North American Association for the Study of Religion (NAASR), I can report that, for a number of years, he would annually (and privately) write a check to NAASR that the organization would then use to double its yearly dues to the IAHR.

But such an orthodox document would also have to make mention of his long-time role in the American Academy of Religion (AAR—significantly, though, never as its President),[13] the SBL (just mentioned),[14] and NAASR (where he also served as President, from 1996–2002). It would be noted that he earned two honorary degrees (one from McGill in 1996 and the other from Queen's University in 2008—both, curiously, in Canada) and that he was also a member of the American Academy of Arts and Sciences (elected to its Philosophy and Religious Studies section in 2000) and the recipient of both the University of Chicago's Quantrell Award for Excellence in Undergraduate Teaching (in 1986) as well as the Yale University Graduate School's most prestigious honor, the Wilbur Cross Medal (in 2015). A typical recounting would observe that after first holding the University of Chicago College's William Benton Chair in Religion and the Human Sciences (beginning in 1975) he was later (in 1982) named the Robert O. Anderson Distinguished Service Professor of the Humanities at the University of Chicago, a position without the usual requirement of a departmental affiliation (also the emeritus status that he held once he retired in 2013). That he was the onetime Program Coordinator of the Religion and the Humanities would doubtless be included, as well as such roles as those he played in the Early Christian Literature program at the University of Chicago College along with the University's Committee on the Ancient Mediterranean World and the Committee on the History of Culture.

Such a traditional remembrance would surely also point out that he was not only a prolific and inventive essayist (his piece on Jonestown still stands out as an important and early contribution to taking so-called new religious movements seriously; see Smith 1982) but a dedicated teacher—one who placed special emphasis on the importance not just of undergraduate education (though he preferred not to call such students "undergraduates") but, more specifically, Core Curriculum or General Education courses that were in the service of helping students, *regardless their majors and future careers*, to learn to read, write and argue; in fact, it could be said that the traditional distinction between teaching and research/publication was one that he did not sanction, for, at least to this reader, *all* of his writings had a pedagogical engine driving them, whether they were explicitly on teaching or not.[15] And we'd surely learn that from 1973 to 1982, he even served for a decade as a university administrator (first as an Associate Dean and then, for five years, as Dean of the University of Chicago College).

Alongside those accomplishments such a standard celebration of his life and work would surely also note that there are now six collections of his essays in print, with many more articles, chapters, introductions, and replies left uncollected (not to mention the unpublished work of which we're not now aware). Mention might be made that his first published essay in the field (placing the origins of logion 37 of the Gospel of Thomas in "archaic Christian baptismal practices") was published in 1966 by Chicago's *History of Religions* and that he later co-edited the same journal for a decade (1970–1980) but we'd likely also learn that, 30 years later, he edited *The HarperCollins Dictionary of Religion* (1995), a resource in which he himself wrote no less than 487 unattributed entries (see pages 397–400 of *Relating Religion* for the complete list).[16] And we'd more than likely be told that his various roles over the years on advisory boards, the book reviews that he wrote, and the invited lectures that he offered at universities around the world were simply too numerous to begin to catalogue (or even for him to itemize systematically on his own C.V.). Such a familiar summary of his career would also include the various fellowships he held as a student (including the Woodrow Wilson [1960] and Kent [1962]), his year as an Instructor at Dartmouth College (1965–1966) and his early and lasting friendship with both Jacob Neusner (1932–2016), whom he already knew, and Hans Penner (1934–2012), whom he met there that year—the former playing a key role in the publication of Jonathan's second scholarly essay (in a 1968 collection in honor of E. R. Goodenough that Jack edited) as well as his own first book, with Brill, and the latter playing a key role in his then developing sense as a scholar of religion.

Finally, such a remembrance would, of course, not be complete without referencing his relationship with Mircea Eliade (1907–1986), whom he reported first meeting on, of all times, Valentine's Day 1968, while Eliade was a Visiting Professor at Santa Barbara and when Jonathan had just returned from his own job interview at Chicago—"I count my association with him as one of the great gifts in my life," Jonathan wrote (2004: 13).[17] In fact, it would certainly have to be remarked that, despite their disagreements, among his last major pieces of writing was the introduction that he wrote to the fiftieth-anniversary edition of Eliade's *The Myth of the Eternal Return* (2005), a book whose descriptive chapters have, in Jonathan's words there, "stood the test of time."[18] And, in this same vein, such an account would have to make mention of Jonathan's resignation from his initial appointment to the Divinity School (where he served from 1968–1979)[19] but also his eventual acceptance, some years later, of a re-appointment as one of Swift Hall's associate faculty members—an appointment that facilitated his work with graduate students despite his career-long and often-stated preference for working with B.A. students, especially those in their first two years of college.

But, while necessarily linking him to Eliade—whether as a critic or friend—such an orthodox article would also, at some point, surely have to connect Jonathan to his now (in)famous line from the opening pages of *Imagining Religion* concerning the creation of religion in the scholar's study. "If I had a nickel for every time that sentence has been quoted," he once remarked in an interview, "I could have retired forty years ago." But, as he then went on to add:

> But I have to say that sometimes the way the quote is used is defamiliar to me! I wasn't saying we should abolish the term, for example. I didn't think I was saying anything very significant when I wrote that. I thought it was a self-evident proposition and I just went on.[20]

It is not difficult to find scholars who now push back on his once provocative line, criticizing Jonathan as overlooking the so-called real people on the ground who daily use the category (with an implied critique, it would seem, of some sort of elitism in his work). However, I think such a reading misses the situation in which he first used the line, i.e., in the introduction to a book directed toward scholars of religion and thus as part of an invitation for them to enhance their own critical self-consciousness as they go about their work (which includes their use of the category religion, among others)—i.e., reading the rest of the paragraph where he wrote those words strikes me as rather important. If we add to that the argument that the modern category (emphasizing belief, faith, feeling, and private experience over public action, structure, and organization) was deployed and refined in moments of contact, by European scholars along with administrators, missionaries, and bureaucrats, etc., to make sense of unexpected similarities and differences, then I think his point still stands (as he also elaborates in his chapter "Religion, Religions, Religious" in Taylor 1998). That the category's utility has, subsequent to this refinement, been seen by yet others as useful, and that by today it has been widely adopted in a variety of daily acts of self-designation across wide swaths of European-influenced society does not, I would argue, take away from his point. In fact, with just his point in mind, we may have a model currently right before our eyes of how this all works, e.g., the technical use of "the Nones" or "spiritual but not religious" (SBNR) as part of a conclusion reached by pollsters and scholars to explain what started as Pew polling results with regard to just a few questions on a 2012 survey but which has now been widely adopted among not just scholars but the media and the population at large, as if it names an actual and coherent sub-group of people whose class, gender, regional, and racial traits can be measured and who behave (e.g., vote) in predictable patterns.[21]

But having documented such field-shaping accomplishments, with which many of his readers, to varying degrees, may already be acquainted (many of which, by the way, took place just as the academic study of religion was taking hold for the first time across North American public universities), and thereby offering a testament to him "in the proper and customary manner,"[22] what still remains to be explored is the unfamiliar; and for me, given the person who I came to know, that comprises two things: his generosity and his wit.

With regard to the first, I recall him coming to Alabama to be the second annual lecturer invited by our Department, in the 2003/4 academic year. We were then a little and rather inconsequential undergraduate Department of just four faculty members, one that had very recently been on the brink of closure and which was then at the start of what would turn out to be a long (but successful) road toward reinvention. When I first contacted him with the invitation to come to Alabama to lecture,[23] I delicately broached the topic of a speaking fee, since I had recently learned just how finicky some academics could be about not just their fees but also the details of their trip.[24] To my timid question about whether he had a fee he not only offered a simple "No" but then, to my query about what all he might be willing to do when he visited our university, he replied: "Use me as you wish; I'm there to work." That's exactly how I remember our conversation going.

It says something noteworthy about him, as a person and as a scholar, that he not only accepted whatever we offered but that—despite his reliance on that cane even then—he worked non-stop while visiting with us. He lectured to a full house in the evening but visited classes during the day, met with faculty, and was even whisked off to a lunch downtown by some of our B.A. students. (In fact, one still tells the story of driving him and chatting all the way.) He even had dinner with our Dean and Associate Dean, the latter of whom happened to be the son of Jonathan's own first Department chair (the late Robert S. Michaelsen [1919–2000]) and whom Jonathan remembered as a little boy back in his Santa Barbara days. He therefore modeled for all of us, in the way that he accepted our invitation and how he worked when with us, what it was to be a scholar—one who was a generous and public intellectual long before the term was invented and constrained to signify only TV appearances.

With regard to the second—his humor—I think that many fail to read his work with a sufficient sense of irony, failing to "get" the joke that he occasionally made in his lectures and writings,[25] as a result of his having put two seemingly unlike things beside each other in some novel manner. (That's just what comparison was, for him: placing unexpected items together within the confines of a scholar's imagination, in pursuit of his or her own curiosities; on this see Smith 1990: 115.) After all, as he himself reported, he went on to study religions "[b]ecause they're funny ... They relate to the world in which I live, but it's like a fun house mirror: Something's off. It's not quite the world I live in, yet it's recognizable. So that gap interested me."[26]

Religions, then, as Jonathan understood them, are both familiar and strange, and holding that seeming (but inevitable) contradiction in tension often results in our being surprised by the things that we see or read about when we study them—and, as scholars, that ought to make us curious and provoke us to dig a little deeper. So in the midst of the serious and the erudite (for some, he was undoubtedly intimidating) scholar whom he was widely known to be (by all reports, though patient, he did not suffer fools gladly—to borrow an old phrase from 2 Corinthians 11:19) there remained not just his generosity but the mischievous and often undetected jest.[27] But in my reading, none of these were simply a *bon mot*; instead, they were always indicative of some larger, theoretical point: they were each an e.g., as he might have phrased it, something interesting not in and of itself but only inasmuch as we could relate it to something else, thereby establishing a relationship to something that we, as scholars, have seen before, such as the playful (sometimes maddeningly so) ambiguity of language and of social life.[28]

So I recall the time that my good friend and frequent collaborator, Willi Braun, and I walked up to the main conference hotel, after just arriving for the start of the annual AAR/SBL meeting in Philadelphia, back in late November of 2005. We just happened to meet Jonathan outside, where he was taking a break and, yes, having a cigarette; sooner or later the conversation turned to the terrible storm and flooding that had hit New Orleans just the previous August and from which the city was still reeling. Jonathan spoke of the televised news coverage of Katrina that he'd been watching and how, upon hearing the reporter note that "the Levys had fallen" (thereby mistakenly pronouncing the term "levee" as if it instead were the classically Hebrew-derived surname), he said, in an incredulous voice raised loudly for effect:

My people have stood for 5,000 years and *now* they've fallen?!

And then he laughed, as we did as well.

This is the Jonathan whom I choose to remember—knowledgeable and rigorous, sure, at times maybe even intimidating, but also generous and witty.[29] He was the one who not only saw each item of knowledge as illustrative of some wider point but, because of that, understood knowledge as a playful, temporal thing, something that *we* produce when *we* put unlike things together in our own surprising, maybe even accidental, manner (such as a Levy and a levee). Moreover, that anecdote illustrates so nicely to me that, while devoting a lifetime to studying religion, none of it ever really was about religion, at least as I understand him; instead, the various things commonly designated *as* religion (such as those things scholars call myths or rituals, canons and symbols) provided him with opportunities to talk about people from the past, who happened to leave things behind that made us curious—people who, just like us, were themselves trying to address the gaps in their worlds, devising ways to manage the distance between us and them, the proper and the improper, the tame and the wild, the ideal and the routine, the planned and the accidental or just here and there, now and then or, yes, even the familiar and the strange. It was in that gap's playful, *but always consequential*, middle space where this thing we just generalize as culture takes place (a point so nicely made by Smith's Christian origins colleague, Burton Mack [1991: 19–20]), and it was in that same ambiguous, middle space in which I see Jonathan's life and work to have taken place—often with a wink, sometimes a laugh or even a scowl (though playful, the stakes were always high and he certainly didn't fear letting you know that), never by means of a computer's black box and, whether teaching or conversing, always with plenty of shrugs and gestures.

Russell T. McCutcheon is University Research Professor and longtime Chair of the Department of Religious Studies at the University of Alabama; he has published widely on a variety of topics in the history of the field and on the tools that scholars use when going about their work.

Acknowledgments

This chapter is a substantial revision of a piece originally invited by American Academy of Religion's former executive director, Jack Fitzmier (and which then appeared on the website of *Religious Studies News* on January 5, 2018) which was then enlarged as a result of an invitation by the President of the International Association for the History of Religions (IAHR), Tim Jensen, for publication in *Numen* (McCutcheon 2018). My sincere appreciation therefore goes to both Jack and Tim for such generous requests. Also, readers should be warned that, in places, I have followed Smith's own habit concerning his "characteristic deployment of the lengthy footnote, going far beyond mere citation of authorities— a practice that strives to fulfill the maxim proposed by the old Isaac D'Israeli: 'Digressions are never more agreeable than when they become dissertations ...'. For me, a footnote is least interesting when it authorizes; it is at its best when it exposes, explores, and perhaps, mediates, conflicts of interpretations; for me, the chief goal of scholarship'" (Braun and McCutcheon 2018: 122).

Notes

1   This quotation is taken from an interview conducted by Alfred F. Benney, of Fairfield University, on November 21, 1999, in Boston, MA, a transcript of which is included in Braun and McCutcheon (2018). See all of the videotaped interviews by searching for "Jonathan Z. Smith" at http://digitalcommons.fairfield.edu (accessed March 13, 2018). The interviews of Smith are part of Benney's larger American Scholars of Religion Video Project.

2   For those exclusively interested in an overview of his scholarly contributions, consult either my own Introduction or the various essays included in the *Festschrift* published in Jonathan's honor, originally contracted and published by Equinox Publishing but now published by Routledge (Braun and McCutcheon 2008).

3   Of interest is the number of times scholars report using his "Religion, Religions, Religious" essay, from Taylor (1998: 269–285), in classes; as reported to me by the press, it is the most-used essay from that wordbook (judging by permission requests to reproduce it in course packets).

4   For example, he not only used a manual typewriter (tracking progress by how many bells he heard that day) but he considered the cell phone "an absolute abomination" and saw the computer as a way for workers (i.e., writers) to be alienated from their production (see Braun and McCutcheon 2018: 1, 2). Moreover, as he went on to state: "I've never seen the Internet. And my son endlessly explains to me that I should say that rather than 'I've never seen the Web.' I haven't seen that one either!" (ibid: 17).

5   "We never look at one thing; we always look at more than one thing. Even years ago when I used to teach a course, Bibles in Western Civ, which was then a Western Civ requirement, for three quarters I would do the Hebrew Bible, the New Testament, the Koran, and the Book of Mormon as 'the Bibles of the West.' Because it doesn't have just one Bible, it has a bunch of Bibles, and we might as well take a look at them. Even that makes it simpler than it is, because it depends on whose New Testament you look at, whether it has 24 books, 27 books, or 38 books, and so on. I think that's what got me interested in grass, how many kinds of grass there are. I'm fascinated by how many kinds of religions there are, how many kinds of Bibles there are" (Braun and McCutcheon 2018: 5).

6   Enrolled in all but the practical ministry courses of their Bachelor of Divinity degree, he was "interacting on a daily basis with tribal Protestants" which, he went on to say, "was analogous to an anthropologist's fieldwork" (2004: 7). As for how he came to go to Yale after his Bachelor's degree, he would often tell a story as follows: "So I asked my favorite philosophy teacher where I should go to get a degree in Greek mythology, and he told me I should go to Yale Divinity School and study the New Testament because it was the biggest piece of Greek mythology around. And I, being very serious, did not understand he was joking, so I went to Yale Divinity School and studied the New Testament" (Braun and McCutcheon 2018: 27-8).

7   Shortly after his death, the University of Chicago Press made this essay available free online; see: http://press.uchicago.edu/books/excerpt/2018/Smith_Relating_Religion.html (accessed March 12, 2018).

8   Gary, the onetime Chair of the History of Consciousness program at UC Santa Cruz, was himself a longtime contributor to the IAHR, serving as its treasurer (1997–2008); see Donald Wiebe and Luther Martin's obituary for Gary in *Numen* 55 (2008): 337–339. On more than one occasion, Jonathan cited Gary's still infamous sacrifice. As he phrased it in the already mentioned *Chicago Maroon* interview from 2008:

> I have a friend, who recently died, but he actually decided to show kids what a sacrifice looks like, so he sacrificed a lamb at Easter time. "We talk about it so much—here's what it looks like!" Half the class puked, half the class had angry letters from mommy and daddy. But he did demonstrate that it's not just a metaphor. It's a messy and not altogether pleasant process. (Braun and McCutcheon 2018: 6)

9 Collecting these letters and publishing them would be an interesting exercise, well worth the effort, I'd argue, especially given his own comment that "the published collections of scholars' correspondence are better at revealing the tenor of their thought and practice than are the autobiographies by the very same figures" (quoted from his last AAR plenary address, delivered on October 31, 2010, a transcription of which is included, along with Ann Taves's introduction of him, in Braun and McCutcheon 2018: 110).

10 Find the full interview at: www.chicagomaroon.com/2008/06/02/full-j-z-smith-interview (accessed March 13, 2018). As quoted above, this is also included in Braun and McCutcheon (2018)—a volume whose author's royalties, I feel I should add, go directly to Jonathan's estate (as per a document he signed in the summer of 2017) and not the editors.

11 Tim Jensen relates a story of writing an old fashioned letter to Jonathan to inform him of the honor (given that he did not use computers, let alone email); it was sometime later that he learned of Jonathan's habit of asking a secretary to store his incoming mail in brown bags that were then hung in a closet; eventually, the unanswered mail would turn out to be so old, as Jensen heard it, that Jonathan would be relieved not to have to answer it. Eventually, Jensen managed to get through to a family member, and also to a good friend of Jonathan's, to convey the news.

12 SBL's full affiliation awaits action of the General Assembly at the IAHR's next World Congress—though the 2020 meeting in New Zealand has been cancelled due to COVID-19 concerns.

13 His absence among its leadership was explicitly named by Taves—herself AAR President at the time—as being one of her reasons for inviting him to deliver what turned out to be his last AAR plenary paper in 2010 (the text of which is also included in Braun and McCutcheon 2018).

14 Jonathan's role in helping to establish (e.g., see his 1975 essay on the topic) and then participate in the SBL's innovative, multi-year project to redescribe how scholars discuss Christian origins (doing so in a way that avoids reproducing common participant claims on its founding and earliest development) deserves special mention here. See the papers from the group's initial session—entitled Ancient Myths and Modern Theories of Christian Origins—published in *Method & Theory in the Study of Religion* 8 (1996) as well as the published collections from the group (e.g., Cameron and Miller 2004, 2011; Crawford and Miller 2017).

15 As many have learned, it would be an error to fail to see that the datum (a word from which he did not shy away in his writings, by the way) with which any one of his essays works was merely an opportunity—often a detailed and involved opportunity, to be sure—for him to demonstrate how to go about doing what it is that we as scholars do at a variety of sites, e.g., describe or compare things.

16 A favorite is his disarmingly simple and succinct entry for god: "common term for a male deity" as well as his entry for God, Goddess: "common term for the supreme deity" (1995: 389)—the latter asks reader to "see also" the so-called term question, an entry that briefly describes a debate among nineteenth-century Protestant missionaries to China concerning how best to translate such words.

17 The meeting is not mentioned in the second volume of Eliade's published journals (only that his wife, Christinel, was reading A. J. Symons's *The Quest for Corvo* "that I found in Jonathan Smith's library" [February 28, 1968]), though reference to it may certainly appear in Eliade's unpublished papers, of course. Of interest to those who see the two men as representing diametrically opposed views in the field—making them, and not just their positions, antagonists—may be the friendship they shared (though not without its ups and downs, to be sure), e.g., Eliade noting in the third published journal volume that he and his wife celebrated their 25th anniversary at a party hosted in their home by Jonathan and Elaine (see the entry for January 25, 1975).

18 Gentle but succinct indications of his disagreement with aspects of the work are also included, to be sure. Concerning Jonathan's thoughts on the 50th anniversary of yet another of Eliade's enduring works—*Patterns in Comparative Religion*—see his two-part essay (Smith 2000a; also reproduced in Smith 2004), originally delivered as two lectures at the University of Chicago's Divinity School; see also Smith 2010 concerning his detailed effort to determine if Eliade's multivolume (yet unfinished) *A History of Religious Ideas* (the title of its English translation) can correctly be understood as what had once (and repeatedly) been described by Eliade as his intended follow-up to *Patterns in Comparative Religion*. Notably, in this essay, Jonathan identifies a variety of (sometimes significant) English mistranslations or additions by the translator in work Eliade originally published in French.

19 In a very interesting remembrance (included in this volume), Peter Grieve, editor of *The Chicago Maroon* (Grieve 2018), reproduced Jonathan's letter to Eliade, dated November 21, 1980, in which he recollects his decision, in December 1979, to resign from "what was being called 'History of Religions' in the Divinity School" as well as from his role on the editorial board of *History of Religions*. It opens as follows: "Dearest Mircea, I have just received your letter dated November 12. I am pained that you—who I love and revere—should have had to become touched by my frustration and rage. I had the naïve hope that you and I could continue as if nothing had happened …" After outlining his plan to resign, and also leave the University of Chicago (which, obviously, did not happen), he closes with "I still persist in my naïve hope that, for us, none of this has happened. With deep affection …"

20 See Braun and McCutcheon (2018: 69); the interview, involving Jensen along with Satoko Fujiwara, Tom Pearson, and Eugene Gallagher, took place in Smith's home in November 2012 and was originally published in *Teaching Theology and Religion* 17/1 (2014): 61–77.

21 See the panel discussion, from the 2013 annual meeting of the AAR, as an example of scholars critically aware of this development, thus knowing that "the Nones" is not a descriptive but a constitutive term: https://vimeo.com/82109794 (accessed March 13, 2018).

22 As one of his own epigraphs, taken from George Bernard Shaw, once put it; see the opening to his now classic essay "The Bare Facts of Ritual" (included in Smith 1982).

23 His essay, "God Save This Honourable Court: Religion and Civic Discourse," had yet to be published (see the final chapter of *Relating Religion*), so this was the lecture that he delivered, having earlier given it as the second annual Ninian Smart Memorial Lecture at the University of California, Santa Barbara (a lecture widely available online).

24 I recall not only what I still see to have been exorbitant speaking fee requests but also the scholar who would only do two things while visiting, given what we paid—not three and certainly not four. So it was either a public lecture *and* a class visit *or* a meal with students …

25 Perhaps not unlike how, as already mentioned, Smith himself routinely reported how he himself missed the joke when he was told by a philosophy professor that he ought to go to Yale Divinity School to study the myth of the New Testament.

26 See the opening to the previously cited *Chicago Maroon* interview.

27 For example, that often quoted line about religion being "the creation of the scholar's study" is, to me, a crafty *double entendre* that few, I think, detect, inasmuch as it references both our work and the place in which we do it—an effect also achieved by his preference for gerunds (as evidenced in many of his book titles; on his fondness for gerunds see Braun and McCutcheon 2018: 117).

28 For, as he often remarked, nothing could be interesting, or even known, if it was so unique as to be self-contained and thus incomparable. As he made plain in his essay, "Classification" (Smith 2000b: 43): where we cannot compare things by means of classifying them, then there thought ends.

29 I would hope that readers keep in mind, as he told us on more than one occasion (such as in the concluding lines of his dictionary's Note on Transliteration), that what might at first appear as descriptions are always a translation that inevitably bears the marks of the translator, and so are never to be treated as an idle presentation of some pristine original (and thus that unavoidable gap reappears once again). That others will have different memories should be evident from this point, such as Lofton's reflections on her memories as one of his undergrad students (2014).

References

Braun, Willi and Russell T. McCutcheon (eds.) (2008). *Introducing Religion: Essays in Honor of Jonathan Z. Smith*. New York: Routledge.

——. (2018). *Reading J. Z. Smith: Interviews and Essay, 1999–2013*. New York: Oxford University Press.

Cameron, Ron and Merrill P. Miller (eds.) (2004). *Redescribing Christian Origins*. Society of Biblical Literature Symposium Series, vol. 28. Leiden: Brill.

——. (2011). *Redescribing Paul and the Corinthians*. Society of Biblical Literature Early Christianity and its Literature Series, vol. 5. Atlanta, GA: Society of Biblical Literature.

Crawford, Barry S. and Merrill P. Miller (eds.) (2017). *Redescribing the Gospel of Mark*. Society of Biblical Literature Early Christianity and its Literature Series, vol. 22. Atlanta, GA: Society of Biblical Literature.

Eliade, Mircea (2005). *The Myth of the Eternal Return: Cosmos and History*. Willard R. Trask (trans.) and Jonathan Z. Smith (intro.). Bollingen Series, XLVI. Princeton, NJ: Princeton University Press.

Grieve, Peter (2018). "Jonathan Z. Smith (1938–2017): The College's Iconoclastic, Beloved, Chainsmoking Dean," *The Chicago Maroon* (March 23); www.chicagomaroon.com/article/2018/3/23/jonathan-z-smith-dean-of-college-university-of-chicago (accessed March 14, 2019).

Hamerton-Kelly, Robert G. (ed.) (1988). *Violent Origins: Walter Burkert, René Girard, and Jonathan Z. Smith on Ritual Killing and Cultural Formation*. Stanford, CA: Stanford University Press.

Lofton, Kathryn (2014). Review of *On Teaching Religion: Essays by Jonathan Z. Smith*, *Journal of the American Academy of Religion* 82/2: 531–542. https://doi.org/10.1093/jaarel/lfu027

Mack, Burton (1991). *A Myth of Innocence: Mark and Christian Origins*. Philadelphia, PA: Fortress Press.

McCutcheon, Russell T. (2018). "A Life and Career: Jonathan Z. Smith (1938–2017)," *Numen* 65: 441–455. https://doi.org/10.1163/15685276-12341507

Smith, Jonathan Z. (1975). "The Social Description of Early Christianity," *Religious Studies Review* 1: 19–25.

——. (1978). *Map Is Not Territory: Studies in the History of Religions.* Leiden: Brill.

——. (1982). *Imagining Religion: From Babylon to Jonestown.* Chicago, IL: University of Chicago Press.

——. (1987). *To Take Place: Toward Theory in Ritual.* Chicago, IL: University of Chicago Press.

——. (1990). *Drudgery Divine: On the Comparison of Early Christianities and the Religions of Late Antiquity.* Chicago, IL: University of Chicago Press.

—— (gen. ed.). (1995). *The HarperCollins Dictionary of Religion.* New York: HarperSanFranciso.

——. (2000a). "Acknowledgements: Morphology and History in Mircea Eliade's Patterns in Comparative Religion (1949–1999), Parts 1 and 2, *History of Religions* 39: 315–331, 332–351. https://doi.org/10.1086/463599

——. (2000b). "Classification," in Willi Braun and Russell T. McCutcheon (eds.), *Guide to the Study of Religion*, 35–44. London: Bloomsbury.

——. (2004). *Relating Religion: Essays in the Study of Religion.* Chicago, IL: University of Chicago Press.

——. (2009). "Religion and Bible," Presidential Address, Society of Biblical Literature, *Journal of Biblical Literature* 128: 5–27. https://doi.org/10.2307/25610162

——. (2010). "The Eternal Deferral, 215," in Christian K. Wedemeyer and Wendy Doniger (eds.), *Hermeneutics, Politics and the History of Religions: The Contested Legacies of Joachim Wach and Mircea Eliade*, 215–237. New York: Oxford University Press.

——. (2013). *On Teaching Religion: Essays by Jonathan Z. Smith.* Christopher Lehrich, ed. New York: Oxford University Press.

Taylor, Mark (ed.) (1998). *Critical Terms for Religious Studies.* Chicago, IL: University of Chicago Press. https://doi.org/10.7208/chicago/9780226791739.001.0001

Part I

Essays

AMERICAN ACADEMY OF RELIGION'S COMPARATIVE STUDIES IN RELIGION UNIT PANEL

This section, containing Chapters 1–6, is composed of papers presented at the Comparative Studies in Religion Unit Panel at the 2018 American Academy of Religion Annual Meeting in Denver, Colorado. The panel was entitled "Remembering Jonathan Z. Smith: Shaping Our Field and Our Work in the Comparative Study of Religion."

Chapter 1

Introduction: Remembering Jonathan Z. Smith— Shaping Our Field and Our Work in the Comparative Study of Religion

Kathryn McClymond

"Which religious studies theorist has shaped your thinking the most, and why?" This was the opening question in the AAR Employment Center interview that led to my career at Georgia State University. Jonathan Herman—trained at Harvard Divinity School—was asking me—trained at UC Santa Barbara—and I answered, "Jonathan Z. Smith."

Flash back six years to my first semester at UC Santa Barbara. As part of the required pro-seminar, I was asked to discuss the work of Mircea Eliade. It quickly became clear that I could not talk about Eliade without discussing Jonathan Z. Smith. Specifically, I was drawn to Smith's essay "In Search of Place," the first chapter in Smith's landmark *To Take Place: Toward Theory in Ritual*. Not only did this essay transform my thinking about Eliade; it also gave me a ringside seat to a dynamic intellectual bout between two religious studies heavyweights, wrestling over the nature of our work as scholars. Smith not only argued for a different take on the Tjilpa myth; he carefully crafted a scholarly "take down" of Eliade's interpretation that ignited the field of religious studies for me. *This*, I thought, is where I want to be: in the center of sharp, passionate argument, with nothing less than the understanding of how human beings make sense of the world at stake. This was my initiation into comparative research.

A few years later I was given my first opportunity to teach—undergraduates, of course. I was eager but unsure how to engage a large lecture class. Someone told me about J. Z. Smith's approach. (All of us acted as if we knew him well enough to call him "J. Z.") I used techniques that he recommended (whether he actually used them or not), distributing index cards to students at the end of each class session, asking them to summarize one thing they learned in class and one question the discussion had sparked for them. I'm not sure if this index card exercise improved student learning, but it gave me insight into what students cared about when we talked about religion. And I learned to teach informed by what my students brought to the conversation.

Six years later, during my job interview, Jonathan Z. Smith naturally came to mind. In the years to come, I heard him lecture and saw him from afar at AAR conferences, usually smoking, and always involved in deep conversation. I engaged his work in my own writing, ultimately disagreeing with him on some points, but never losing my appreciation for how he fueled debate. We celebrate Smith's work today because even when you disagreed with him—even if you never met him—you had to contend with him. In the essays to follow, Hugh Urban, Oliver Freiberger, Eric Mortensen, Kurtis Schaeffer, and Kimberley Patton speak to the ways in which Eliade fed their comparative work and, more fundamentally, how he shaped them as scholars. He was and will continue to be one of the handful of scholars who shapes how we comparativists launch, structure, and articulate our arguments, how we imagine the comparative enterprise. Because of this, even with his passing, religious studies scholars will continue to contend with "J. Z."

Kathryn McClymond is Associate Dean for Faculty Affairs and Professor in the Department of Religious Studies at Georgia State University. Her current work examines how veterans deal with moral injury by drawing on world cultures' ritual traditions.

Chapter 2

The Poetics and Politics of Comparison: From Revolutionary Suicide to Mass Murder

Hugh B. Urban

Comparison does not necessarily tell us how things "are" ... [L]ike models and metaphors, comparison tells us how things might be conceived, how they might be "redescribed."
—Jonathan Z. Smith (1990: 52)

They were just fucking slaughtered ... There was nothing dignified about it, it had nothing to do with revolutionary suicide, it had nothing do with making a fucking statement. It was just senseless waste, senseless waste and death.
—Jonestown survivor Tim Carter (Nelson 2007)

From the outset of this short article, I should probably confess that, although I was a graduate student at the University of Chicago during the 1990s, I never actually had a chance to work with Jonathan Z. Smith personally. During that period, Smith actually worked with very few graduate students and was known to us more as a distant, elusive, and iconic figure whom we might occasionally glimpse fleetingly across campus but whose works still permeated our thinking about the comparative study of religion. After my graduation from Chicago, however, I wrote an article about Smith's work, which focused primarily on his method of comparison, and I decided—on a whim—that I would send him a draft copy for his feedback. Much to my surprise, Smith sent me a detailed reply (typed, of course, on an old-school manual typewriter) with some critical but overall very constructive feedback. It is in part this draft and Smith's original feedback that forms the basis of the article that follows, supplemented with some of my own recent research on new religious movements.[1]

Although Smith's work is wide-ranging and multi-faceted, I want to highlight just two key points in my brief remarks here; and I will conclude with one, more critical comment about some potential weaknesses in his comparative methodology. For the sake of space, I will focus primarily on his 1982 collection, *Imagining Religion* and his well-known essay from that volume, "The Devil in Mr. Jones."

One of the most basic but vitally important points that Smith makes is the observation that the scholar of religions must be "relentlessly self-conscious." As he famously put it, the category of religion—as an abstract, cross-cultural ideal— is itself largely an "imagined" category, that is, the product of academic discourse and of our own second-order, imaginative acts of comparison and analysis. For this reason, we must be critically aware of the ways in which we define and represent religion, and most especially, we need to be mindful of the real-world effects those definitions will inevitably have upon the human beings whom we study: in short, "the student of religion, and most specifically, the historian of religion, must be relentlessly self-conscious. Indeed, this self-consciousness constitutes his expertise, his foremost object of study" (Smith 1982: xi).

As we see in the legacies of colonialism, imperialism, and the conquest of other cultures, our imaginings of religion have often had profound and sometimes violent effects on real human bodies and communities. Because much of my own early work has focused on religions of India, particularly during the British colonial period, I have always been acutely aware of the many ways in which our imaginings of Indian religions have had material effects on the human beings whom we study; and the effects of our imaginings have obviously continued in the context of late capitalism, neo-liberalism, and the ongoing exoticizations and exploitations of the mysterious Orient in the twenty-first century (Urban 2003; Inden 1990; King 1999). The rampant commodification and commercialization of yoga and Tantra—much of it rooted in American and European scholarship on these traditions—is only the most obvious and latest example of this trend (Jain 2014; Carrette and King 2004). Thus, the need for a J. Z. Smithian sort of self-consciousness and critical self-reflection in the imagining of religions is today perhaps more necessary than ever.

The second key contribution of Smith's work that I want to highlight is his revitalization of comparison as a methodological tool in the study of religion (Smith 2004: 29–30; Gill 1998; Patton and Ray 2000; Segal 2005). For much of the nineteenth and twentieth centuries, comparison had often been a flawed and problematic enterprise. On the one hand, for many British and European anthropologists of the nineteenth century, comparison went hand in hand with the projects of empire and colonialism; that is, the comparative study of the "primitive," the Oriental, and the exotic served as a useful handmaiden to the conquest of Africa, Australia, much of South Asia, and the Americas (see Hughes 2017; Lincoln 2018; Urban 2004).[2] On the other hand, for more sympathetic historians of the twentieth century such as Mircea Eliade, comparison had become a means to absorb all of the world's many diverse religious traditions and historical exempla into one universal approach to "the Sacred." Yet in Eliade's ambitious and omnivorous approach, any sense of historical difference and cultural nuance was largely lost amidst universal archetypes and comparative patterns (Eliade 1958).[3]

Smith's comparative method offers a profoundly original and refreshing alternative to both the colonialist and the universalist methods. Rather than seeking grand universals or archetypes, Smith is more interested in comparison as a *pragmatic tool*—that is, as a subtle, playful juxtaposition of diverse phenomena in order to generate fresh insights into larger categories in the academic imagining of religion. One of his most important discussions of comparison is his 1990 book, *Drudgery Divine*, in which he suggests that comparison works best like a kind of *metaphor*. Just as a good metaphor (such as "her face is a rose") does not imply a simple equation between the two terms (her face is not actually a rose), so too, a good comparison does not imply that the two terms are exactly the same. Rather, like a metaphor, it suggests that we can gain some new insight by juxtaposing the two terms (such as face and rose) and playing upon their obvious differences and subtle similarities in order to gain a new insight into some third thing that we are interested in (such as her beauty, her fragile delicacy, her impermanence). As Smith put it, borrowing some insights from Max Black's work on metaphor:

> Comparison does not necessarily tell us how things are ... [L]ike models and metaphors, comparison tells us how things might be conceived, how they might be "redescribed," in Max Black's useful term. A comparison is a disciplined exaggeration in the service of knowledge ... Comparison provides the means by which *we* revision phenome as *our* data in order to solve *our* theoretical problems. (Smith 1994: 52; see Black 1962).

Smith engaged in this sort of metaphoric comparison throughout his work, often in extremely creative and provocative ways. However, one of the most famous—and also, I will argue, most problematic—examples is his essay on the tragic case of the Peoples Temple movement and its mass murder-suicides in 1978, when over 900 men, women, and children died in Guyana. While most of the media at the time immediately described Peoples Temple as a bizarre, brainwashing "cult of death" (Time 1978), most of the academy was stunned into silence by the event. Smith, however, took this as a challenge to try to make sense of the event, placing it within the broader framework of the history of religions.

In classic J. Z. fashion, Smith juxtaposed Peoples Temple and Jonestown with two other, completely unrelated historical examples; and he did so, not in order to say that they are "the same" in a universal or archetypal sense, but rather to suggest that they can be used like *metaphors* to shed new light on this complex incident.

Thus, he first compared Jim Jones's controversial sexuality, promiscuity, and transgressions to the sexuality of other transgressive religious movements, most notably the Dionysian or Bacchic cults of ancient Greece and Rome. Second, he then compared the mass deaths and destruction at Jonestown to the mass destruction and slaughter that took place among some of the so-called "Cargo Cults" of Oceania (Smith 1982: 102–120). Citing the example of a Cargo Cult from the New Hebrides Islands in 1944, Smith recounted the way in which the indigenous community destroyed all of their crops, houses, and livestock in response to the European colonizers. In metaphoric fashion, Smith then juxtaposed the Cargo Cult example with Jim Jones's own act of destruction:

> Jones and Peoples Temple had labored mightily, at extraordinary cost, to achieve their vision of radical equality. And they had failed ... What was left was a gesture—a gesture designed to elicit shame, a gesture that the mixed rhetoric of Jonestown termed a "revolutionary suicide." By destroying all, by giving their all, they sought to call forth a reciprocal action. They would show the world ... In death, they would achieve a corporate picture of peace and harmony ...
>
> They failed; as the cargo cults failed, but we may catch a glimpse of the logic of their deed, aided by familiarity gained from Oceania. (Smith 1982: 120)

While I generally appreciate Smith's comparative method, I would argue that it is precisely here that we also see the potential problems in this model of comparison as metaphor. In order for the comparison to be effective and illuminating, the metaphoric examples chosen must be really *good* ones. But at least in Smith's reading of the Jonestown case, I would argue, they were ultimately *not* very good ones. By comparing the Jonestown suicides to Oceanic Cargo Cults, Smith basically accepted Jones's own description of the deaths as a form of "revolutionary suicide protesting the conditions of an inhumane world" (Nelson 2007; Smith 1982: 127–131), and so fell into the common media narrative that the deaths were largely voluntary; at the same time, he also implied that they were somehow even tragically heroic, if only in a failed sense, like the failed Cargo Cults. This narrative of revolutionary suicide was subsequently accepted by other scholars, such as David Chidester, who compared Jonestown to the deaths of the Sicarii Jews at Masada in 73 BCE, to the Japanese rite of seppuku, and to other cases of voluntary "religious suicides" (Chidester 1991; see Wessinger 2000).

In the decades since the tragedy, however, a great deal of evidence has come forth suggesting that the Jonestown deaths were not all—and probably not even *mostly*—voluntary, but instead cases of murder, in which many members died against their will.[4] One of the most outspoken Jonestown survivors is Tim Carter, who has written extensively about his experience in the movement and is adamant that this was *not* a mass suicide but instead primarily a case of mass murder (Carter 2015; see Urban 2015). Based on his observations of the scene, he believes that by far the majority of the deaths were either children and seniors who were forced to drink cyanide against their will or adults who were forced at gunpoint and/or injected with the poison. Carter counts 246 children, 180 seniors and at least 125 adults who had signs of needle injection, in addition to those who may have been coerced by threat of force (other observers have put the number of children closer to 300; see Dieckman 2018).[5]

To be sure, Carter acknowledges that the community had engaged in the infamous "White Nights," which were emergency drills that involved preparations for some imminent, dramatic threat to the community; and on a few occasions, these included "practice suicides" in which members were instructed to drink poison.[6] Yet even taking into account those adults who may have died voluntarily, Carter argues, most of those at Jonestown clearly died against their will: "Mass suicide? Or mass murder? While some did commit suicide, the vast majority of those who perished in Jonestown were murdered. Jonestown should always be considered a mass murder, with some suicide" (Carter 2015). Other Jonestown survivors echo Carter's assessment. In the words of Stanley Clayton, one of the few members who was able to flee the camp and live to talk about it, "I ain't never used the term suicide, and I'm not gonna never use the term suicide. That man was killing us" (Nelson 2007).

As Carter recounted in an interview with me in 2015, he witnessed his own infant son—like many other small children—have cyanide poured down his throat; and he argued persuasively that redefining Jonestown as a mass murder rather than a suicide completely changes the way we think about the entire Peoples Temple movement and its members. If reframed as a mass murder, Peoples Temple might look not so much like a brainwashing cult (as the media portrayed it) or as a group of tragic, failed martyrs (as Smith portrays it); instead it would look like a very complex and internally divided religious movement, most of whose members sincerely believed in the utopian community they were creating, but whose ideals were violently hi-jacked by Jones and a small number of his inner circle:

> People want to focus on Jim Jones. But the story of Peoples Temple is the people. It's not Jim Jones ... What made the temple dynamic and successful and *mainstream* was the people—because we were as mainstream as it could get in terms of the progressive movement of the Bay Area. We were not freaks. We were not cultists. We were mainstream ...
>
> If you look at the ending as suicide, then it really was a waste. But if you look at the ending as *murder*, then some of the things we did do still have meaning. (Urban 2015: 260)

As such, Smith's choice of an Oceanic cargo cult as his metaphoric foil arguably obfuscates rather than illuminates the case of Jonestown, framing the deaths (in Jones's own terms) as voluntary acts of revolutionary suicide rather than as some other form of involuntary violence. Personally, I have to admit that I have trouble thinking of a *better* metaphoric comparison for the tragic case of Jonestown; but it seems to me to be perhaps closer to a suicide bombing or a mass shooting or a terrorist attack than it is to a "revolutionary suicide."

One reason for Smith's failure in the case of the Jonestown tragedy, I think, is his avowed commitment to a kind of Enlightenment rationality, one that refuses to leave any phenomena outside the grasp of reason and intelligibility. As he famously put it at the beginning of the Jonestown essay:

> *The academic study of religion is a child of the Enlightenment...* Rediscovering the old tag, "Nothing human is foreign to me," the Enlightenment impulse was one of tolerance and...one which refused to leave any human datum, including religion, beyond the pale of understanding, beyond the realm of reason...As students of religion, we have become stubbornly committed to making the attempt (even if we fail) at achieving intelligibility. (Smith 1982: 104)

It is this commitment to rationality, I think, that leads Smith to his comparison with examples of revolutionary suicide and Cargo Cults—examples that make Jonestown seem intelligible and familiar. But it also prevents him from considering the element of the *irrational*, from taking seriously acts and motivations that may lie well outside the pale of reason.

In 1978, Smith's call to reason was understandable and probably appropriate. This was, after all, a time when new religious movements were still not really taken seriously in the academy, when the "cult scares" were very much alive and well in the United States, and when the Jonestown event had unleashed a media feeding frenzy on "brainwashing death cults." Yet in 2018, in light of much more evidence about the Jonestown events and an academic context in which the study of new religions is much more developed, we probably need to consider different approaches.

Perhaps the academic study of religion in the twenty-first century needs to reconsider its attachment to Enlightenment rationality and take more seriously the darker, more frightening prospect of the *non-rational* aspects of religious behavior. And here I mean not simply suicide bombers and terrorist hi-jackers but also the Anders Breiviks, the Marshall Applewhites, the Shoko Asaharas, and others whose acts of violence appear to fundamentally defy rationality and perhaps call for *other* modes of analysis. This is not to suggest that we can say nothing at all about such figures or movements, but rather that we might need to resort to other forms of critical interrogation that take us beyond the familiar frameworks of religious studies and deeper into the very "foreignness" that Smith refuses to concede.

For example, a serious analysis of Jim Jones and his Peoples Temple would also need to take account of Jones's own serious drug addiction and mounting paranoia (Maaga 1998; Moore and McGehee 1978), as well as the sheer depth of horror experienced by those present at the scene. A transcript of a *survivor's* account such as Tim Carter's or Stanley Clayton's would be necessary to counter-balance the transcript of Jones's account that Smith includes in the appendix to his essay; and it might well make the deaths look much less like familiar examples such as "Cargo Cults."[7] Likewise, an analysis of Breivik's terrorist rampage would need not simply to comprehend his neo-Crusader's religious worldview, as authors such as Mark Juergensmeyer have (2017: 21-24); it would also need to delve deeply into the dark current of racism, fear, hatred, and xenophobia that drives so much of the white supremacist violence now spreading across Europe and the United States (see Berry 2018). An account of Marshall Applewhite's UFO movement might require not simply understanding his apocalyptic worldview; rather, it would also mean grappling with his wildly postmodern pastiche of science fiction, popular culture, computer technology, and cyberspace—a pastiche that bears more resemblance to Jean Baudrillard's hyper-reality and simulacra than it does to Enlightenment rationality (see Urban 2000b).

Such a critical rethinking of the academic study of religion, I submit, would be in perfect keeping with Smith's own call for "relentless self-consciousness" in our ongoing imagining and re-imagining of religion.

Hugh B. Urban is a Distinguished Professor in the Department of Comparative Studies at Ohio State University. He is the author of numerous books and is currently finishing a book on religion and secrecy.

Notes

1 My original correspondence with Smith took place in 1999-2000. Some of Smith's feedback was also incorporated into an early article of mine (Urban 2000a).
2 On the construction of categories such as the "primitive," see Kuper (1988) and Long (1986: 79-113).
3 There are innumerable critiques of comparative Eliade's method; see for example Strenski (1987), McCutcheon (1997), Dubuisson (2014) and Smith's own work (e.g. Smith 1993: 88-103).

4   There is a great deal of debate on the murder vs. suicide question. See Moore (2018a: 7). For a series of articles on both sides, see San Diego State University (2018). Perhaps the most balanced assessment among these is Moore (2018b), which argues that the deaths of the children and seniors should certainly be considered murders, while the deaths of at least some of the adults could be considered suicides: "I initially called all the deaths suicide ... I later came to change my own conception of the deaths, however, once I faced the logical impossibility of children committing suicide. In addition, the seniors found dead in their housing units—injected with cyanide—do not appear to be suicide victims."

5   It should also be noted that autopsies were performed on only seven of the bodies, so the official cause of death in most cases is unknown. See Moore (2018c: 106–107).

6   On the White Nights and "practice suicides," see Moore (2018c: 75–76) and Reiterman (2008: 391). Reiterman notes that even during a practice suicide that took place in 1978, there was intense resistance to the idea, and Jones himself put a stop to it.

7   For interviews with survivors, see Nelson (2007), San Diego State University (2018), Urban (2015: 247–249), Layton (1999) and Maaga (1998).

References

Berry, Damon (2018). *Blood and Faith: Christianity and White Nationalism.* Syracuse, NY: Syracuse University Press. https://doi.org/10.2307/j.ctt1pk86c2

Black, Max (1962). *Models and Metaphor.* Ithaca, NY: Cornell University Press.

Carrette, Jeremy and Richard King (2004). *Selling Spirituality: The Silent Takeover of Religion.* New York: Routledge. https://doi.org/10.4324/9780203494875

Carter, Tim (2015). "Murder or Suicide: What I Saw," *Alternative Considerations of Jonestown and Peoples Temple,* San Diego State University; https://jonestown.sdsu.edu/?page_id=31976 (accessed June 24, 2019).

Chidester, David (1991). *Salvation and Suicide: Jim Jones, The Peoples Temple, and Jonestown.* Bloomington, IN: Indiana University Press.

Dieckman, Josef (2018). "Murder vs. Suicide: What the Numbers Show," *Alternative Considerations of Jonestown & Peoples Temple,* San Diego State University; https://jonestown.sdsu.edu/?page_id=31969 (accessed June 24, 2019).

Dubuisson, Daniel (2014). *Twentieth Century Mythologies: Dumézil, Lévi-Strauss, Eliade.* London: Routledge. https://doi.org/10.4324/9781315711324

Eliade, Mircea (1958). *Patterns in Comparative Religion.* New York: Sheed and Ward.

Gill, Sam (1998). "No Place to Stand: Jonathan Z. Smith as *Homo Ludens*: The Academic Study of Religion *Sub Specie Ludi*," *Journal of the American Academy of Religion* 66/2: 283–312. https://doi.org/10.1093/jaarel/66.2.283

Hughes, Aaron (2017). *Comparison: A Critical Primer.* Sheffield: Equinox.

Inden, Ronald (1990). *Imagining India.* Oxford: Blackwell.

Jain, Andrea (2014). *Selling Yoga: From Counterculture to Pop Culture.* New York: Oxford University Press. https://doi.org/10.1093/acprof:oso/9780199390236.001.0001

Juergensmeyer, Mark (2017). *Terror in the Mind of God: The Global Rise of Religious Violence.* Berkeley, CA: University of California Press.

King, Richard (1999). *Orientalism and Religion: Postcolonial Theory, India and the Mystic East.* New York: Routledge.

Kuper, Adam (1988). *The Invention of Primitive Society: The Transformations of an Illusion.* London: Routledge.

Layton, Deborah (1999). *Seductive Poison: A Jonestown Survivor's Story of Life and Death in the People's Temple.* New York: Anchor.

Lincoln, Bruce (2018). *Apples and Oranges: Explorations In, On, and With Comparison.* Chicago, IL: University of Chicago Press. https://doi.org/10.7208/chicago/9780226564104. 001.0001

Long, Charles H. (1986). *Significations: Signs, Symbols and Images in the Interpretation of Religion.* Philadelphia, PA: Fortress Press.

Maaga, Mary McCormick (1998). *Hearing the Voices at Jonestown.* Syracuse, NY: Syracuse University Press.

McCutcheon, Russell (1997). *Manufacturing Religion: The Discourse of Sui Generis Religion and the Politics of Nostalgia.* New York: Oxford University Press.

Moore, Rebecca (2018a). "Jonestown: Forty Years On," *Nova Religio* 22/2: 3–14. https://doi. org/10.1525/nr.2018.22.2.3

——. (2018b). "The Sacrament of Suicide," *Alternative Considerations of Jonestown & Peoples Temple,* San Diego State University; https://jonestown.sdsu.edu/?page_id=31985 (accessed June 20, 2019).

——. (2018c). *Understanding Jonestown and Peoples Temple.* Santa Barbara, CA: Praeger.

Moore, Rebecca and Fielding M. McGehee III (eds.) (1978). *The Need for a Second Look at Jonestown.* Lewiston, NY: Edwin Mellen Press.

Nelson, Stanley, director (2007). *Jonestown: The Life and Death of Peoples Temple.* PBS Frontline.

Patton, Kimberley C. and Benjamin C. Ray, eds. (2000). *Magic Still Dwells: Comparative Religion in the Postmodern Age.* Berkeley, CA: University of California Press.

Reiterman, Tim (2008). *Raven: The Untold Story of Jim Jones and His Peoples Temple.* New York: Tarcher Perigee.

San Diego State University (2018). "Should the Deaths in Jonestown be Considered as Suicides or Murders?" *Alternative Considerations of Jonestown & Peoples Temple,* San Diego State University; https://jonestown.sdsu.edu/?page_id=35427 (accessed June 19, 2019).

Segal, Robert A. (2005). "Classification and Comparison in the Study of Religion: The Work of Jonathan Z. Smith". *Journal of the American Academy of Religion* 73/4: 1175–1188. https://doi.org/10.1093/jaarel/lfi120

Smith, Jonathan Z. (1982). *Imagining Religion: From Babylon to Jonestown.* Chicago, IL: University of Chicago Press.

——. (1990). *Drudgery Divine: On the Comparison of Early Christianities and Religions of Late Antiquity,* Chicago, IL: University of Chicago Press.

——. (1993). *Map is not Territory: Studies in the History of Religions.* Chicago, IL: University of Chicago Press.

——. (2004). *Relating Religion: Essays in the Study of Religion.* Chicago, IL: University of Chicago Press.

Strenski, Ivan (1987). *Four Theories of Myth in Twentieth Century History: Cassirer, Eliade, Lévi-Strauss, and Malinowski.* Iowa City, IA: University of Iowa Press.

Time. (1978). "Cult of Death: The Jonestown Nightmare: A Religious Colony in Guyana Turns into a Cult of Death," *Time Magazine* (December 4); http://content.time.com/ time/subscriber/article/0,33009,912249-1,00.html (accessed June 24, 2019).

Urban, Hugh B. (2000a). "Making a Place to Take a Stand: Jonathan Z. Smith and the Poetics and Politics of Comparison," *Method and Theory in the Study of Religion* 12/3: 339–378. https://doi.org/10.1163/157006800X00247

——. (2000b). "The Devil at Heaven's Gate: Rethinking the Study of Religion in the Age of Cyber-Space," *Nova Religio* 3/2: 268–302. https://doi.org/10.1525/nr.2000.3.2.268

——. (2003). *Tantra: Sex, Secrecy, Politics and Power in the Study of Religion*. Berkeley, CA: University of California Press.

——. (2004). "Power Still Dwells: The Ethics and Politics of Comparison in *A Magic Still Dwells*," *Method and Theory in the Study of Religion* 16/1: 24–35. https://doi.org/10.1163/157006804323055182

——. (2015). *New Age, Neopagan and New Religious Movements: Alternative Spirituality in Contemporary America*. Berkeley, CA: University of California Press.

Wessinger, Catherine (2000). *How the Millennium Comes Violently: From Jonestown to Heaven's Gate*. New York: Seven Bridges.

Chapter 3

The Magus: J. Z. Smith and "the Absolute Wonder of the Human Imagination"

Kimberley C. Patton

Supriya Sinhababu: What got you interested in the religions that you study?
J. Z. Smith: Because they're funny. They're interesting in and of themselves. They relate to the world in which I live, but it's like a fun house mirror: Something's off. It's not quite the world I live in, yet it's recognizable. So that gap interested me. ... I mean, you ask me what I get out of it. ... I get a feeling of the absolute wonder of the human imagination. It's unstoppable. It's funny, it's sort of a game among analytic philosophers when they discuss religion to invent something crazy and then talk about how you could invent it. And I always ask them, "Why are you working so hard to invent something? I could show you a hundred crazier things than you could come up with that are in somebody's most sacred writings." It's mind-boggling.

And the one who challenged me on it was someone who had a living rock. It could only go "woo!" or "uh." And how do you work out the grammar of "woo!" and "uh"? And I said, "You don't tell me how the woos got there. You don't tell me how these woos and uhs got there. I mean, you're a shitty mythmaker!" So I just picked up one yesterday—the world is a spider web, formed of the dripping, green semen of another spider that goes down the various parts of the web—I don't know what you call them, filaments—and congeals here and there. So now you want to talk about rationality—man, you deal with that. To hell with your woos and uhs. And that's only the first paragraph. The myth goes on for I think about 700 paragraphs actually. It's a Brazilian native myth. Wow! I look at that, I've never taught it, but I look at that ... it's not that I want to understand it so much. I just want to say, "Hats off to you kids! You sold it to generations and generations! Woo! Terrific! Wonderful!" That's what I like about religion, it never fails to surprise me. Whenever you think you've seen it all, you find something like this that—"Whoops, back to the drawing board. My definition has not been broad enough. I have to get this one in too." It's good. It's good subject matter. It doesn't conclude, and that's good too.

—Sinhababu (2008)

It was hard not to notice that he was becoming a wizard—consciously, it seems. Shortly after the death of Jonathan Z. Smith on December 30, 2017, Brett Colasacco wrote that his University of Chicago professor of *Introduction to Religious Studies* had been "a tall old man in a vintage suit, with shoulder-length white hair, a beard, and an ancient-looking walking stick. Gandalf the wizard, only with large glasses and a less pointy hat" (Colasacco 2018). "I'm going to invent myself as this old guy!" he said to Charles Long when his black hair began to turn white (Grieve 2018). Self-occulting like Merlin, hard to contact. No computers, no email, no cell phones—"an abomination." Self-archaizing.

Of the cane—"liberated" by his uncle from the Great Smoky Mountains National Park, "that crazy stick he walked with in recent years" (Wendy Doniger in Grieve 2018), "that tree-trunk of a cane" (McCutcheon 2018)—its owner said to Supriya Sinhababu in 2008:

> Well, I'll tell you about this thing, because it's botanical. This is a rhododendron. It grows from mama, it grows from under the ground, and gets out from underneath mama—this is a parable—and it comes out from underneath. So it's a natural cane. And what I didn't know, from the spindly, shitty rhododendrons that we have around here, that they grow to this length. I've seen photographs of them in England and they grow to be like trees. Feel it, it's very heavy! That's not my picture of a rhododendron. (Sinhababu 2008)

For a scholar who suggested that Eliade's *axis mundi* was a "wobbling pivot" (Smith 1978a: 88), it was his own terrestrial-celestial link, over whose crook he would cross his wrists, eyes closed, listening, listening. Close to a decade later, Sinhababu herself reflected, "He died at 79, but in my head he's at least like a thousand. He really feels like a legendary figure" (Grieve 2018).

We indulge rather than seriously attend to interviews with scholarly icons: *ad hoc*, oral, they are marginalia that leaven the written corpus. But like the "damn richness" of a religious tradition, a lifespan of thought should be considered in its entirety—not only what is curated in writing, but also what is said when the thinker asked point-blank *why* or *what about ...?* Interviews can reveal the paradox that has been, for years, beating at the heart of the matter. As the responses of Levinas to Nemo in *Ethics and Infinity* or Lévi-Strauss to Eribon in *Conversations* startle, so those of Smith to Sinhababu testify to the heuristic power of dialogue. To expect congruency between what J.Z.S. wrote and what he said, or even what he believed, is to make the classic disciple's error. He was, after all, a champion of incongruity in the study of religion, in particular comparative religion. "It is difference that generates thought, whether at the level of data or of theory. *Thus, a model gains its cognitive power by not according in all respects to that which it models.* 'Map is not territory' and is, therefore, of intellectual value ..." (Smith 2002a: 4, italics added). The one who drew this map: "For the self-conscious student of religion, *no datum possesses intrinsic interest.* It is of value only insofar as it can serve as an exempli gratia of some fundamental issue in the imagination of religion" (Smith 1982: xi), responded, when asked why he studied the religions he did: "Because they're funny. *They're interesting in and of themselves*" (Sinhababu 2008; italics added). The one who called the procedure of comparison "homeopathic" and comparative theory "built on [Frazerian] contagion" elegantly finessed his own comparative archetype about the discovery of archetypes:

> The discovery of the archetype, as represented in the [morphological] literature, has a visionary quality; it appears to be the result of a sudden, intuitive leap to

simplicity. Characteristic of morphological presentations will be a dated account of the vision—Goethe gazing at a palmetto in an Italian botanical garden on 17 April 1787; Lorenz Oken accidentally stumbling over a deer's skull while walking in the Harz Forest in the spring of 1806. To these, and others that might be cited, can now be added Mircea Eliade in a London bomb shelter in the fall of 1940. (Smith 2004b, citing Smith 1982)

Bottling the Genie: Appropriating J.Z.S.

Sadly now bracketed by two dates, Smith's metamorphic *vita* backlit religion neither as a miasma of power relationships nor as a matrix for the negotiation of identity, despite how both are trending at the moment. For him it was not *not* these, but it was also (arguably above all else) a parallel universe, funny, "one-off"; like the Looking-Glass or Diagon Alley—in his words, wonder-ful. Myth-making, he said, is an inexhaustible activity. The move to distill religious history to one or even several concepts is a mistake. Paradigms must always evolve. The urge to conclude, to cauterize, any valuable enquiry is also a mistake. "I don't joke about dropping dead in the middle of class any longer. But I always try to—and I don't always succeed—to end the last class on an incomplete sentence. And that to me is important. Don't come to an ending." Like the Sinhababu interview itself, "It [religion] doesn't conclude, and that's good too." Everything flows. Nothing is ever over and done.

Over the years we have tended to press his superbly erudite thinking into the service of whatever colors we are currently waving at the barricade. Smith's platform seems so nicely to dovetail with postmodern epistemology and critical theory: religion as a second-order phenomenon; comparison as a set of privately juxtaposed associations "brought ... together within the space of the scholar's mind for the scholar's own intellectual reasons" (Smith 1990: 51), hence easily coopted by colonialist ideas; map that is claimed to be, but is not, territory; ritual slippage and mythic incongruity; "universal" archetypes that collapse under scrutiny, that do not in practice center the world, and never did, not even close. Only differences were of real interest to him, while similarities were close to unreal, of value only as strategy, never indicative of " 'natural' affinities or processes of history" (ibid.: 51). *Pace* the ambiguity in Eliade, "there is nothing that is inherently sacred or profane. These are not substantive categories, but rather situational or relational categories, mobile boundaries which shift according to the map being employed. There is nothing that is sacred in itself, only things sacred in relation" (Smith 1982: 55). These facets of Smith's intellectual project apparently bolster our current preoccupations, dis-oriented and disenchanted as we have become. Because like Long, Foucault, Lincoln, Asad, Bell, and Agamben, among others, he cross-examined and demystified transcendentalized aspects of religious ideologies and practices in the context of history, because he so fiercely deconstructed generalization, many of us consider him an ancestor and an ally, standing as we do "OTSO-JZS" ("on the shoulders of Jonathan Z. Smith"; White 2000: 53).

A "Distinctively Human World": The Mobile Magician

This however is a distortion. Validated by what Smith said was *not* possible, we may overlook what he said *was* possible. Even if religion is stripped of its theological dimensions or its universal applicability, its nature as constructive human activity makes our obligation to account for its scope and mystery no less pressing. He felt that "to portray rather than explain" should be the goal, citing Goethe at the start of his "Acknowledgement" of the contribution of Eliade's *Patterns in Comparative Religions* (Smith 2004b: 80). Often such portrayal meant destabilizing Eliadean constructs, like the broken *axis mundi* of the Aranda (Arrernte) in *To Take Place*:

> The central ritual connection between the ancestor and his "place," between the ancestor and the kind of individual Aranda, the central mode of celebrating and signifying objectification, is not dramatization, but recollection. In the words of Gurra [an Aranda elder reported in Strehlow], "My elders kept on repeating these ceremonies time and time again in my presence: they were afraid I might forget them ... Had I forgotten them, no one else would now remember them." In such a system, rupture does not occur by breaking poles linking heaven to earth; rupture occurs through the human act of forgetfulness. (Smith 1987: 13)

His portrayals were sometimes more explanatory than he averred. In his critique of the role of the "sky-pole," for example, one can discern his own preference for memory over what he calls "dramatization." The subject, however, is cultural oblivion avoided through the ceremonial maintenance of story-lines laid down by the Culture Hero Ulamba (Rain). Hence recollection is arguably not opposed to, but rather enacted by dramatization. *iIf I forget thee, O Jerusalem, Let my right hand forget her cunning."*

With Cassirer, Smith believed that "language 'creates' the world; it does not merely reflect it" (Smith 2004a: 4). To that "distinctively human world, our 'second environment,'" created by language, belongs religion itself. The right place of the scholar of religion is not on the shore of religion as a spectator, or even as a "cold-blooded ... analytical" critic (Doniger in Grieve 2018), but in the midst of the oceanic, ongoing co-creation of that second-order world: "Religion is solely the creation of the scholar's study" (Smith 1982: xi).

While the motivations of wizards are enigmatic, their operations are precise: in conjuring worlds, they care both about intricate details and about consequences. JZS was agnostic—or better, apathetic about metaphysics—yet his commitment to the theoretical analysis of metaphysical arrangements was intense: "The Church of the Holy Sepulchre requires relations of equivalence, indeed, of identity; there is no room in its systematic articulation for homologies, let alone for relations of difference" (Smith 1987: 86). Exactly right, but who else has argued this so unapologetically, and from a non-confessional stance? Remaining "shy of a quest for 'deeper' meaning" (Smith 2004a: 4), and through his reading of Cassirer, allegiant "(as Durkheim would later confirm), to neo-Kantianism and its relationship to aspects of the Enlightenment project" (5), he nevertheless continued to work in Hellenistic and Late Antique magic (see, *inter alia*, Smith 1978b, 1978c, 2002b, 2003). Words generated from **magh*, "power," characterize his affinities: Persian *mágoi*, who Pliny said wielded a deep combined knowledge of medicine, religion, and astronomy; the Greek *mágoi* condemned by Plato but sought out by everyone else to bind lukewarm lovers and protect the *polis* gates; *máchesthai*, the power of argument, combat, or struggle, especially the kind of power that calls stampeding sacred cows to halt, to self-examination. Above all, *imagination*, a word also deriving from **magh*, but more recently from the Latin *imaginari*, "to picture oneself" in reflexive, interior world-creation.

It is enlightening to read him on Thessalos the Greco-Egyptian magician or Simeon Stylites the Syrian saint, as his words may reveal as much about how he saw the academic study of religion as they do about his take on Mediterranean Late Antiquity:

> the cosmos has become anthropologized. Rather than a sacred place, the new center and chief means of access to divinity will be a divine man [*theios anēr*], a magician, who will function, by and large, as an entrepreneur without fixed office ... Rather than celebration, purification, and pilgrimage, the new rituals will be those of conversion, of initiation into the secret society or identification with the divine man ... only those elements which contribute to this new, anthropological, and and highly mobile understanding of religion will be retained. (Smith 1978b: 187–188)

Overlay this onto the shift over the past 120 years from *Bet Din, Ecclesia, ʿUlamāʾ* and Faculty of Dogmatic Theology to our own field, with its Enlightenment-vectored, fungible view of religion and its cult of personality: the congruence is striking.

Kaleidoscopic Comparison

As Sam Gill wrote, Jonathan Z. Smith was about "raising questions, demolishing unquestioned categories, insisting that discerning difference is fundamental to comparison"; the theory these moves produced "might well be understood in terms of play" (Gill 1998: 283). Smith's work has been called magisterial—but he himself was *magister ludi*. Like the first-century wonder-worker Apollonius of Tyana, whose "free, playful, and utterly transcendent intervention in specific situations which allow for a moment the possibility of another point of view" that Smith celebrated (Smith 1978c: 197), the comparative religionist is the ultimate magus:

> Comparison does not necessarily tell us how things "are." ... [L]ike models and metaphors, comparison tells us how things might be conceived, how they might be "redescribed."... A comparison is a disciplined exaggeration in the service of knowledge ... an active, even a playful, enterprise of deconstruction and restitution which, kaleidoscope-like, gives the scholar a shifting set of characteristics with which to negotiate the relationship between his or her theoretical interests and data stipulated as exemplary. (Smith 1990: 50–53 *passim*)

I once believed that Smith meant this as wholesale critique. In *A Magic Still Dwells*, I countered that the right framework for comparative religion was not "play" without objective correlative, but analogous disciplines such as comparative anatomy or linguistics (Patton 2000: 160). But I now wonder whether what he called the "magic" of comparison was the burn it appeared to be.

Perhaps he viewed our work as resembling that of the dreamer of the *Brihadaranyaka Upanishad* 4.3.9–10, which Doniger (1984) discusses in *Dreams, Illusion, and Other Realities*: a way to destroy and remake one's own mirror-worlds, one's own "chariots, harnessings, and roads" through magical practices like the juxtaposition of historically unrelated cults, like miniaturization, like the self-conscious creation of structures. His Durkheimian outlook and analytical rigor may have led us to misclassify him as a skeptic. Substitute the word "theory" for his "myth" in this epic quotation from *Map is Not Territory*, and I think we come closer to Smith's view of what we do:

> There is something funny, there is something crazy about myth for it shares with the comic and the insane the quality of obsessiveness. Nothing, in principle, is allowed to elude its grasp. The myth, like the diviner's objects, is a code capable, in theory, of universal application. But this obsessiveness, this claim to universality is relativized by the situation. There is delight and there is play in both the fit and the incongruity of the fit between an element in the myth and this or that segment of the world or of experience which is encountered. It is the oscillation between "fit" and "no fit" which gives rise to thought. (Smith 1978d: 300)

Like most great thinkers, he willingly engaged the thought of many with whom he radically disagreed. He held in respect and affection his older Chicago confrère Huston Smith, whose autobiography was called *Tales of Wonder: Adventures Chasing the Divine* (2009), and whose approach to the study of religion is often cast as the polar opposite of his—the perennialist popularizer of the school of what Bruce Lincoln has called "a-temporal expressions of eternal truths" versus the critical humanist who "re-theorized religion as something human and thereby opened it up to critical investigation" (Shimron 2018). As Arvind Sharma tells it, when asked to "write something that is true" by a student after a lecture, Huston Smith wrote, "Absolute perfection reigns and it is our job to conform our lives to that fact" (Sharma 2017). Could any stance have been further from that of Jonathan Smith's? Stark binaries, however, ought to be viewed with suspicion—as they both believed. Strangely, they died exactly a year apart, on December 30, in 2016 (H.S.) and 2017 (J.Z.S.). Their respective gazes were trained on different levels of the ziggurat. Wonder animated them both.

Gifts of the Magus

Smith left many gifts at our threshold. As is remarked often: Intellectual accountability, methodological rigor, and self-conscious scholarship. The indispensability of investigating the history, culture, and context of religious phenomena; the need for granular description and re-description. The commitment to continuously "rectifying" our theoretical models—to widening, never narrowing, our paradigms. The refusal to suppress religious incongruity; instead, an insistence on its catalytic energy: "Myth is ... a self-conscious category mistake. That is to say, the incongruity of myth is not an error, it is the very source of its power" (Smith 1978d: 299). A reclamation of chaos as generative rather than as profane.

As ought to be remarked more: A view of myth as evolved philosophy, whose sophistication still far exceeds the interpretive capability of analytical philosophy. Brave, even sometimes perverse willingness to flip the script, to honor complexity and eschew finality. Genuine rather than dismissive engagement with ideas that do not mirror ours. Humor; delight in religion's wealth of strangeness, the "crazy" ultimacy of its claims. A vision of "the absolute wonder of the human imagination" animating both the myths and the mythmakers, including religion scholars. Awareness of the crazy ultimacy of our own claims.

"Wizard and Wand"

All wizards have magical staffs. His was weird and twisty, un-orthodox ("not-straight"), carved from a flowering Appalachian plant growing wild, far from Chicago. "The wand chooses the wizard," Ollivander tells Harry Potter both at the beginning and then again near the end of his ordeal.

> If you are any wizard at all you will be able to channel your magic through almost any instrument. The best results, however, must always come where there is the strongest affinity between wizard and wand. These connections are complex. An initial attraction, and then a mutual quest for experience, the wand learning from the wizard, the wizard from the wand. (Rowling 1998: 82; 2009: 474)

In his honor, I visited some magnificent rhododendron bushes "as big as trees," of the kind that grew his cane, blooming on an abandoned estate near my home. I found one regally decked out in fuchsia. I checked my phone camera battery: 8%. Low, but more than enough to snap a photo; I've taken pictures at 1%. I clicked. The phone instantly went dead.

Exhaling in frustration, I looked up from the dark screen. To the absolute wonder of the rhododendron in front of me.

"I think the cell phone is an absolute abomination."

Yes, you do, Jonathan. What was I thinking?

Woo!

> For we have learned, from the Tjilpa narratives, that loss does not necessarily represent a "rupture," a "fall," a plunge into the "chaos" of "nonbeing." Instead, loss can provide the beginning of a complex process of modulation and change in that which was, but is no longer, and yet remains present. Yet through this very process of change, of being displaced from his "self" and being emplaced in an "other"—an object, a person, or a mark—the ancestor achieves permanence. He remains forever accessible. (Smith 1987: 12)

May you remain forever accessible. We miss you dearly.

Kimberley C. Patton is Professor of the Comparative and Historical Study of Religion at Harvard Divinity School. Her research is in ancient Greek religion and archaeology, particularly ritual studies, sanctuaries, and iconography.

References

Colasacco, Brett (2018). "How I Failed J. Z. Smith," The Martin Marty Center for the Public Understanding of Religion, The University of Chicago Divinity School, January 4; https://divinity.uchicago.edu/sightings/how-i-failed-j-z-smith (accessed June 24, 2019).

Doniger, Wendy (1984). *Dreams, Illusion, and Other Realities*. Chicago, IL: University of Chicago Press.

Gill, Sam (1998). "No Place to Stand: Jonathan Z. Smith as Homo Ludens, the Academic Study of Religion Sub Specie Ludi," *Journal of the American Academy of Religion* 66/2: 283–312. https://doi.org/10.1093/jaarel/66.2.283

Grieve, Peter (2018). "Jonathan Z. Smith (1938–2017): The College's Iconoclastic, Beloved, Chainsmoking Dean." *The Chicago Maroon* (March 23); www.chicagomaroon.com/article/2018/3/23/jonathan-z-smith-dean-of-college-university-of-chicago (accessed June 24, 2019).

McCutcheon, Russell (2018). "Let's Get to Work" (December 31, 2018); https://religion.ua.edu/blog/2017/12/31/lets-get-to-work (accessed June 24, 2019).

Patton, Kimberley (2000). "Juggling Torches: Why We Still Need Comparative Religion," in Kimberley Patton and Benjamin Ray (eds), *A Magic Still Dwells: Comparative Religion in the Postmodern Age*, 153–171. Berkeley, CA: University of California Press.

Rowling, J. K. (1998). *Harry Potter and the Sorcerer's Stone*. New York: Scholastic.

——. (2009). *Harry Potter and the Deathly Hallows*. New York: Scholastic.

Sharma, Arvind (2017). "In Memoriam: Huston Smith (1919–2016)," *Religious Studies News* (January 19); http://rsn.aarweb.org/memoriam-huston-smith-1919-2016 (accessed June 24, 2019).

Shimron, Yonat (2018). "Religion Historian Jonathan Z. Smith Dies." January 2, 2018; https://religionnews.com/2018/01/02/religion-historian-jonathan-z-smith-dies (accessed June 24, 2019).

Sinhababu, Supriya (2008). "Full J. Z. Smith Interview," *The Chicago Maroon* (June 2); www.chicagomaroon.com/2008/06/02/full-j-z-smith-interview (accessed June 24, 2019).

Smith, Huston (2009). *Tales of Wonder: Chasing the Divine, an Autobiography*. New York: HarperOne.

Smith, Jonathan Z. (1978a). "The Wobbling Pivot," in *Map is Not Territory: Studies in the Histories of Religion*, 88–103. Chicago, IL: University of Chicago Press.

——. (1978b). "The Temple and the Magician," in *Map is Not Territory: Studies in the Histories of Religion*, 172–189. Chicago, IL: University of Chicago Press.

——. (1978c). "Good News is No News: Aretalogy and Gospel," in *Map is Not Territory: Studies in the Histories of Religion*, 190–207. Chicago, IL: University of Chicago Press.

——. (1978d). "Map is Not Territory," in *Map is Not Territory: Studies in the Histories of Religion*, 289–310. Chicago, IL: University of Chicago Press.

——. (1982). *Imagining Religion: From Babylon to Jonestown*. Chicago, IL: University of Chicago Press.

——. (1987). *To Take Place: Toward Theory in Ritual*. Chicago Studies in the History of Judaism. Jacob Neusner, William Scott Green, and Calvin Goldscheider (eds.). Chicago, IL: University of Chicago Press.

——. (1990). *Drudgery Divine: On the Comparison of Early Christianities and the Religions of Late Antiquity.* Chicago, IL: University of Chicago Press.

——. (2002a). "Religion Up and Down, Out and In: The Relationship of Text to Artifact," in B. M Gitlin (ed.), *Sacred Time, Sacred Space: Archaeology and the Religion of Israel*, 3–10. Winona Lake, WI: Eisenbrauns.

——. (2002b). "Great Scott! Thought and Action One More Time," in P. Mirecki and M. Meyer (eds.), *Magic and Ritual in the Ancient World*, 73–91. Religions in the Graeco-Roman World, 141. London: E. J. Brill.

——. (2003). "Here, There, and Anywhere," in S. Noegel, J. Walker, and B. Weeler (eds.), *Prayer, Magic, and the Stars in the Ancient and Late Antique World*, 21–36. Magic in History 8. University Park, PA: Pennsylvania State University Press.

——. (2004a). "When the Chips are Down." In *Relating Religion: Essays in the Study of Religion*, 1–60. Chicago, IL: University of Chicago Press.

——. (2004b). "Acknowledgements: Morphology and History in Mircea Eliade's Patterns in Comparative Religion [1949–1999]," in *Relating Religion: Essays in the Study of Religion*, 80–100. Chicago, IL: University of Chicago Press.

White, David Gordon (2000). "The Scholar as Mythographer: Comparative Indo-European Myth and Postmodern Concerns," in Kimberley Patton and Benjamin Ray (eds.), *A Magic Still Dwells: Comparative Religion in the Postmodern Age*, 47–54. Berkeley, CA: University of California Press.

Chapter 4

Citing Smith

Kurtis R. Schaeffer

Man is a very curious animal, and the more we know of his habits, the more curious does he appear. He may be the most rational of all beasts, but certainly he is the most absurd. Even the saturnine wit of Swift, unaided by a knowledge of savages, fell far short of the reality in his attempt to set human folly in a strong light.
—George Frazer, *Psyche's Task* (1911), as quoted by J. Z. Smith (1969: 377)

How Should We Read Collected Works?

At what point in the life of the writings of significant authors should communities to which this writing matters begin to read their works in a different way? How are authors' works cited, evoked, or deployed once those works begin to form a closed canon? Jonathan Z. Smith has probably had as large a share of readers in religious studies as any academic scholar of religion has had in the last several decades. Typically works that take some sort of direction from Smith, either as a track to follow or depart, reference a portion of his work, focusing mostly on particular passage, sometimes a single article, or in passingly few cases a single volume. This makes a certain sense. As Smith says of his writing style, "I am an essayist, which makes me more elusive and indirect than a writer of monographs. I tend to do my work in explicit relation to others. I tend not to speak my mind, but to speak my mind in relation to another mind" (Smith 1987a: 206). Most authors cite other authors in relationship to a particular topic, and so focus on that topic within the cited author's work. Smith wrote about so many topics from places and time around the world and across millennia throughout his five decades of publishing, and few scholars seem to follow his lead in this. What value would there be in reading across all five of his central volumes (*Maps, Imagining, Place, Drudgery*, and *Relating*, for short), across their forty-seven articles, five prefaces, and all of those notes? And what would be gained adding his essays on higher education, both the thirteen published in *On Teaching Religion* and those that remain uncollected, his encyclopedia entries, or his publications since 2004, when *Relating Religion* was published, to the bibliography of the big five volumes?

For people interested in a particular time or place that Smith touches upon in one or another of his writings, probably not much. His historical and philological work are typically in the foreground of his essays, while methodological statements, arguments on theory, and an explicit sense of scholarly lineages he might call his own, remain in the background (certain counterexamples notwith-standing). Yet if anything in Smith's works might merit a broad reading strategy, it would be his work on the term religion and what reflection upon this term could entail for the study of religion. He continues from the above quote: "I would say that the first question that interests me is: for the purposes of academic dis-course, is it possible to construct a generic theory of religion?" (Smith 1987a: 206).

And so I asked myself "When might it be to one's advantage to read across Smith's corpus?" This question came up as I was reading two recent books in the field of animals and religion, namely Aaron Gross's *The Question of the Animal and Religion* and Donovan Schaefer's *Religious Affects: Animality, Evolution, Power*. Both books use Smith's writing to set up an academic sense of religion that they largely proceed to critique. Both books have a publication date of 2015, though *Religious Affects* quotes *The Question of the Animal and Religion*. *Religious Affects* also happens to quote *The Question of the Animal and Religion* specifically about Smith, so they make a great pair for the present conversation. Both books are thoughtful, pro-vocative, and have helped me to get into a scholarly literature that I have not had much experience in, and for that I am grateful. In what follow's I'll read the rele-vant passages (in possible contradiction with my above statement about reading widely across an author's works, with its implicit suggestion that that is what one *should* do) in both books, asking "How do these authors cite Smith?" In other words, how do they read, refer to, and in effect reconstruct Smith's work in order to write their own contributions to the study of religion and related fields? Along the way I'll offer some possible readings of themes relevant to Gross and Schaefer that can be found across Smith's writings.

Aaron Gross's *The Question of the Animal and Religion*

Aaron Gross's book, *The Question of the Animal and Religion*, sets out to "expose the absent presence of animals in the history of the study of religion and clear a space for their future—inside and outside the academy" (Gross 2015: 7). Gross's book argues that, in the study of religion and in society writ large, "[w]e require a way of speaking about the depth dimension we share with animate life that does not overconfidently think we can simply make animals full present by coming into physical proximity with them" (ibid.). The book does not begin with Smith, though in chapter 3 it does include Smith within a survey of ostensibly influential writers on religion: Durkheim, Cassirer, Eliade, and Smith. Gross argues that Smith's goal was to place the study of religion on the human side of a human-divine binary, but that he failed in this attempt because he did not reckon with the question of the animal and religion (ibid.: 82). He writes, "Perhaps the only way to truly create a study of religion that would be properly distinct from the divine sciences is to open the question of animal participation in the phenomenon of religion" (ibid.: 83).

Probably unfairly, and possibly undermining my own argument here, I'll skip over Gross's thoughtful reading of Smith's 1972 essay, "I am a Parrot (Red)" (in Smith 1978), and linger on the first part of the Smith section of chapter 3 in which he evokes Smith to tell his story of the humanistic study of religion in the twentieth century. Gross cites what is likely the most quoted sentence in Smith's collected works, and does what many writers do with it, moving quickly past the "staggering amount of data" clause, settling on the "no data" clause, and setting out from there to attach the particular problem one is concerned with to this apophatic mantra: No data, no data, no data, "there is no data for religion." Much love and hate has been heaped upon this phrase, though *The Question of the Animal and Religion* refreshingly avoids that dichotomy. The famous quote in Gross's citation begins "while there is a staggering amount of data ... that might be characterized ..." (This reading of the passage also occurs in Gross's 2013 article in the volume *Animals as Religious Subjects*.) The ellipsis slides over three terms: phenomena, human experiences, and expressions. The whole sentence reads "That is to say, while there is a staggering amount of data, of phenomena, of human experiences and expressions that might be characterized in one culture or another, by one criterion or another, as religious—there is no data for religion" (Smith 1982: xi). I don't recall reading an analysis of the first part of the sentence, though given the amount of heated exegesis of the last part in academic writing since its publication in 1982, there might be some merit in returning to it. At any rate, the key word I want to highlight is "experience."

Experience is not a word I normally think of as being part of the glossary of Smithian religious studies. But in working through how Gross and Schaefer's books portray Smith's work, it caught my eye. It caught my eye because a part of Gross's implicit argument, and part of Schaefer's explicit argument, is that Smith's version of religious studies cannot successfully consider the role of experience in religion due to its focus on either language or reason. Gross (2015: 82) cites Waldau and Patton (2006: 12) to argue that a failure to take into account "animal subjectivities" has hampered the Smithian study of religion achieve its goal, a human science distinct from and complete without a divine science, because the human/animal dichotomy is false, and because if we overcame that dichotomy we would actually learn more about human religion, and therefore, I presume he would say, about human experience. I am tempted to say that the ellipsis of the triad phenomena-experience-expression (itself a powerful starting point for theories of both religion and religious studies) serves Gross's argument a bit too well. At the least, if we put 'experience' back in the quote, and consider it to be a serious part of Smith's most famous sentence, the conversation might get more interesting.

To establish some depth for the notion of experience in Smith's corpus, I would look to another of Smith's well-known plays upon words, the move from Eliade's *homo religiosus*, humans as inherently religious, to *homo faber*, humans as, by definition, makers of tools (I think it is possible, that in addition to likely referencing Eliade's essay, "Homo Faber and Homo Religiosus" (Eliade 1974), Smith also alludes to the term as developed by Hannah Arendt, or possibly that he reaches further back in the intellectual history of anthropology, but that a question for another time). I do not think that Smith would have objected to equating tool making and using, or building, as experience, but honestly I've yet to do the work on this so I stand to be corrected. But if we grant this, then *homo faber* becomes useful not just for its critique of Eliadian theory, but for how we might take the term to connect to other concerns Smith treats.

This requires a certain amount of playfulness, but such play could result in some useful insight if taken seriously. In a note to chapter 1 of *Relating Religion*, Smith relates *homo faber* to ritual conceived of as work (2004: 52–53 n. 85). The opening chapter of his most extended writing on ritual, *To Take Place*, character-izes the work of ritual as a form of building. And here is where things may get interesting for readers of Gross and Schaefer's books. In a note to the discussion on ritual as building, Smith asks the reader to "Recall that, in some sense, ani-mals build." And he references a work on animals and building, saying "See the thoughtful work by H. Hediger, 'How Animals Live'" (1987b: 133, n. 70). As with so many references in Smith's work, he does not summarize the content of Hediger's essay (Hediger 1974); whatever one might think of Heini Hediger's mid-century work on zoo biology, one needs to read it oneself to assess how it might relate in a more explicit way to Smith's discussion.

Homo faber does some conceptual heavy lifting from its almost unnoticed place in the final sentence of "The Unknown God," where it intimates a redefinition of human nature as "makers": "By placing it [the Maori text on the god Io] back within its context, the historian of religion may begin to perceive its labors, its strains, its achievements. Such a study may allow us to begin to interpret properly and appreciate *homo religiosus* as being, preeminently, *homo faber*" (Smith 1982: 89) If we take the reference to animals in *To Take Place* with an equal measure of seri-ousness, and synthesize it with the quote from "The Unknown God," it becomes less easy to say, as does *The Question of the Animal and Religion*, that for Smith "the study of religion is, at bottom, the study of the human." Reading these admittedly disparate threads across Smith's essays together, we might say that if ritual is work, and if both humans and animals work, *and* if working is work is part of what makes humans human--all claims which Smith makes--then animals and humans in fact share in a defining feature of being. In this reading of Smith we might be close to actively considering work such as ritual as belonging to the animal. Even such things as dancing in front of waterfalls becomes approacha-ble within the context of Smith's study of religion. Which brings us to Donovan Schaefer's book, *Religious Affects*.

Donovan Schaefer's *Religious Affects*

Religious Affects brings two fields together, the study of animal religion and the study of affect theory. The book defines affect as "the flow of forces through bodies outside of, prior to, or underneath language" (Schaefer 2015: 4). It opens with a retelling of Jane Goodall's famous account of chimpanzees dancing at a waterfall (to be found reprinted in Waldau and Patton 2006: 653). Goodall suggests that the chimpanzees might dance because they feel awe in the presence of the waterfall, and that this feeling may be a cause of religion in both chimpanzees and humans. *Religious Affects* takes the awe in Goodall's account to be an example of affect. As such, awe is a good example of the kind of religious phenomena that cannot be understood through the study of language. If we want to understand the awe of the chimpanzees, we cannot begin with language.

Religious Affects holds Smith to be the developer of a "linguistic template," that is operative in the study of religion today. A key example of this template at work is Stephen Prothero's book, *God is Not One*, in which, Schaefer argues, Prothero "builds on" Smith's linguistic template. There are four Smiths mentioned in *God is Not One*––Ninian, Huston, Joseph, and Wilfred Cantwell––but no J. Z., so it is not clear that Prothero developed his approach on the basis of this Smith's work (Prothero 2010). That aside, the larger issue is to what extent it is useful to think of Smith's work as advancing such a claim. According to Schaefer, "Smith's work lays out the contours of this template for religious studies by focusing on religions as text-like technologies of social control," which gives rise, at least in the context of the study of religion, to a "linguistic fallacy":

> The linguistic fallacy misunderstands religion as merely a byproduct of language, and misses the economies of affect––economies of pleasure, economies of rage and wonder, economies of sensation, of shame and dignity, of joy and sorrow, of community and hatred––that are the animal substance of religion and other forms of power. (Schaefer 2015: 9–10)

The linguistic fallacy entails other restrictions, including reason, rationality, rational actor theory, and cognition more generally. As "the most prominent theorist in the study of religion for the last forty years," Smith appears in the account of *Religious Affects* as the scholar largely responsible for limiting the study of religion to these domains. Affect theory, on Schaefer's account, supplements the linguistic turn, presumably keeping it from becoming a fallacy, by overcoming Smith's theory of religion, which "suggested that we view all religion as a formation of human thought" (ibid.: 10).

It may be that Schaefer captures something of Smith here, though in this last phrase I might replace "religion" with 'scholarship about religion', for that is more often than not what Smith is referring to, what he is interested in:

> I stand squarely in the rationalist tradition. I have an uncompromising faith in reason and intellection. My intellectual ancestors are the Scottish Enlightenment figures. Not surprisingly, I accord religion no privilege. It's ordinary, common-sense, and usually boring. (I often wonder what the study of religion would look like if it weren't a product of Protestant seminaries.) As I said before, there are no data as given. Data are what I choose for my argument. Neither is there a given text; it's all commentary. There is no primordium; it's all application. Everything is elaboration. (Smith 1987a: 206)

This perhaps plays very well into Schaefer's account of Smith. But I think that flattening the term religion out so that it always one-dimensionally refers to both experience and its linguistic referent is to miss something interesting in Smith's work. He is not talking about religion here, but rather the strengths and limits of a particular tradition of thought that he counts himself in, the study of religion. Religion (no quotes) is often far less interesting to Smith than "religion," where the quotes signify that the term refers to a category of scholarship rather than a phenomenon. But this does not mean that religion (no quotes) is absent from Smith's inquires, or absent, in Smith's view, from the world: Recall the three words often left out in the most famous Smithian quote, "while there is a stagger-ing amount of data, of phenomena, of human experiences and expressions that might be ..."

As is the case with Gross's work, a key sticking point in Schaefer's assessment of Smith's portrayal of religion seems to be the place of experience as opposed to thoughts about experience or verbal expressions of experience. On Schaefer's account, Smith privileges language to such an extent that his scope of analysis precludes any substantive reference to experience. As I alluded to above, Smith's work mentions experience in different ways. Given Schaefer's portrayal of Smith's work, and the prominence of that portrayal in the opening section of *Religious Affects*, it may have been interesting to put affect theory, as well as the animal studies, in closer conversation with Smith's work rather than leave Smith's work as the representative of a form of scholarship that either has nothing to say about or is actively against talk of experience. Beyond citing the full quote of the "no data" sentence, there are other places in his work to which one could have, and probably should have, referred in order to argue with him about emotion, expe-rience, reason and by extension debates about animals and religion. The entirety of chapter 2 of *To Take Place*, for instance, treats what Smith identifies in Kantian thought, and to a certain extent in Durkheim and Mauss's attempts to transcend Kant, as "the extraordinary priority granted to the autonomy of the singular mind and experience, whether in the cognitive or the affective mode..." (Smith 1987b: 35). Or one might turn to chapter 3 of *Drudgery Divine*, where Smith addresses the "experience of direct, non-mediated communication" (Smith 1990: 55). The first paragraph of that chapter sets up, through the citation of a Hebrew pun, a discussion of centuries-long debates about language and experience in a wonder-fully ambiguous way. Or one might read "Sacred Persistence" with an eye toward Smith's comments on experience, where he notes that his call for scholarly focus on canon as a human practice "implies that historians of religion will not lose their freedom to study the all but limitless horizon of human religious experi-ence and expression and objects of religious concern, but that they will take as a prime interpretative and comparative task the understanding of the surrender of that freedom by the communities they study and the rediscovery of that freedom through the community's exercise of ingenuity within their self-imposed limits" (Smith 1982: 44).

This assemblage of quotes is not to imply that Smith will find agreement in affect and animal studies. However, that spent his career writing more about language does not necessarily imply dismissive views about experience on his part, or that he did not think through such issues. There is a way to read Smith, here and elsewhere, as suggesting that communication goes all the way down, and that experience (and thus affect) goes all the way up so thoroughly that language-and-experience should be approached as a synthetic whole. A renewed emphasis on the mention of experience in the first half of his most famous sentence, as I suggested above, might be a good starting point for this. A broader read of his work on experience and language might portray him as a more philosophically engaged historian of the history of religion that we see at first glance, one that offers a productive challenge in contemporary discussions.

It is perhaps no wonder that histories and analyses of debates about experience suffuse Smith's works from almost beginning to end, for he writes that such debates animate the contemporary study of religion. For Smith, the study of religion is, in this era, concerned with a "larger question as to whether knowledge and experience, of any sort, are always mediated or whether they can be immediate—a debate I have described elsewhere as being between re-presentation and presence. This question divides the academic study of religion in ways that thoroughly cross-cut old, quasi-political divisions such as the warfare of theology with the history of religions" (Smith 2010: 1156). Given that both the study of animals and religion and affect and religion both hinge on longstanding deliberations about experience and representation (though neither are reducible to this), in may be of value to locate the places in Smith's work where he charts this territory in the history of the study of religion, rather than too quickly reducing his contribution to ahistorical caricature, in which the delimited tool of the trade, "religion," is routinely conflated with the subject of the work, religion (no quotes), which for Smith is perhaps better characterized as that "all but infinite nature of the plenum which confronts man in his religiousness" (Smith 1982: 41).

How Should We read Smith's Collected Works?

When is it good to read Smith as a whole? Should reading for theme and argument across his corpus be a thing that we do, now that the canon is relatively fixed? I tend to think so, and I find myself wishing that *The Question of the Animal and Religion* and *Religious Affects* did so, because these two books eloquently raise issues about which I think Smith's corpus as a whole has relevant and engaging things to say in the context of the contemporary study of religion. I also wonder, reading these two books, if Smith's work might tend to enable in its readers a tendency to produce a caricature of the practice of argument that it is relatively easy to cite and dismiss, rather than invite synthesis and engagement. I like to think that the latter was what he was after in his readership. As he says, "I am an essayist, which makes me more elusive and indirect than a writer of monographs." If he is by his own admission elusive and indirect, how do we engage him. If we take seriously his statement that "I tend not to speak my mind, but to speak my mind in relation to another mind," then we will want to look at his corpus as a whole to explore what other minds he is speaking with. For instance, if we want to take him at his word that his "intellectual ancestors are the Scottish Enlightenment figures," then we might ask who they are and what they thought as we investigate and portray, as part of our own intellectual agendas, Smith's "mind in relation to another mind." Along the lines of the former experiment with connecting disparate passages in Smith's work to form an image of a useable, useful whole, we might look deep into the footnotes of his 1969 work, "The Glory, Jest, and Riddle," where we find an extended bibliography of ... Scottish Enlightenment figures (Smith 1969: 114–115, n. 18). The last mention in this list is John Gregory (1724–1773), who may not be irrelevant to the present issues. For in the book that Smith cites—Gregory's publication of a paper delivered in 1758, *A Comparative View of the State and Faculties of Man, with those of the Animal World*—he states:

> Man has been usually considered as a Being that had no analogy to the rest of the Animal Creation.—The comparative Anatomy of Brute Animals has indeed been cultivated, with some attention—; and has been the source of the most useful discoveries in the Anatomy of the Human Body: But the comparative Animal Oeconomy of Mankind and other Animals, and comparative Views of their States and manner of life, have been little regarded.—The pride of man is alarmed, in this case, with too close a comparison, and the dignity of Philosophy will not easily stoop to receive a lesson from the instinct of Brutes.—But this conduct is very weak and foolish.—Nature is a whole, made up of parts, which tho' distinct, are intimately connected with one another. This connexion is so close, that one Species often runs into another so imperceptibly, that it is difficult to say where the one begins and the other ends. (Gregory 1766: 8–9)

Gregory's argument echoes Gross's assertion, cited earlier, that "[w]e require a way of speaking about the depth dimension we share with animate life that does not overconfidently think we can simply make animals full present by coming into physical proximity with them," therefore highlighting a thread that has run through the study of religion not for three decades, but for three centuries. Through wide reading in Smith's corpus, in other words, those interested in such fields as animal religion or the study of emotions in humans and other animals, and their intersections with the current study of religion, might find an engaging history of discussion and debate about related, if not in some cases identical, issues, a long history in which to place their own contributions.

As he has told his readers, Smith is an essayist first and foremost. He does not foreground his theoretical pronouncements with a topical background; it is the other way around. Smith tends to "show his work" first through micro studies, and then offer clipped suggestions on how one might think about the implications of those studies. The well-known mantra at the beginning of *Imagining Religion* is the exception to the rule, which is perhaps why readers go to those lines again and again without much moving past them. There is much in Smith's work that is challenging to tease out because of his style. To make matters more challenging, there are essays that are relatively difficult to find because they have not been collected, and because we don't have a great bibliography of his work after 2003. Neither Gross nor Schaeffer, for instance, cite Smith's uncollected 1974 essay "Animals and Plants in Myth," where he offers a historical perspective on debates over the distinction between human and animal, which presumably would have something to say to animal studies. More noticeable is the absence in Gross's book of Smith's 1987 article, "The Domestication of Sacrifice" (collected in *Relating Religion*), and its uncollected yet extended discussion section (Smith 1987a). In this article and the ensuing discussion Smith undertakes his most extensive study of animals in relation to sacrifice and domestication, the former a key topic for Gross and the latter a potentially key topic for understanding the history of the study of emotions in animals. If these essays were to be anthologized, perhaps we would more readily read them? Consider them to be a part of a canon that deserves, at some level, a comprehensive strategy of reading? So the question becomes not just "How do we read Smith's corpus as a whole?" but "How will be create that corpus in the years to come?"

Kurtis R. Schaeffer is the Frances Myers Ball Professor in the Department of Religious Studies at the University of Virginia; focusing on the study of the Buddhist traditions of Tibet, his interests center on the literary history of life-writing, poetry, philosophy, and the cultural history of intellectuals.

References

Eliade, Mircea (1974). "Homo Faber and Homo Religiosus," in Joseph Kitagawa (ed.), *The History of Religions: Retrospect and Prospect*, 1–13. New York: Macmillan.

[Gregory, John] (1766). *A Comparative View of the State and Faculties of Man, with those of the Animal World*, 2nd ed. London: J. Dodsley.

Gross, Aaron (2013). "The Study of Religion after the Animal," in Celia Deane-Drummond, Rebecca Artinian-Kaiser, and David L. Clough (eds.), *Animals as Religious Subjects: Transdisciplinary Perspectives*. London: Bloomsbury.

——. (2015). *The Question of the Animal and Religion: Theoretical Stakes, Practical Implications*. New York: Columbia University Press.

Hediger, Heini (1974). "How Animals Live," in Joseph Klaits and Barrie Klaits (eds.), *Animals and Plants in Historical Perspective*, 21–35. New York: Harper & Row.

Prothero, Stephen (2010). *God is Note One: The Eight Rival Religions that Run the World*. San Francisco, CA: HarperCollins.

Schaefer, Donovan (2015). *Religious Affects: Animality, Evolution, and Power*. Durham, NC: Duke University Press. https://doi.org/10.1215/9780822374909

Smith, Jonathan Z. (1969). *The Glory, Jest and Riddle: James George Frazer and the Golden Bough*. Ph.D. dissertation, Yale University.

——. (1978). *Map is Not Territory: Studies in the History of Religions*. Leiden: E. J. Brill.

——. (1982). *Imagining Religion: From Babylon to Jonestown*. Chicago, IL: University of Chicago Press.

——. (1987a). "The Domestication of Sacrifice" and "Discussion," in Robert G. Hamerton-Kelly (ed.), *Violent Origins: Ritual Killing and Cultural Formation*, 191–238. Redwood City, CA: Stanford University Press.

——. (1987b). *To Take Place: Toward Theory in Ritual*. Chicago, IL: University of Chicago Press.

——. (1990). *Drudgery Divine: On the Comparison of Early Christianities and the Religions of Late Antiquity*. Chicago, IL: University of Chicago Press.

——. (2004). *Relating Religion: Essays in the Study of Religion*. Chicago, IL: University of Chicago Press.

——. (2010). "Tillich['s] Remains ..." *Journal of the American Academy of Religion* 78/4: 1139–1170. https://doi.org/10.1093/jaarel/lfq087

——. (2013). *On Teaching Religion*. Christopher I. Lehrich (ed.). New York: Oxford University Press.

Waldau, Paul and Kimberley Patton (eds.) (2006). *A Communion of Subjectivities: Animals in Religion, Science, and Ethics*. New York: Columbia University Press.

Chapter 5

J. Z. Smith on Comparison:
Insights and Appropriations

Oliver Freiberger

In their introduction to a recently published collection of interviews with Jonathan Z. Smith, Willi Braun and Russell T. McCutcheon relate how they discovered Smith's work in graduate school in the late 1980s. Since then, they note, his writings had become "virtually canonical in the field" (Braun and McCutcheon 2018: vii–viii). In Germany, where I was trained, things were—and still are—slightly different. As a student I may have read two or three of Smith's essays, but he was only one of many contemporary North American scholars we studied, quite a number of which seemed not only more accessible but also more relevant to our discussions (Donald Wiebe, Luther Martin, Bruce Lincoln, Rodney Stark, Gary Lease, Benson Saler, and Harvey Whitehouse, to name a few). Equally, if not more, important for our training were contemporary European theorists of that generation whose oeuvres, with some exceptions, still await proper recognition from the broader North American discourse (e.g., Kurt Rudolph, Burkhard Gladigow, Hans G. Kippenberg, Fritz Stolz, Michael Pye, Ulrich Berner, or Hubert Seiwert). To me, Smith's work did not seem to stand out in any particular way and was certainly not more relevant than that of other theorists.

That J. Z. Smith had gained a somewhat special status, at least in North American and wider Anglophone circles, I first realized in the year 2000 at the world congress of the International Association for the History of Religions in Durban, South Africa, when his plenary address was transmitted to the congress from Chicago by video broadcast. Smith, about 30 feet tall, spoke down at us from a gigantic screen in the great ballroom, illustrating, as it were, that he had become a larger-than-life figure in the field. The organizers were proud that the technology, which seemed rather innovative at the time, worked. They had bent over backwards to make it happen for a man who, allegedly, did not attend in person because all flights to South Africa were non-smoking flights. The colleague sitting next to me quipped that Smith's appearance and mannerism resembled that of a prophet in ancient Israel. The second and last time I saw J. Z. Smith in person was ten years later, in 2010, when he delivered the plenary address at the annual meeting of the American Academy of Religion in Atlanta, Georgia. About thirty minutes in, the colleague next to me whispered that she could not stand listening to Smith for more than half an hour, and left.

These two anecdotes reflect two attitudes towards J. Z. Smith that I keep observing. To some, he is a scholarly hero who ought to be revered and even venerated. Each of the learned societies that met in Denver in November 2018—the American Academy of Religion, the Society of Biblical Literature, and the North American Association for the Study of Religion—memorialized him in panel sessions; the *Journal of the American Academy of Religion* recently published seven essays devoted to Smith; and the present volume, which has a similar goal, will likely not be the last effort to honor his legacy. Other scholars, by contrast, do not find his work particularly outstanding and are put off by what they feel is hero worship, or they recognize his reputation largely for pragmatic reasons. I know scholars who find Smith's writings obscure and his style pretentious. For them, his name has become synonymous with convoluted writing that students ought not to emulate (quote: "Don't pull a J. Z. Smith in your essay!"). And I have heard professors say that in order to "spice up" a dissertation theoretically, the student should add some of Smith's articles to the bibliography. How exactly these would support the work was of minor importance, given Smith's preeminent reputation in the field. Even those who do not care much for Smith's work recognize that citing him will look good. It is almost like quoting scripture. Recalling Braun and McCutcheon's observation, it seems that to some, Smith's work is not only "virtually" canonical.

I find such canonization both disrespectful and dangerous. Disrespectful because it precludes a critical discussion of his work's content (although I might reveal a protestant bias here). Dangerous because congealed canonical scholarship can be easily (mis)used to legitimize deviant agendas. I will give examples below. On the other hand, it is almost inevitable that canonization triggers iconoclasm and protest against the new "establishment" among scholars of the next generation. As Braun and McCutcheon rightly observe, young scholars "now question the gains that his work helped the field to achieve" (Braun and McCutcheon 2018: ix), especially his insights about the researcher's constitutive role in identifying religion. For example, the ways in which some scholars speak about an agency of objects display an interesting similarity with the notion of having direct access to "the sacred."[1] Such approaches seem to challenge, implicitly or explicitly, Smith's idea of how religion should be studied and conceptualized.

Academic disciplines might need heroes and villains for self-affirmation, but in order to properly engage with Smith's work we ought to resist all forms of hero worship and, instead, read Smith as critically as we read other scholars. Thus let me start by making a few remarks with which some readers might take issue. First, I am not a fan of Smith's writing style. I find his articles difficult to read, and often unnecessarily so. At times I am unable to suppress the feeling that he is showing off, for example when he claims that he had surveyed 2,500 years of comparative literature (Smith 1982a: 22). Really? Or when he quotes, as he often does, scholars from unrelated fields whose works are rather tangential to his argument. And who, for goodness' sake, gives an essay a title that is entirely in Latin ("Adde Parvum Parvo Magnus Acervus Erit," Smith 1978)? Worse, even translated into English this title needs a robust explanation: "When you add a little to a little, the result will be a great heap." No wonder the essay is rarely quoted. I find this rather annoying, especially because this article is very important for the debate about the comparative method. In it, Smith proposes and discusses four problematic modes of comparison that he identifies in earlier comparative studies: the ethnographic, the encyclopedic, the morphological, and the evolutionary mode. I suggested elsewhere that these modes, slightly adjusted, can serve as useful heuristic tools in the analysis of comparative studies (Freiberger 2016). I suspect that one reason for why they have rarely been utilized as such is the entirely unnecessary Latin title of the article. Some of Smith's fans might try to sell this style as "witty" or "playful rhetoric," but in my view obscurity is not a virtue in scholarship—clarity is. Another issue is that although Smith gives the impression that he is extremely meticulous in his scholarship, a closer look reveals occasional citation errors and mistakes.[2] To be sure, nobody is perfect. I mention this only to remind us that Smith was a human being and that he deserves to be read critically, with all the meticulousness that he rightly demanded from all students of religion. Only thus can we truly appreciate his contributions to scholarship—and identify misleading interpretations of his work.[3]

In the following I wish to discuss what I regard as two misinterpretations of Smith's views about comparison in the study of religion. As far as I can see, few scholars have engaged deeply and critically with his comparative *methodology*—Burton Mack and Hugh Urban are notable exceptions (Mack 1996; Urban 2000)—but many invoke Smith to legitimize their respective approaches when it seems convenient. Here I will discuss (1) the notion that Smith questioned the very possibility of comparison as a method and (2) the assumption that he endorsed homological and rejected analogical comparison.

The Very Possibility of Comparison

J. Z. Smith had fundamental insights—often expressed in highly quotable lines—that are truly important for the comparative study of religion. Aside from some unnecessary loops in his essays, he developed extended arguments that sometimes neither fans nor critics have the patience to follow in all details. One example is his article "In Comparison a Magic Dwells" (Smith 1982a), which has become a go-to work for critics of comparison. It is rarely acknowledged that this piece is, first and foremost, a follow-up to the above-mentioned article, "Adde Parvum" (Smith 1978). Smith analyzes three more recent comparative approaches and concludes that these constitute variants of the four comparative modes presented in "Adde Parvum." While seventy-five percent of the article (twelve of sixteen pages) are devoted to this analysis, few readers seem to pay attention to this discussion. Most focus on the roughly three-and-a-half pages on which Smith allegedly formulates a fundamental criticism of comparison and allegedly identifies it as an act of magic (Frazer's homoeopathic magic), not of science. These three-odd pages have earned him the reputation of being a major critic of comparison. They also elevated the essay to a status of extraordinary importance, inspiring the title of a whole volume, *A Magic Still Dwells* (Patton and Ray 2000a), in which it was reprinted as the "prologue." Kimberley Patton and Benjamin Ray, the editors of that volume—which is, by itself, a milestone in the debate about comparison in the study of religion—express a wide-spread view when they say that Smith's article was "the most cogent and eloquent challenge to the very possibility of responsible comparison" (Patton and Ray 2000b: 3) and that it provided an "unequivocal assessment (and rejection) of the possibility of a valid comparative approach" (ibid.: 12).

I feel that this reading does not quite capture the spirit of Smith's article. Rather than claiming that comparison was, on principle, a form of magic, he merely holds that earlier comparative efforts in the study of religion resembled the Frazerian idea of homeopathic magic insofar as they were associative "recollection[s] of similarity." He states that "*thus far*, comparison appears to be more a matter of memory than a project for inquiry; it is more impressionistic than methodical" (Smith 1982a: 22, my emphasis). At the end of the article Smith concludes:

> Each of the modes of comparison has been found problematic. Each new proposal has been found to be a variant of an older mode. ... We know better now how to evaluate comparisons, but we have gained little over our predecessors in either the method for making comparisons or the reasons for its practice. ... These matters will not be resolved by new or increased data. In many respects, we already have too much. It is a problem to be solved by theories and reasons, of which we have too little. So we are left with the [Wittgensteinian] question: "How am I to apply what the one thing shows me to the case of two things?" The possibility of the study of religion depends on its answer. (Smith 1982a: 35)

Note the urgency in the final sentence, which also concludes the whole essay. If we fail to find a better way of comparing, he says, the study of religion will not be possible. But Smith is not suggesting that we ought to give up the study of religion. Nor is he saying that we cannot or should not compare. His criticism of earlier comparative approaches is analytical and retrospective rather than programmatic and substantial. The problems are real, but they cannot be solved by abandoning comparison. Rather, we must *improve* the comparative method.

For this endeavor J. Z. Smith laid important groundwork himself. First, he pointed out that in the most basic model of comparison—which holds that two things (the comparands) are compared in view of a third thing (the *tertium comparationis*, or "third of comparison")—this third thing deserves particular attention. Comparing an apple and an orange in view of size yields a different result than comparing them in view of taste. In view of size they may be similar, in view of taste they are different. This common aspect in view of which we compare—size, taste—is a theoretical construct, says Smith. "In the case of an academic comparison, the 'with respect to' is most frequently the scholar's interest, be this expressed in a question, a theory, or a model" (Smith 1990: 51). Like picking the comparands, choosing a *tertium comparationis* is therefore a deliberate scholarly act that serves a particular research interest. He notes: "Comparison provides the means by which *we* 're-vision' phenomena as *our* data in order to solve *our* theoretical problems" (ibid.: 52). Again, this is not a critique or an accusation but an analysis. It is how religious studies works. All the technical vocabulary of this highly theorized discipline is metalinguistic and therefore comparative—from the category "pilgrimage" to the category "embodiment," from "life-cycle ritual" to "hybridity." When Smith speaks about solving "our theoretical problems," he refers to questions surrounding these and many other theoretical categories. We compare *cases* of pilgrimage, of embodiment, of life-cycle rituals, of hybridity in order to refine the categories and enrich our theories. That the study of religion is in the business of classification was an insight that Smith discussed various times in his essays on classification and taxonomy (see, e.g., Smith 2000a, 2004). And every classificatory act is, by definition, comparative.

J. Z. Smith also outlined activities that constitute the comparative process: the *description* of the items that will be compared, the *comparison* of the items in view of differences and similarities, the *redescription* of those items on the basis of insights gained from the comparison, and the *rectification* of metalinguistic categories (Smith 2000b). And he conducted his own comparative studies, including cross-cultural ones such as the comparison of the People's Temple in Jonestown with Dionysiac cults of antiquity and an early twentieth-century cargo cult in the South Pacific (Smith 1982b).

All those constructive and productive reflections show that Smith was not a critic of the comparative method. On the contrary, he was convinced that studying religion as an academic enterprise is simply not possible without it. He did criticize the ways in which scholars had compared but only to insist that we need to find better ways. Invoking him as a key critic who fundamentally questioned the possibility of comparison does not seem to do justice to his work.

Homological and Analogical Comparison

As Smith noted too, since Darwin's days biologists have distinguished between homologies and analogies in their comparisons. Homologies are similarities that result from being related and having a common ancestor, while analogies are similarities that are caused by environmental circumstances. For example, unlike sharks, dolphins and whales are mammals and have horizontal tail fins. This similarity is a homology. At the same time, both dolphins and sharks have a streamlined body shape, flippers, and fins, all of which allow them to swim faster when they hunt prey. Since dolphins and sharks are not related, these common body traits evolved independently. That is an analogy. While in biology the value of both homological and analogical comparisons seems self-evident, in the study of religion the question is rather controversial. Should we only compare items that are related to each other? Or may we also compare items that are located in entirely different contexts, thereby grouping them under a category that we create? While some recent works champion both activities,[4] other scholars— many of whom engaged in postcolonialist critiques—express deep skepticism toward analogical comparison. They fear that the categories of Western scholarship are being imposed on non-Western cultures and will inevitably distort them. Instead, they suggest, we ought to restrict our comparisons to homological—or, as they prefer to call it, genealogical—inquiry, tracing terms and concepts within (and also beyond) local contexts. Important for them is that the compared items are related, and it is this relation that they analyze.[5]

A recent manifesto of the latter approach is Aaron Hughes's book *Comparison: A Critical Primer* (Hughes 2017). In it, Hughes repeatedly asserts that he is indebted to J. Z. Smith, a sentiment that he also expresses as the editor of a collection of essays in Smith's honor in the *Journal of the American Academy of Religion* and in his introduction to this collection (Hughes 2019). Despite his apparent familiarity with Smith's work, he endorses the problematic narrative discussed above, citing Smith's "In Comparison a Magic Dwells" as evidence for his claim that some scholars "doubt the utility" of comparison: "[C]omparison in our chosen field has been used for a host of apologetic and often highly ideological ends. So much so that many now doubt its utility (e.g., Smith 1982a; Patton and Ray 2000b: 1–4)" (Hughes 2017: 10).[6] As noted above, while Smith criticizes various *forms* of comparative research, he does not question comparison as such. On the contrary, for Smith it is precisely its *utility* that makes comparison essential for the survival of the study of religion.

Smith's alleged doubts about the utility of comparison are not mentioned in Hughes's more recent praise of his comparative approach: "Smith's comparison is a 'higher' type of comparison, one attentive to small details, the complexity of social formation, and the nuances of philology. ... As someone who works on the intersection of Islam and Judaism, I have benefitted immensely from Smith's endorsement of this high-level comparison" (Hughes 2019: 20). Considering this praise of Smith's "high-level" comparison (Hughes's term, not Smith's, if I am not mistaken), it might surprise some readers that at the outset of his book, Hughes programmatically dismisses analogical, cross-cultural comparison altogether:

> If comparison is to be an effective method it must be historical and not phenomenological, local and not global. By this, I mean that while cross-cultural comparisons may appear eye-catching or useful ('*x* in Hinduism,' for example, 'is like *y* in Christianity'), such results are at best idiosyncratic, that is, contingent on the particular needs of the comparativist, and rarely if ever verifiable. (Hughes 2017: 12; emphasis in the original)

What he means by "verifiable" here is quite unclear, especially when we follow Smith's observation that *every* comparative act—no matter if it is historical, phenomenological, local, or global—has a specific purpose that is determined by the comparativist. To repeat Smith's quote: "Comparison provides the means by which *we* 're-vision' phenomena as *our* data in order to solve *our* theoretical problems" (Smith 1990: 52). Interestingly, but by now not unexpectedly, Hughes quotes and endorses this very line from Smith elsewhere in the book (Hughes 2017: 46). Unfortunately, he does not seem to apply its insight to his own approach. Let me return to his programmatic statement, which continues as follows:

> A much more useful type of comparison is one that emerges from those places where contiguous or overlapping social groups speak the same literal language and think with the same metaphorical vocabulary. (Hughes 2017: 12)

In other words, for Hughes all comparison in the study of religion ought to be homological (or genealogical)—only comparands that are contextually related can be meaningfully compared. By contrast, analogical, cross-cultural comparison is idiosyncratic, misleading, and of little use.[7]

Elsewhere Hughes expresses this same view in a way that seems to leave no room for ambiguity: "For me, comparison cannot be cross-cultural, comparing texts or phenomena from different times and places" (Hughes 2018b: 72).[8] It is worth asking if this approach in fact undermines the academic mission of religious studies, a discipline whose entire theoretical and metalinguistic vocabulary is based on analogical comparison. One may argue that if we give that up, the discipline will mutate into fragmented area studies of myriad locations, each with its "same literal language" (Hughes). Restricting our research in this way seems not only unnecessary but also renders theorizing about religion impossible. And I dare to say that J. Z. Smith would not have endorsed it. Note what he wrote in 2000:

> Many students of religion, with their exaggerated ethos of localism and suspicion of generalization, tend to treat their subject in an Adamic fashion as if they were naming entities, often exacerbated by their insistence on employing native terminology which emphasizes the absolute particularity of the data in question rather than deploying a translation language which already suggests that the data are part of a larger, encompassing category.... Such approaches give every appearance of rejecting explicit taxonomic enterprises, although the use of geographical or linguistic nomenclatures, the deployment of categories such as 'living religions,' 'monotheism' or 'mysticism' suggest the presence of implicit taxonomies. (Smith 2000a: 36).

I doubt that Smith would have shared Hughes's optimism that by restricting ourselves to comparing genealogically and only within local contexts we could somehow escape the epistemological challenge that Smith identified, namely that every comparative act, no matter how locally restricted, is governed by the comparativist's interest and shaped by his or her theorization of the *tertium comparationis*. Smith writes:

> In the case of the study of religion, as in any disciplined inquiry, comparison, in its strongest form, brings differences together within the space of the scholar's mind for the scholar's own intellectual reasons. It is the scholar who makes their cohabitation—their "sameness"—possible, not "natural" affinities or processes of history. Taken in this sense, "genealogy" disguises and obscures the scholar's interests and activities allowing the illusion of passive observation. (Smith 1990: 51)

As Smith notes, even when we study homologies or genealogies in a local context, the moment we compare them we place them in the same category and have thus identified an analogy. "Similarity and difference are not a given. They are the result of mental operations. In this sense, *all comparisons are properly analogical*" (Smith 1990: 51; emphasis in the original). In the final analysis, there is merely a gradual, not a qualitative difference between contextual, genealogical comparison and cross-cultural, analogical comparison.

In seems unlikely that restricting our comparisons to the exploration of similarities in local contexts will change the fact, noted by Smith, that we look through *our* lenses and try to "solve *our* problems." Put more broadly, one of those problems scholars of religion face is that we are confronted with a countless number of phenomena—around the globe, past and present—that we identify as religious and are eager to study. I would claim that analyzing and classifying those phenomena is one primary purpose of religious studies. The academic discourse of this discipline constantly discusses, evaluates and re-adjusts the metalinguistic, analogical categories by means of which we do this work and without which the discipline would not exist. In this discourse we certainly need homological and genealogical studies, but analogical comparison seems even more essential because it enables us to theorize about religion more generally.

Conclusion

As noted above, there are aspects of Jonathan Z. Smith's work that I cannot agree with or find annoying and others that I consider insightful and important for our discipline. Remembering him as a scholar cannot mean that we treat his work as sacred or canonical and merely quote memorable lines whenever we need a motto for a chapter. Here I fully agree with Hughes, when he refers to "what I call the trope of 'Jonathan Z. Smith' that is invoked frequently and for all kinds of purposes in the academic study of religion, often in ways that are contradictory" (Hughes 2019: 21). And, I might add, we ought not to invoke his work for agendas that are not in line with his own approach. The best way to honor the legacy of this important thinker is to engage with his arguments, to criticize him for his shortcomings, to adopt relevant insights, and to develop them further. J. Z. Smith left us important reflections about the problems of comparison and about its fundamental functions for the study of religion. It is up to us to develop and refine a methodology for responsible and productive comparisons.[9]

Oliver Freiberger is Professor of Asian Studies and Religious Studies at the University of Texas at Austin. Aside from his work on early Buddhism and asceticism, he studies the methodology of comparison in the study of religion.

Notes

1   For a revealing survey of approaches that view objects as agents, here primarily in anthropology and archeology, see Jones and Boivin (2010). At a religious studies conference in 2017, a young anthropologist of religion who sought to explore "the expressions of 'other-than-human-persons' (location, nature, geography, ecology, etc.) as active agents," reported that during his fieldwork in Japan a particular cave—a local site of worship—spoke directly to him. When asked during the Q&A if he meant this metaphorically, he asserted that the cave literally spoke to him and that he arrived at his scholarly conclusions by means of this method. Some might call this a textbook case of a hierophany.

2   To give only one important example, in his chapter on comparison in *Drudgery Divine* Smith says that "like models and metaphors, comparison tells us how things might be conceived, how they might be 'redescribed,' in Max Black's useful term" (Smith 1990: 52). The term "redescription" is indeed crucial to Smith's conceptualization of the comparative process (see Smith 2000b, and below). But on the pages of Black's book to which Smith refers here (Black 1962: 236–238) this term is not discussed or even mentioned—nor in the whole chapter on "Models and Archetypes" that includes the cited pages (ibid.: 219–243).

3   In the discussion after the panel session "Remembering J. Z. Smith" at the AAR meeting 2018, some suggested that Smith's work was self-contradictory and that those contradictions were perfectly acceptable because of his playful approach to scholarship. I do not claim to have a comprehensive grasp of Smith's entire oeuvre, but my impression is that his views about comparison, at least, are fairly coherent.

4   For example, Egil Asprem advocates for applying the term "esotericism" not only to Western but also to non-Western contexts, thereby calling for various forms of comparison, including analogical and cross-cultural ones. Concluding with a striking parallel from evolutionary biology, he notes that studying bats—the only winged mammals—synchronically and diachronically in their evolutionary development (i.e., homologically) seems as important as comparing them (analogically) with birds and flying insects. Only thus can one explore the environmental constraints and selection pressures that might explain the evolutionary development of wings (Asprem 2014: 27–30).

5   Michael Bergunder makes a comprehensive argument for this approach (see Bergunder 2016). See also, in the same spirit, Bergunder (2014) for a discussion of the term "religion."

6   Citing Patton and Ray here might be misleading too. Patton and Ray, in their introduction to *A Magic Still Dwells*, describe a common postmodernist and postcolonialist critique of comparison, but they are firmly opposed to it.

7   In his book Hughes equates analogical comparison with the approach of the classical phenomenology of religion, indulges in phenomenology-bashing that brings back memories of the 1980s and '90s, and takes no notice of substantial comparative studies of recent decades (before 2017), for example monographs by Holdrege, Doniger, McClymond, Manning, Bornet, Shushan, Freidenreich, Weddle, Patton, or Taves, and articles by Asprem, Bynum, Lubin, Pasche Guignard, Rondolino, or Thomas, to name only a few, most of which are written in English and easily accessible to any North American scholar interested in comparison. None of these works are even mentioned in Hughes's book. What is discussed, and highly criticized as a mere continuation of classical phenomenology, is a recent book by Michelle Voss Roberts, a comparative theologian (Hughes 2017: 102–105). Ignoring the disciplinary boundary between religious studies and theology and disrespecting the disciplinary discourse of theology, Hughes criticizes the book for having a theological agenda. Even more confusing, he claims that it exemplified current comparative work in religious studies (not theology), a conclusion that would have been hard to draw after a quick glance at some of the above-listed works. For these and other problems of Hughes's book see also the thoughtful review by Michael Stausberg (2018).

8   This quote is from a response to panelists who discussed an essay of his that he labels "a microcosm of my *Comparison: A Critical Primer*" (Hughes 2018a: 31). Interestingly, later on the very same page he seems to reintroduce ambiguity in his positive comment about Andrew Durdin's engagement with his work. Hughes's example was from the

Eastern Islamic Empire in the eighth and ninth centuries, while Durdin is an expert on ancient Rome. Hughes notes: "What he has done is use my discussion of empire, society, and religion to think about his own material. Sometimes my framework works for him and sometimes it does not. But, reading his response, the point is that we find common ground with which to illumine one another's work. This, for me, is comparison—again, I am not even sure how comfortable I am using this term—done properly (Hughes 2018b: 72). For someone who, earlier on that page, quite comfortably dismissed "comparing texts or phenomena from different times and places," he seems surprisingly at ease with doing exactly that and even praising this analogical(!) comparison between phenomena in the late Umayyad/early Abbasid empire and in ancient Rome as "comparison done properly." Which one is it? a reader may ask.

9   For some suggestions that owe much to J. Z. Smith's work see Freiberger (2019).

References

Asprem, Egil (2014). "Beyond the West: Towards a New Comparativism in the Study of Esotericism," *Correspondences* 2/1: 3–33.

Bergunder, Michael (2014). "What Is Religion? The Unexplained Subject Matter of Religious Studies." *Method and Theory in the Study of Religion* 16: 246–286. https://doi.org/10.1163/15700682-12341320

Bergunder, Michael (2016). "Comparison in the Maelstrom of Historicity: A Postcolonial Perspective on Comparative Religion," in Perry Schmidt- Leukel and Andreas Nehring (eds.), *Interreligious Comparisons in Religious Studies and Theology: Comparison Revisited,* 34–52. London: Bloomsbury.

Black, Max (1962). *Models and Metaphors: Studies in Language and Philosophy.* Ithaca, NY: Cornell University Press.

Braun, Willi and Russell T. McCutcheon (2018). "Introduction," in Willi Braun and Russell T. McCutcheon (eds.), *Reading J. Z. Smith: Interviews and Essays,* vii–xiii. New York: Oxford University Press.

Freiberger, Oliver (2016). "Modes of Comparison: Towards Creating a Methodological Framework for Comparative Studies," in Perry Schmidt-Leukel and Andreas Nehring (eds.), *Interreligious Comparisons in Religious Studies and Theology: Comparison Revisited,* 53–71. London: Bloomsbury.

——. (2019). *Considering Comparison: A Method for Religious Studies.* New York: Oxford University Press.

Hughes, Aaron W. (2017). *Comparison: A Critical Primer.* Sheffield: Equinox.

——. (2018a). "Comparison," in Brad Stoddard (ed.), *Method Today: Redescribing Approaches to the Study of Religion,* 15–35. Sheffield: Equinox.

——. (2018b). "Response," in Brad Stoddard (ed.), *Method Today: Redescribing Approaches to the Study of Religion,* 70–5. Sheffield: Equinox.

——. (2019). "Introduction," "Roundtable on Jonathan Z. Smith: Whence and Whither the Study of Religion?" *Journal of the American Academy of Religion* 87/1: 18–21. https://doi.org/10.1093/jaarel/lfy046

Jones, Andrew M. and Nicole Boivin (2010). "The Malice of Inanimate Objects: Material Agency," in Dan Hicks and Mary Carolyn Beaudry (eds.), *The Oxford Handbook of Material Culture Studies,* 333–351. Oxford: Oxford University Press.

Mack, Burton (1996). "On Redescribing Christian Origins," *Method and Theory in the Study of Religion* 8/3: 247–269. https://doi.org/10.1163/157006896X00350

Patton, Kimberley C., and Benjamin C. Ray (eds.) (2000a). *A Magic Still Dwells: Comparative Religion in the Postmodern Age*. Berkeley, CA: University of California Press.

——. (2000b). "Introduction," in Kimberley C. Patton and Benjamin C. Ray (eds.), *A Magic Still Dwells: Comparative Religion in the Postmodern Age*, 1–19. Berkeley, CA: University of California Press.

Smith, Jonathan Z. (1978). "*Adde Parvum Parvo Magnus Acervus Erit*," in *Map Is Not Territory: Studies in the History of Religions*, 240–264. Chicago, IL: University of Chicago Press.

——. (1982a). "In Comparison a Magic Dwells," in *Imagining Religion: From Babylon to Jonestown*, 19–35. Chicago, IL: University of Chicago Press.

——. (1982b). "The Devil in Mr. Jones," in *Imagining Religion: From Babylon to Jonestown*, 102–120. Chicago, IL: University of Chicago Press.

——. (1990). "On Comparison," in *Drudgery Divine: On the Comparison of Early Christianities and the Religions of Late Antiquity*, 36–53. Chicago, IL: University of Chicago Press.

——. (2000a). "Classification," in Willi Braun and Russell T. McCutcheon (eds.), *Guide to the Study of Religion*, 35–44. London: Cassell.

——. (2000b). "The 'End' of Comparison: Redescription and Rectification," in Kimberley C. Patton and Benjamin C. Ray (eds.), *A Magic Still Dwells: Comparative Religion in the Postmodern Age*, 237–241. Berkeley, CA: University of California Press.

——. (2004). "A Matter of Class: Taxonomies of Religion," in *Relating Religion: Essays in the Study of Religion*, 160–178. Chicago, IL: University of Chicago Press.

Stausberg, Michael (2018). Review of Aaron Hughes, *Comparison: A Critical Primer*," *Numen* 65: 437–440. https://doi.org/10.1163/15685276-12341506

Urban, Hugh B. (2000). "Making a Place to Take a Stand: Jonathan Z. Smith and the Politics and Poetics of Comparison," *Method and Theory in the Study of Religion* 12: 339–378. https://doi.org/10.1163/157006800X00247

Chapter 6

Wrestling with Angels and Heavy Books

Eric D. Mortensen

I will divide my remarks today into three themes. First, I am going to revisit some of the ideas of Smith's with which I find I continually wrestle. Specifically, I will address the notion of magic in the historical and comparative study of religion.

Second, I will touch upon the influence of Smith's writings on my own field-work and research in southeastern Tibet. I can identify with confidence several methodological priorities that I really learned, or at least internalized, from reading and rereading Smith's writings. I must admit, the book *Imagining Religion* is the only book I have ever actually thrown across a room in frustration ... and the reason I did so was because I did not want him to be right. The honest self-reflexive critique that some of Smith's cautionaries have necessitated remain with me and have grown to be valued tools as I engage in folklore fieldwork in the mountains of Gyalthang.

Third, I will briefly bring us back into the classroom, where I do the preponderance of my work. I teach at Guilford College—a small Quaker liberal arts college in Greensboro, North Carolina, and for sixteen years the majority of my life-energy has been dedicated to teaching small classes wherein the works of Smith are our main meal, and where Smith's ideas are requisite for understanding the comparative projects into which my students delve. I'll detail a bit of what I find most valuable about the effects Smith's theoretical entreaties—again, surrounding methodology—have on the larger project of leading students to challenge themselves toward augmented cultural relativism, toward valuing radical taxonomy, and toward questioning modalities and mechanisms of causality in projects of comparison. Many of us know Smith best through his writings, but it is worth noting—indeed worth celebrating—his passions as a classroom teacher and mentor to undergraduate students.

The first one-on-one conversation I had with Jonathan Smith was on a windy street-corner in some city hosting the Annual Meeting of the American Academy of Religion about eighteen or so years ago. Kimberley Patton had invited him to Harvard to speak with a seminar of graduate students a year or so earlier, so I knew what he looked like. That was the seminar in which we eager students tried to push him to articulate why he studied what he studied, and specifically how he identified his own comparative topics, given his own condemnation of comparisons generated by the comparative scholar's tendency to see similarities between phenomena. In his seminal 1982 essay "In Comparison A Magic

Dwells," Smith writes (and I suspect some of you here today have this passage memorized):

> the scholar has not set out to make comparisons. Indeed, he has been most frequently attracted to a particular datum by a sense of its uniqueness. But often, at some point along the way, as if unbidden, as a sort of déjà vu, the scholar remembers that he has seen "it" or "something like it" before ... This experience, this unintended consequence of research, must then be accorded significance and provided with an explanation. In the vast majority of cases in the history of comparison, this subjective experience is projected as an objective connection through some theory of influence, diffusion, borrowing, or the like. It is a process of working from a psychological association to a historical one; it is to assert that similarity and contiguity have causal effect. But this, to revert to the language of Victorian anthropology, is not science but magic ... We are left with a dilemma that can be stated in a stark form: Is comparison an enterprise of magic or science? Thus far, comparison appears to be more a matter of memory than a project for inquiry; it is more impressionistic than methodical. (Smith 1982: 26)

And he concludes the essay:

> We must conclude this exercise in our own academic history in a most unsatisfactory manner. Each of the modes of comparison has been found problematic ... We know better how to evaluate comparisons, but we have gained little over our predecessors in either the method for making comparisons or the reasons for its practice. There is nothing easier than the making of patterns ... We are left with the question, "How am I to apply what the one thing shows me to the case of two things?" The possibility of the study of religion depends on its answer. (Smith 1982: 40–41)

We, the graduate students in the seminar, thought we had him cornered. "Why do you study what you study?" His answer: "Because I think it is interesting." Period.

So, I knew what he looked like, and he was standing with his hair blowing in the city wind, holding his gnarled staff (which I still think he stole from Radagast), repeatedly pressing the crosswalk button to no avail, and muttering something to himself under his breath. I walked up to him and said: "Hi professor Smith." When I got close enough I could tell he was muttering a continual stream of F-bombs. He looked at me, still pressing the crosswalk button, and said "these things stopped working when Kennedy was shot."

In "Trading Places," the intro chapter in Marvin Meyer and Paul Mirecki's brilliant specialist edited volume *Ancient Magic and Ritual Power*, Smith takes on the term and concept of "magic":

> if the purpose of a model in academic discourse—if the heart of its explanatory power—is that it does *not* accord exactly with any cluster of phenomena ('map is not territory'), by what measurement is the incongruency associated with those phenomena labeled "magical" by scholars (rather than, say, "religious") judged to be so great as to require the design and employment of another model? (Smith 1995: 14)

It is in this essay that Smith blessedly addresses the work of Stanley Tambiah, and where Smith dismisses the utility of the term "magic," he writes: "I see little merit in continuing the use of the substantive term 'magic' in second-order, theoretical, academic discourse" (ibid.: 16).

Now, I have not—ever—hurled this particular book across a room. It is a heavy book, although the essay is reprinted in the slightly smaller but even heavier collection of Smith's essays *Relating Religion* (2004). I get his points about the problematic triangulation of magic, science, and religion. However, in his 1998 work "Religion, Religions, Religious" he ends his essay by celebrating the multiplicity of definitions of religion:

> The moral ... is not that religion cannot be defined, but that it can be defined, with greater or lesser success, more than fifty ways ... "Religion" is not a native term; it is a term created by scholars for their intellectual purposes and therefore is theirs to define. It is a second-order, generic concept that plays the same role in establishing a disciplinary horizon that a concept such as "language" plays in linguistics or "culture" plays in anthropology. There can be no disciplined study of religion without such a horizon. (Smith 2004: 193–194)

Could one muster the political will to say the same of magic, per se? I wonder about the degree to which Smith thought of the horizon as a circle, or as just a perspective view, as watching the sunrise. Can one turn around and look at the opposite horizon? Magic is not a native term, it is a product of the colonial imaginary, a term created by scholars and thus theirs to define. Magic is no less exclusion-worthy from the triangulation than science or religion. It is a second-order concept, can be defined more than fifty ways, and, when as scholars we do what we do either because we are privileged to get to do so or maybe because it is a necessity and urgent, we find that magic is interesting.

There are other places I wrestle with Smith's work. Religion, for example, is perhaps not only a human project. Note, for example, Kimberley Patton's *Religion of the Gods* (another heavy and notably unthrowable tome ... not that I would ever ...) where she emphasizes the divine reflexivity of gods sacrificing to themselves—and sacrificing themselves—and argues for an understanding of religion as the purview of gods (Patton 2009). In holding aloft the importance of culturally relativistic and anti-colonialist valuing that the truth claims of different peoples worldwide are equally possibly true, we have also seen a sea-change in the academic opening to the possibilities of non-human animals as religious subjects. In a 2009 AAR paper titled "The Problem: if Subjects, then Themselves Religious," I argued—in conversation with Aaron Gross, Kimberley Patton, and others—that "If we are to attribute subjectivity and its correlative agency to non-human animals, then why are we not, or are we, comfortable attributing to animals such things as religiosity?" Kurtis Schaeffer's paper today about the engagement with Jonathan Z. Smith in Gross and Shaffer's groundbreaking books further illustrates some important queries we can offer to Smith's humanist stance on religion.

We wrestle with this better angel, Jonathan Z. Smith, while doing our own work. We probably all do. All fields of study should be so lucky as to have a healthy critic like Jonathan Z. Smith, and not all do. Kurtis Schaeffer is right about the philological rigor of Smith's vast corpus, and we value these priorities too.

Even today, in our venerable Comparative Studies in Religion Program Unit of the American Academy of Religion, the preponderance of the panels is populated with individual papers which, when taken together as thematic panels, perhaps prove provocative to the inquiring comparativist mind. But the individual papers are only extremely rarely themselves comparative projects. We cannot be paralyzed by Smith's raising of the hurdles on the racetrack of comparison, and many of us have engaged with Smith's work in valuable critical ways, as per Kimberley Patton and Benjamin Ray's inestimable edited volume *A Magic Still Dwells* (2000).[1] Even Jonathan Z. Smith was himself a comparer, after all—just a very careful one.

My own fieldwork takes me into the granite mountains of Gyalthang in southern Khams, in what is today northwestern Yunnan Province of Southwest China. Even though Smith was not a Tibetologist, his wisdom about methodology plays a central role in how I envision and proceed with my analysis of the variant folk stories I collect and analyze about wildman monsters and invisible villages, about casters of poison, and animal divination. My studies of raven augury and invisible villages, for example, both augment the importance of these phenomena beyond their local proportional importance, as per an important point Smith made in "Trading Places," noting the work of Susan Stewart, and elaborated upon by Laurie Patton.

Folklorists (to whom Smith, in his "Epilogue" in *A Magic Still Dwells*, actually gives the thumbs up in terms of genealogical comparative method) and mythographers from Albert Lord to Gregory Nagy to Vladimir Propp have long been aware of the folly of seeking an "original." Smith's objection to the morphological approach in his 1982 essay "In Comparison a Magic Dwells" is based on an assessment that "Morphology allows the arrangement of individual items in a hierarchical series of increased organization and complexity ... Allows the morphologist to compare the individual with the generative 'original element' (the archetype)" (Smith 2000: 28).

In my research on folk stories, comparison of data is grounded on concepts of version, not of relationship with an implied archetype (or spider),[2] or "original" tale or ritual. Rules of difference become vital. Micro-distinctions must prevail. I suppose the best way to put this is that Smith's work has served as a reminder of the necessary care one must take when studying the dynamics of ritual taxonomy, local explanations or lack thereof of performative efficacy, of the processes of meaning-making and of reasons for laughter in the sharing of stories, not just their content. For this, Jonathan Z. Smith will always have my thanks.

Finally, my students in my classes at Guilford College are doing comparative projects. In our *Witches, Ghosts, & Demons* course (aka *Defense Against the Dark Arts*) this semester, for example, student teams created interactive digital entries for a bestiary, and each team (we called them "cults" ... the "cult of the naga," "cult of the dragon," etc.) was required to be "comparative." First, we read Smith (and Tambiah, Doniger, and others). What the students are discovering is that their comparative projects are wickedly difficult. The cults have universally tightened the scope of their comparisons to phenomena—to data—that are causally linked, based on student concerns about falling into the quagmire of Victorian magical methodology. Perhaps influenced by my own biased disagreement with Smith's critique of the "morphological" "mode or style" of comparison, some cults have decided to get more edgy and take some intellectual risks. Overall, they are wrestling with method, but they have not been pinned. They have not been paralyzed. They are being careful, and rigorous. It is awesome. They are awesome.

Smith was famously devoted to teaching undergraduates. I don't avoid graduate students, I just don't have access to them. I still pretend it is a choice, though. Smith was seemingly unconcerned with whether peoples, communities of practice, all over the globe, had and have (Smith's focus was on both ancient and present) truth claims that were indeed true—for he did not pass such judgements, postmodern in attitude as he was. But he did indeed focus on how "true" the scholarship about these communities' truth claims was and is. He went right for the jugular of Eliade on accuracy of data, for example, but his passions seemed to lie on a critique of method, and it is here where I think Smith's legacy will persevere.

I did not know him as well as did many of you in this room, and I'm sorry for your loss. I value the conversations we did have, and now I make my students buy his heavier books.

Eric D. Mortensen is a Professor of Religious Studies at Guilford College. He recently completed a Fulbright U.S. Scholars Program fellowship conducting research on the performances of folk stories in Tibetan communities in China.

Notes

1   Smith's chapter is reprinted in the edited volume, and following the chapters assessing his work, Smith offers a valuable "Epilogue: The 'End' of Comparison: Redescription and Rectification" (2000: 237–242).
2   Here I'm drawing on and adapting Wendy Doniger's metaphor (Doniger 1998).

References

Doniger, Wendy (1998). *The Implied Spider: Politics & Theology in Myth.* New York: Columbia University Press.

Mortensen, Eric D. (2009) "The Problem: If Subjects, Then Themselves Religious?" Paper presentation, American Academy of Religion Annual Conference, Montreal, Quebec, CA, November 22.

Patton, Kimberley C. (2009). *Religion of the Gods.* Oxford: Oxford University Press. https://doi.org/10.1093/acprof:oso/9780195091069.001.0001

Patton, Kimberley C., and Benjamin C. Ray (eds.) (2000). *A Magic Still Dwells: Comparative Religion in the Postmodern Age.* Berkeley, CA: University of California Press.

Smith, Jonathan Z. (1982). *Imagining Religion: From Babylon to Jonestown.* Chicago, IL: University of Chicago Press.

——. (1995). "Trading Places," in Marvin Meyer and Paul Mirecki (eds.), *Ancient Magic and Ritual Power.* Leiden: Brill.

——. (1998). "Religion, Religions, Religions," in Mark C. Taylor (ed.), *Critical Terms for Religious Studies*, 269–284. Chicago, IL: University of Chicago Press

——. (2000). "Epilogue: The 'End' of Comparison: Redescription and Rectification," in Kimberley C. Patton and Benjamin C. Ray (eds.), *A Magic Still Dwells: Comparative Religion in the Postmodern Age*, 237–242. Berkeley, CA: University of California Press.

——. (2004). *Relating Religion: Essays in the Study of Religion*. Chicago, IL: University of Chicago Press.

SOCIETY OF BIBLICAL LITERATURE
WISDOM OF THE AGES PANEL

This section, containing Chapters 7 and 8, is composed of papers presented at the 2018 Society of Biblical Literature Annual Meeting in Denver, Colorado. They were part of a Wisdom of the Ages Section panel entitled "In Memory, Gene M. Tucker (1935–2018) and Jonathan Z. Smith (1938–2017)."

Chapter 7

Introduction: In Memory of Gene M. Tucker (1935–2018) and J. Z. Smith (1938–2017)

Zev Garber

We welcome you to a discussion of the myriad professional issues represented among SBL members. With the hope of establishing recurring sessions, this group will focus on the academic and professional wisdom of SBL's elders and provide opportunities for transferring such wisdom, cultivating mentoring relationships, and engaging the generational gamut in the processes of reflection and preparation. Our hope is that scholars and teachers "wise in years" would join us to discuss the current state of the profession, sharing information and techniques across generations, and mentoring scholars and teachers as they shape their own insights and felt-needs. Previous years embraced the wisdom of honorees Barukh Levine, Lawrence Schiffman, Lester Grabbe, Peter Machinist and a panel discussion on Z. Garber's edited book, *Teaching the Historical Jesus: Issues and Exegesis* (Routledge, 2015).

This year we honored the memory of two former SBL Presidents, Gene M. Tucker (1996) and Jonathan Z. Smith (2008), who died within days of each other. Short presentations by former colleagues and students reviewed the life and scholarship of Tucker and Smith. Ehud Ben Zvi reflected on the personality and biblical scholarship of Tucker; second presenter, former SBL Executive Director Kent Richards and close friend of Tucker was not able to attend. Ron Cameron and Jorunn J. Buckley discussed Smith as an educator, innovator and influencer in the study of comparative religions, focusing on primary influences and lasting priorities.

Capsule C.V.

Jonathan Z. Smith completed his B.A. degree in philosophy at Haverford College (1960), B.D. from Yale Divinity School and Ph.D. in history of religions from Yale University (1969), with a thesis focusing on the anthropological and religious thought of J.G. Frazer entitled "The Glory, Jest and Riddle: James George Frazer and the Golden Bough." He taught at Dartmouth and UC Santa Barbara before his permanent appointment at the University of Chicago Divinity School (assistant professor, 1968; full professor, 1975; appointed Robert O. Anderson Distinguished Service Professorship in Humanities, 1982–2008; served as head of the Humanities Collegiate Division, 1974–1977; and as Dean of the College, 1977–1982). He retired in 2013, and among his last classes that he instructed, "Introduction to Religious Studies," a lasting testimony to his first love, teaching and engaging students to enjoy, understand, and imagine Religion (texts, belief, behavior). Smith's stellar academic career as a foremost historian of religion in his generation was molded by rigorous methodological research and teaching pedagogy. His staunch academic accomplishments, professionalism (teaching and writing), and leadership are rightly acknowledged in distinguished awards and recognition he received, including the Quantrell Award for Excellence in Undergraduate Teaching (1986), membership in the American Academy of Arts and Sciences, past president of the Society of Biblical Literature (2008) and the North American Association for the Study of Religion, and honorary lifetime membership in the International Association for the History of Religions (2013).

Description, comparison, and interpretation of religious texts and sources are the hallmark of Smith's scholarly acumen. Primarily an essayist, his engaging style and innovative approach embrace topics of Christian origin, Hellenistic religions, cultic imagery, and pedagogy. His essay on "Religion, Religions, Religious" in M. C. Taylor, *Critical Terms for Religious Studies* (University of Chicago Press, 1998), typifies his methodology and his interest in desperate religions. Noteworthy collections *Map is not Territory: Studies in the History of Religions*, University of Chicago Press, 1975 (paperback 1993); *Imagining Religion: From Babylon to Jonestown*, University of Chicago Press, 1982 (paperback 1988); *To Take Place: Toward Theory in Ritual*, University of Chicago Press, 1987 (paperback 1992); *Drudgery Divine: On the Comparison of Early Christianities and the Religions of Late Antiquity*, University of Chicago Press, 1990 (paperback 1994); and *Relating Religion: Essays in the Study of Religion* (University of Chicago Press, 2004).

The Z Spot

Language is a reciprocal tool: it reveals and, at the same time, it is revealing. That is, not only do we use language to explain the things that define our world, but, by the same token, the way we use language also necessarily discloses how we explain and define ourselves within that world. In general, everyone can instinctively grasp how a given word or phrase is used to demarcate, even create that small bit of universe which it encompasses in linguistic terms. But the subtle aspects of how this same word or phrase might disclose a part of our own identities is less obvious and is less consciously considered. *Weltanschaung* (worldview) is understood by scholars to mean wo/man's cultural and intellectual world, not the world of nature. Smith innovates that it is the inner relationships of the "elements," their system, their interior logic and coherence that validates 'worldview' not conformity to nature (*Imagining Religion* [1982: 26]). On the prominence and preeminence of Jonathan Z. Smith, *yēš wā-yēš* (there is a lot to go around). Kudo/s abound from University of Chicago colleagues, Margaret Mitchell and Wendy Doninger: indomitable intellectual, mentor, teacher; challenging, inspiring, witty, brilliantly erudite, and utterly devoted to a life of learning and teaching. Neo-Kantian thinkers, such as Ernest Cassirer and Émile Durkheim, and James George Frazer left their mark on Smith's approach to and study of religion. But it is his innovative paradigms and theoretical formulations that instrumentally affect contemporary study of comparative religion (as identified by Doninger). In sum, Smith's public life and private self are enshrined in his teaching rhetoric: Religion is a mythic statement on man by man and how he sees the environment in which he lives, functions, and dies. All else is commentary and *boubkis*, including, *kudos.* Etymologically speaking, the final "s" in "kudos" is voiceless, which is hardly observed in spoken English, which pronounces it as a voiced "z." And in more formal contexts, both *kudo* and *kudos* are seen as incorrect. *A zei geht!*

There was no funeral or memorial services to honor the life and superb achievements of Jonathan Z. Smith. Why so? Jonathan so insisted, his widow, Elaine B. Smith, shared with me after the Denver conference. Touched by the ubiquitous Z (Zittell [Yiddish] mother's name) in Jonathan Z. Smith's name, I introduced the section honoring him as a *yahrzeit* which triggered personal and religious meaning for Elaine and daughter, Siobhan, who were present at the session. From *yenner welt* Jonathan beamed *chutzpah* and reluctantly approved, he had no choice. A scholars' scholar, publicly appearing iconoclast in academics and personal religion but a caring and supportive husband, father, and grandfather. At the celestial Seder table, I envision Jonathan Z. Smith in the role of the Wise Son who excludes himself from communal responsibility, "What mean the testimonies, and the statutes, and the ordinances which the Lord our God has commanded *you* (not him)?" (Deut. 6:20). Yet ancient versions of the Passover Haggadah state "... which our God has commanded *us*" which is the reading of the Septuagint text. More likely, the Wise Son's dictum directly opposes the Wicked Son's, "What is this service to you (not to him)?" *Tsedek* (righteousness, justice) judges thusly; and Jonathan Z. Smith, a scholar of integrity is honored accordingly. May his memory be for a blessing; and his teaching be an inspiration. The *pintele "Z"* requests so.

Zev Garber is Emeritus Professor and Chair of Jewish Studies and Philosophy at Los Angeles Valley College. He has presented and/or written hundreds of academic articles and reviews and has authored and/or edited 14 academic books.

Chapter 8

A Matter of Interest: In Memory of Jonathan Z. Smith

Ron Cameron

> I am a human being;
> nothing human is alien to me.
> —Terence, *The Self-Tormentor* 77

Jonathan Z. Smith introduces a remarkable, and largely neglected essay concerned with the "discovery" of the Americas, the invention of the category of "race," and western imaginations of difference—of the "other"—by citing an article by Benjamin Franklin that was published in a London newspaper, when Franklin was resident in England, on August 29, 1771. Having heard some report of Captain Cook's first Pacific voyage aboard the HMS *Endeavour* (in 1768–71) about "a brave and generous race, who are destitute"—the Maori of New Zealand—Franklin published a "Plan for Benefiting Distant Unprovided Countries," proposing a subscription to enable "a voyage intended to communicate *in general* those benefits which we enjoy, to countries destitute of them in the remote parts of the globe ... Britain is said to have produced originally nothing but *sloes*," Franklin wrote, but it has:

> become a wealthy and a mighty nation, abounding in all good things. Does not some *duty* hence arise from us towards other countries, still remaining in our former state? Britain is now the first maritime power in the world ... The inhabitants of those [other] countries, our *fellow men*, have canoes only ... little astronomy, and no knowledge of the compass to guide them; they cannot therefore come to us, or obtain any of our advantages. From these circumstances, does not some duty seem to arise from us to them? Does not Providence, by these distinguishing favours, seem to call on us, to do something ourselves for the common interest of humanity? ... A voyage is now proposed, to visit a distant people on the other side of the globe ... to do them good, and make them, as far as in our power lies, to live as comfortably as ourselves ... We may therefore hope, in this undertaking, to be of some service to our country as well as to those poor people, who, however distant from us, are in truth related to us, and whose interests do, in some degree, concern every one who can say, *Homo sum*, &c.[1]

Observing that "there is much of interest here," Smith says that "what caught my eye in the *Proposal* was ... a small detail in the course of Franklin's argument for charity." He wrote that these people, however "distant ... are in truth related to us, and whose interests do, in some degree, concern every one who can say, *Homo sum*, &c."[2] "I am a human, etc.," is "a remarkably abbreviated tag even by eighteenth century standards," Smith notes. The full quotation, "I am a human being; nothing human is alien to me" (*homo sum; humani nil a me alienum puto*), is a line from Terence's *The Self-Tormentor*, composed ca. 163 BCE, which in context was meant as "a defense of gossip" or meddling in the affairs of others, but that was taken as "a sort of Roman version of the 'Golden Rule'" and came to serve as "a motto of Enlightenment cosmopolitanism."[3] Tracing moments in the reception history of the Terentian tag from its possible precursor in Menander (frg. 475), through Cicero (*Off.* 1.9.30) and Seneca (*Ep.* 95.53), and on to Vico, Dumarsais, Voltaire, and Henry Home, Lord Kames, and offering a selection of other translations[4] and paraphrases to clarify the various understandings of the sentence—for example, "One ought to be interested in the least detail concerning fellow human beings"—Smith writes that "each sentence only becomes problematic and, therefore, interesting, if the terms 'human' and 'fellow human' are themselves problematic; if other human beings are not merely different, but in some fundamental way 'alien' though nonetheless 'human.' It will be the burden" of his essay, he continues, "to attempt to isolate the occasion at which this sense of the problematic first emerged and to isolate its first strong theoretical formulation. It is at this moment that the human sciences become intellectually urgent."[5]

Similarly, Smith opens his essay, "A Matter of Class," by appealing to "the redoubtable" Sherlock Holmes, "perhaps the earliest self-conscious methodologist," noting that what "catches my eye"[6] appears to be Holmes's first publication, "Upon the Distinction between the Ashes of the Various Tobaccos"—clearly a matter of interest to Smith. Illustrative of the science of deduction, as described in *The Sign of the Four*, Holmes writes:

> In it I enumerate a hundred and forty forms of cigar, cigarette, and pipe tobacco, with coloured plates illustrating the difference in the ash. It is a point which is continually turning up in criminal trials, and which is sometimes of supreme importance as a clue. If you can say definitely, for example, that some murder had been done by a man who was smoking an Indian lunkah, it obviously narrows your field of search. To the trained eye there is as much difference between the black ash of a Trichinopoly and the white fluff of bird's-eye as there is between a cabbage and a potato.[7]

While the knowledge required of the reader to distinguish between the names of cheroots and types of tobacco is "not uninteresting in itself," Smith says that "what is of interest to me ... is Holmes's enterprise. He uses taxonomy to 'narrow your field,' to arrive at a class of possible offenders, not the individual perpetrator." Taking his clue from Holmes's lead, Smith uses this essay to reflect on "the taxonomic enterprise as it applies to that form of scientific detection known as the academic study of religion,"[8] using his own experience as general editor of *The HarperCollins Dictionary of Religion*.[9] Taking up F. Max Müller's challenge to the study of religion, that "All real science rests on classification, and only in case we cannot succeed in classifying the various dialects of faith, shall we have to confess that a science of religion is really an impossibility," Smith concludes: "we have not yet met his challenge."[10]

And in his reading of the various, early reports of the "White Night" in Jonestown, Guyana, on November 18, 1978, Smith says "my eye was caught by one detail. Not only 914 human deaths, but also all the animals ... The destruction was intended to be total: men, women, children, animals, fish, and water supply—and this destruction alongside a deliberate presentation of utopian harmony—bodies lying together, 'arms around each other,' uniting the sexes, age groups, and races."[11] Arguing that "*the academic study of religion is a child of the Enlightenment*," Smith writes that it is "the mood, the exemplary Enlightenment attitude toward religion that concerns me ... At no little cost, religion was brought within the realm of common sense, of civil discourse and commerce. Rediscovering the old tag, 'Nothing human is foreign to me,' the Enlightenment impulse was one of tolerance and, as a necessary concomitant, one which refused to leave any human datum, including religion, beyond the pale of understanding, beyond the realm of reason."[12] For Smith, "the *skandalon* of Jonestown requires that we make the effort of understanding." For if we "leave it ununderstandable, then we will have surrendered our rights to the academy"; "if we do not persist in the quest for intelligibility, there can be no human sciences, let alone, any place for the study of religion within them."[13]

Smith's interest in the telling detail springs from his conviction that "there is one aspect of scholarship that has remained constant from the earliest Near Eastern scribes and omen interpreters to contemporary academicians: the thrill of encountering a coincidence."[14] "Historians share an uncommon faith in the revelatory power of a telling detail, a small item that opens up a complex whole and that thereby entails a larger set of intellectual consequences. Given the anecdotal nature of their enterprise," Smith writes, "historians are truly the descendants of Herodotus and thereby play the role of 'anthropologists' in Aristotle's sense of the term: people who delight in telling tales (*logoi*) about other folk (*anthrōpoi*), in a word, gossips" (*Eth. nic.* 1125a5).[15] And so, in a study concerned with "Manna, Mana Everywhere," Smith begins with an anecdote from the remote field of textual criticism: "a tiny piece of straw ... embedded in the coarse paper" of a Byzantine manuscript of the Greek text of Euripides, loosened under the heat of ultraviolet light, was found to be the misplaced punctuation mark mistakenly copied in a more expensive vellum manuscript, proving that the latter was dependent on the former. "What interests me most in this narrative," Smith says, "is the denouement ... 'This tiny piece of evidence is now kept, together with an official report, in a strong-box in the [Biblioteca] Laurenziana [in Florence].' As the visual root (*videns/videre*) of the final word, 'evidence,' indicates, the old Herodotean distinction between the probity of 'seeing (for oneself)' over against 'hearing (from an other)' is still in play, augmented by a characteristic positivism that holds such evidence to be self-evident. Hence, the scrupulous preservation of the little relic, the small piece of straw." Of course, Smith wryly observes, "one cannot ... always count on the sheer presence of an object to guarantee its interpretative force. [For] it is not the straw's quiddity, but the character of the argument it entails, that is probative."[16]

In each of these essays, Smith refers to something that caught his eye, that he finds "interesting" or is of "interest" to him, which he uses as a point of entrée and critical leverage for matters of theory and method in the study of religion. Indeed, Smith persistently refers to such matters of interest in his writings,[17] explicitly acknowledging his "interest" in:

- agrostology, or grass breeding[18]
- anthropology[19]
- application[20]
- classification, or taxonomy[21]
- comparison[22]
- processes of complexity[23]
- difference[24]
- discrepancy, incongruity, tension, and the "gap"[25]
- exegetical ingenuity[26]
- generalization[27]
- the Hellenistic period and the religions of Late Antiquity[28]
- Herakles, the Hellenistic cult hero[29]
- history[30]
- Judaism, as exempli gratia for the academic study of religion[31]
- kinship systems[32]
- language[33]
- Late Antique "magical" texts[34]
- method[35]
- myth[36]
- natural history, especially botany[37]
- the question of perfection[38]
- philosophy[39]
- place, "placement," and social locations[40]
- religion, as a generic anthropological category[41]
- ritual, including potlach and the homologous ideological maps in Ezekiel[42]
- the principle of selectivity[43]
- teaching[44]
- theory[45]
- thought.[46]

When discussing the work of others, moreover, Smith regularly refers to what he finds interesting in their scholarship, noting, for example, his particular "interest" in the works of Émile Durkheim,[47] Mircea Eliade,[48] James George Frazer,[49] Immanuel Kant,[50] Claude Lévi-Strauss,[51] Karl Marx,[52] and Marshall Sahlins.[53] What is "interesting" is therefore crucial to Smith—indeed, he says, "it is, perhaps, the most solemn and powerful word I can utter"[54]—inasmuch as the term signifies "matters of 'interest,' queries as to what is 'at stake'"[55] in our various scholarly labors, whether they be concerned with "the central problems for the student of religion,"[56] theory and method,[57] or with questions of explanation and interpretation,[58] negotiating difference,[59] imagining religion,[60] or teaching religious studies to college students.[61] In a lecture concerned with the aims of education, for example, Smith writes:

> Things that are interesting, things that become objects of interest, are things in which one has a stake, things which place one at risk, things for which one is willing to pay some price, things which make a difference. When a book, an idea, an object is found to be interesting in this sense, it is not because it titillates, but rather because it challenges, because it exacts some cost. Ultimately, it is interesting because it challenges the way in which one has construed the world and because, therefore, it may compel one to change ... Such objects of interest require articulation. They call forth speech and discourse ... They provoke argument. As such, they cannot be allowed to stand alone as isolated specimens or to be arranged in superficially pleasing patterns. They must be integrated into a coherent view of the world, or they must challenge previous proposals of coherence and integration. Indeed, things may be most interesting when they are capable of being construed in a variety of ways and when one may tot up the gain or loss of each proposal. Things are *interesting* in the fullest sense of the word when they exemplify, when they signify, when they criticize, when they entail—in short, when they are consequential.[62]

Similarly, in the "Discussion" of his essay on "The Domestication of Sacrifice," at a conference on Ritual Killing and Cultural Formation, Smith says that "the first question that interests me is: for the purposes of academic discourse, is it possible to construct a generic theory of religion?"[63] In response to an observation (from John Lawrence) that Smith's "interest" in ritual is "a scholarly one," which focuses on "the methodology of talking about it, rather than the intrinsic importance of what's talked about," and to the question: "Would you ever wish to be in a position of normatively evaluating a ritual and saying, 'I object to this because I feel that it threatens the continued existence of our species'?" Smith replied:

> I have no interest in the continued existence of our species. I have a deep interest in the continuing existence of the academy. What I'm interested in is the health of academic discourse. What I'm interested in is whether it is in fact possible ... to have academic discourse about religion. That's all I'm asking. As a private citizen, I have some concern for cultural survival, but the only thing that I address as I write and as I work is the health of the academy and the conditions under which responsible discourse can go on in that context. Now, it's not exactly fair to say that the only things I am interested in are things that other people have found interesting.

It is certainly part of what I'm interested in, because I'm an archaeologist, too, but my archaeology is in the academy, not in the field. That really is absolutely true. I am much more interested in the origins of the theory than I am in the origins of a phenomenon—number one, because I think I can get them, and number two, because they have determined us in a way I can find rather than in a way I have to imagine. Obviously, I also say that that which I find interesting is, therefore, interesting, and so I'm not necessarily entirely dependent on what someone else says. I [just] don't see my work as intending to have any particular commentarial function on our times ... What I understand myself to be primarily doing ... is considering how something enters and exits the academic community, which is the only community I have the slightest interest in.[64]

"Biblical studies ought to be of particular interest to students of religion," Smith argues—for the latter is "a generic enterprise" that, necessarily, gives prominence to "questions of theory and method," while the former, by preserving "an unusually thick dossier of the history of its enterprise," provides "an arsenal of test cases, of e.g.s," in his words, "provocative of thought."[65] Taking up Smith's challenge to the academy, I wish to single out for special review three areas of programmatic interest in Smith's scholarly oeuvre.[66] The *first* area of special interest is *theory*. Let me highlight, in particular, the theoretical importance of "translation" for Smith. The White Night of Jonestown, for example, an event that is "a scandal in the original sense of the word," requires that "we make the effort of understanding"; otherwise, Smith writes, "the academy, the enterprise of understanding, the human sciences themselves, become ... impossible in principle since they are fundamentally translation enterprises."[67] Smith focuses on translation as an intellectual operation that necessarily entails difference and discrepancy and, therefore, that constitutes the horizon of both scientific explanation and humanistic interpretation.[68] Translation—"itself the most urgent current intellectual issue within the human sciences"[69]—is "the proposal that the second-order conceptual language appropriate to one domain (the known/the familiar) may translate the second-order conceptual language appropriate to another domain (the unknown/the unfamiliar)."[70] "Central to any proposal of translation are questions as to appropriateness or 'fit,' expressed through the double methodological requirement of comparison and criticism."[71] Smith raises this issue in order to focus on its implications and their consequences. First, "translation, as an affair of language, is a relentlessly social activity, a matter of public meaning rather than one of individual significance."[72] Indeed, "the use of terminology such as 'translation' reminds us that the human sciences have as their preeminent intellectual domain matters of language and of language-like systems and, therefore, study 'eminently social things.'" It follows, necessarily, that "rather than experience preexisting language which then expresses it, we cannot experience the world independently of the conventional, and therefore social, ways in which it is represented."[73] Second, "translation is never fully adequate; there is always discrepancy." Indeed, "the cognitive power of any translation or model," map or redescription "is a result of its difference from the phenomena in question and not from its congruence ... A map which precisely reproduces the territory is useless; a paraphrase," the most common sort of weak translation, "will usually be insufficiently different for purposes of thought."[74] "A theory, a model, a conceptual category, *cannot be simply the data writ large.*"[75]

This problem may be illustrated by Jorge Luis Borges's parable "On Exactitude in Science," which imagines a nation of geographers whose map reproduces exactly the territory it is designed to represent, and which I quote in its entirety:

> ... In that Empire, the Art of Cartography attained such Perfection that the map of a single Province occupied the entirety of a City, and the map of the Empire, the entirety of a Province. In time, those Unconscionable Maps no longer satisfied, and the Cartographers Guilds struck a Map of the Empire whose size was that of the Empire, and which coincided point for point with it. The following Generations, who were not so fond of the Study of Cartography as their Forebears had been, saw that that vast Map was Useless, and not without some Pitilessness was it, that they delivered it up to the Inclemencies of Sun and Winters. In the Deserts of the West, still today, there are Tattered Ruins of that Map, inhabited by Animals and Beggars; in all the Land there is no other Relic of the Disciplines of Geography.[76]

For Borges, Smith writes, "a map without distortion, a map with absolute congruency to its subject matter," is "absolutely useless for second-order intellection ... When map is the territory, it lacks both utility and any cognitive advantage with the result that the discipline which produced it, deprived of its warrants, disappears."[77]

The *second* area of special interest is *method*. The process of comparison is, for Smith, not only "a fundamental characteristic of human intelligence"; comparison "remains *the* method of scholarship ... beyond question."[78] However, though scholars have employed various methods—ethnographic, encyclopedic, morphological, or evolutionary[79]—for making (anthropological) comparisons, when applied to the study of (comparative) religions, comparison has been conceived primarily in terms of similarity and contiguity. "The perception of similarity has been construed as the chief purpose of comparison; contiguity, expressed as historical [borrowing, diffusion,] 'influence' or filiation, has provided the explanation."[80] For the historian of religion, the problem has been to find a way to combine comparative methods with historical disciplines: to discover how to "develop a complex model of tradition and the mechanisms for its transmission" and reinterpretation, and how to "ground comparison and patterns in a historical process" that accounts for the role of continuity and change.[81]

Starting with the observation that every scholar of religion is concerned with "phenomena that are historical in the simple, grammatical sense of the term, that is to say, with events and expressions from the [remote or recent] past, reconceived vividly," Smith concludes that "the scholar of religion is, therefore, concerned with dimensions of memory and remembrance—whether they be the collective labor of society or the work of the individual historian's craft." Elaborating on "the earliest full theory of memory" developed by Aristotle, who introduced terms of difference alongside notions of similarity and contiguity in discussing the relationship of comparison to memory (*Mem.* 451b19–20),[82] Smith argues that "it is the category of the different that marks an advance."[83] This means that comparison, as both a cognitive process and a theoretical discipline, may be described as an intellectual act of invention, "occasioned by surprise." Comparison, "the negotiation of difference to some intellectual end," is "the absolute requirement of responsible thought."[84] This means that "we need to think about the enterprise of comparison under the aspect of difference":[85]

> It is axiomatic that comparison is never a matter of identity. Comparison requires the acceptance of difference as the grounds of its being interesting, and a methodical manipulation of that difference to achieve some stated cognitive end. The questions of comparison are questions of judgment with respect to difference: What differences are to be maintained in the interests of comparative inquiry? What differences can be defensibly relaxed and relativized in light of the intellectual tasks at hand?[86]

As such, comparison "does not necessarily tell us how things 'are,'" but "how they might be 'redescribed'":

> A comparison is a disciplined exaggeration in the service of knowledge. It lifts out and strongly marks certain features within difference as being of possible intellectual significance, expressed in the rhetoric of their being "like" in some stipulated fashion. Comparison provides the means by which *we* "re-vision" phenomena as *our* data in order to solve *our* theoretical problems ... Comparison, in its strongest form, brings differences together within the space of the scholar's mind for the scholar's own intellectual reasons. It is the scholar who makes their cohabitation—their "sameness"—possible, not "natural" affinities or processes of history ... Comparison ... gives the scholar a shifting set of characteristics with which to negotiate the relations between his or her theoretical interests and data stipulated as exemplary ... It is the scholar's intellectual purpose—whether explanatory or interpretative, whether generic or specific—which highlights that principled postulation of similarity which is the ground of the methodical comparison of difference being interesting.[87]

Smith seeks "to situate the comparative enterprise within the overall project of the study of religion, a project entailing definition, classification, comparison, and explanation."[88] Since "the 'end' of comparison cannot be the act of comparison itself," Smith distinguishes "four moments in the comparative enterprise":

> [1] Description is a double process which comprises the historical or anthropological dimensions of the work: First, the requirement that we locate a given example within the rich texture of its social, historical, and cultural environments that invest it with its local significance. The second task of description is that of reception-history, a careful account of how *our* second-order scholarly tradition has intersected with the exemplum. That is to say, we need to describe how the datum has become accepted as significant for the purpose of argument. Only when such a double contextualization is completed does one move on to the description of a second example undertaken in the same double fashion. With at least two exempla in view, we are prepared to undertake their [2] comparison both in terms of aspects and relations held to be significant, and with respect to some category,

question, theory, or model of interest to us [as students of religion]. The aim of such a comparison is the [3] redescription of the exempla (each in light of the other) and a [4] rectification of the academic categories in relation to which they have been imagined.[89]

The *third* area of special interest is *education*. In his pedagogical writing, Smith paraphrases the tradition attributed to Hillel, saying, "If I were asked to define liberal education while standing on one leg, my answer would be that it is *training in argument about interpretations*."[90] Each of these terms is important. *Training* means that education is a learned and learnèd activity, requiring discipline and hard work in order to master the possibilities and the difficult, but solvable problems of critical thought. *Argument* isn't the adolescent "Tastes great ... Less filling" routine of the famous Miller Lite beer commercials—not because, in fact, it doesn't taste great, but because "*it is argument, in particular argument about interpretations, that marks the distinctive mode of speech that characterizes college ... Argument exists for the purpose of clarifying choices*," and "choices are always consequential."[91] "Interpretative decisions must be made," Smith writes, "decisions of judgment which entail real consequences for which one must take responsibility, from which one may not flee by the dodge of disclaiming expertise ... The trained capacity for judgment, for appreciating and criticizing the relative adequacy and insufficiency of any proposal of language and memory," is what liberal learning is all about.[92]

As a proof-text for such an argument, Smith cites a Yiddish vaudeville routine, a tale-type that has many variants within the complex world of Jewish humor, and which goes like this:

Moses came before Pharaoh and said, "Let my people go." Pharaoh, like a good colonial administrator, answered him, "I'd like to, but your people are too dumb to survive off the reservation. But I'll tell you what I'll do. You bring me your wisest man, and I'll question him." So Moses goes out and grabs the first Jew he happens to meet, whose name was Abe ... and brings him before Pharaoh, and the following dialogue ensues. [1] Pharaoh raises his hand; Abe raises his fist. [2] Pharaoh puts up two fingers; Abe puts up one. [3] Pharaoh takes out an egg; Abe takes out an apple. With this, Pharaoh, obviously agitated, cries out, "Stop! I need no more! This is the wisest man I have ever met, wiser than all my sages and magicians. I'm convinced. Your people may go." Abe, being no fool, quickly leaves, but Moses stays and addresses Pharaoh. "I don't understand. What went on?" Pharaoh replies, "Such wisdom I have never seen. [1] I said to him that the world was flat and he said, 'No, it's round.' [2] I said that there were many gods, but he said there was only one. [3] I said to him that the world emerged from an egg, but he said, 'No, it evolved from a seed.'" Moses then goes outside and catches up with Abe. Still puzzled, he asks him, "Abe, what went on in there?" Abe replies, "That son of a bitch Pharaoh. I said to him [that] no matter what he decreed, we'd leave anyway. [1] He said, 'We'll stop you.' I said, 'We'll fight.' [2] He said if we thought we could win we were jackasses. I said, 'Up yours.' [3] Then he saw whom he was dealing with and decided to be friends so ... he showed me his lunch and I showed him mine."[93]

Now, "it is almost a shame to ruin a good story by insisting on drawing a lesson from it," Smith says, "but I shall persevere. That which is 'other,' be it the world, other folk, our own past," is like the activity that takes place, cleverly, in the story. "It sends enigmatic signs ... and our job is to interpret them, to translate them into our language as best we can. This is what both Pharaoh and Abe did, and their respective interpretations, though very different, are each thoroughly satisfying." For us, Smith says:

> the interesting figure ... in the story is Moses (who serves as the paradigm for liberal learning, especially in the human sciences). He has seen the signs, he has heard both interpretations, and now his job is to translate the signs as well as the interpretations, and to decide between the alternative interpretations, to combine or reduce one to the other, or to propose yet a third interpretation of his own. It is, when you stop to think about it, a crazy endeavor, one in which not everything is possible, but one in which there can never ... be [any] certainty. It is an undertaking more closely akin to play than to work ... an undertaking which most closely resembles that which ought to occupy every college classroom.[94]

Such playful acts are what Smith has in mind when, discussing "a fundamental problem in the *study* of religion"—"how to read a religious document"[95]—he writes, "I conceive of the role of the college teacher to be precisely that of insuring that his students have 'wrinkles on their brows,' that they become adept in the 'hermeneutics of suspicion,'"[96] and when, discussing the craft of teaching, he says, "I really want to enable interesting gossip."[97]

Reflecting on the role of courses in religion in the liberal arts curriculum, Smith writes that "to think about an introductory course—any introductory course," including an "Introductory Course in Religion"—"is to think about the nature of liberal education."[98] Because *there is nothing that must be taught*," it follows that "each thing taught is taught not because it is 'there,' but because it connects in some interesting way with something else, because it is an example, an 'e.g.' of something that is fundamental, something that may serve as a precedent for further acts of interpretation and understanding by providing an arsenal of instances, of paradigmatic events and expressions as resources from which to reason, from which to extend the possibility of intelligibility to that which first appears to be novel or strange."[99] Inasmuch as education, in the final analysis, is "argument about interpretations," Smith observes that "interpretation, like translation (the linguistic model on which the humanities [are] finally based), inhabits the playful world of the in-between. It can never be right or wrong, true or mistaken. It can only be more or less persuasive depending on the arguments and their implications." This means that, for Smith, "what we celebrate in college is not rectitude. What we honor, above all else, are playful acts of imagination in the sense stipulated by Wallace Stevens when he wrote, 'Imagination is the power of the mind over the possibilities of things.'"[100] Within the world of the human sciences, "a cognate of the general educational principle, 'no one can be wrong,'" is that "Nothing human is foreign to me." It is this assertion, Smith argues, which is "the ultimate ground of, but also in some sense the pragmatic justification for, the endeavor of humanistic education as discourse with and translation of the 'other,' whether that other be conceived as spatially or temporally different."[101] And so, he concludes, "that old Latin tag from Terence, revived with such force in those Renaissance and Enlightenment academies that gave rise to the study of religion—'Nothing human is foreign to me'—might now be revised: 'Nothing in the human sciences is foreign to me.'"[102]

In one of the very last essays he published, concerned with "matters of theory and method," Smith refers to two consequences that follow from his theoretical commitments:

> The first ... plays the role of a workaday assumption as to "what is the case," leading to an overarching interest in interpreting cultural data in terms of thought and language, and an abiding suspicion of arguments from "experience," as well as a marked disinterest in individualistic formulations of agency, interest, or motivation. The second interest has been an object of persistent engagement in an attempt to frame a more labile model of difference: in intellectual and historical settings, deploying terms such as "gap," "incongruity," or "displacement"; in anthropological constructions, attempting typologies of "difference" or "diverse kinds" in conscious avoidance of the language of the "other" (let alone, the "Other"); in second-order disciplinary discourse, stressing explanation as translation, models as requiring difference from what they model lest they be paraphrases, and comparison as an analogical project across difference. Translated into procedural terms, the question becomes one of working at the possibilities for a responsible integration of morphological and historical studies, with analogical comparison as the privileged site for negotiating these two, often opposed, projects.[103]

This is Smith's response to the urgent question posed by Ludwig Wittgenstein: "'How am I to apply what ... *one* thing shews me to the case of two things?' The possibility of the study of religion depends on its answer."[104]

Ron Cameron is Professor of Religion in the Department of Religion, Wesleyan University, Middletown, Connecticut. He is the author or editor of a number of essays on the Gospel of Thomas and book-length studies of the New Testament and Christian beginnings.

Acknowledgments

Editors' note: In keeping with comments that Smith himself has made concerning his preferred footnoting format not being the social scientific style, which is used throughout this volume (see, e.g., Smith's remarks in *Reading J. Z. Smith: Interviews and Essay*, ed. Willi Braun and Russell T. McCutcheon; New York: Oxford University Press, 2018, 122: "For me, a footnote is least interesting when it authorizes; it is at its best when it exposes, explores, and perhaps, mediates, conflicts of interpretations; for me, the chief goal of scholarship"), this essay honors Smith's memory in part by opting for the Society of Biblical Literature (SBL) format, with full citations in the notes.

Notes

1 Benjamin Franklin and Alexander Dalrymple, "Plan for Benefiting Distant Unprovided Countries," in *The Writings of Benjamin Franklin, Collected and Edited with a Life and Introduction* (10 vols.; ed. Albert Henry Smyth; New York: Macmillan, 1905–1907), 5:340, 341–342, 343 (no. 562), emphasis original. The parts of the proposal written by Franklin and Dalrymple "are easily distinguished" (5:340 n. 1).

2 Jonathan Z. Smith, "Nothing Human is Alien to Me," *Religion* 26 (1996): 297, citing Franklin, "Plan for Benefiting Distant Unprovided Countries," 5:343.

3 Smith, "Nothing Human is Alien to Me," 297, 298.

4 E.g., "The Self-Tormentor (*Heautontimorumenos*)," in *Terence: The Comedies* (ed. and trans. Palmer Bovie; Complete Roman Drama in Translation; Baltimore, MD: The Johns Hopkins University Press, 1992), 84: "I am a man: nothing that is human is foreign to my interests."

5 Smith, "Nothing Human is Alien to Me," 300, adding: "The occasion is the discovery of the Americas; the theoretical formulation is that of race; it is the early theory of the races as separate species of the genus *Homo* that gives rise to the agendum of the emerging human sciences. To bring us to this point we must take the 'long way round,' a detour that is necessarily historical, an element in the complex histories of the western imaginations of difference." For other essays related to these themes, see Smith, "What a Difference a Difference Makes," in *"To See Ourselves as Others See Us": Christians, Jews, "Others" in Late Antiquity* (ed. Jacob Neusner and Ernest S. Frerichs; Scholars Press Studies in the Humanities; Chico, CA: Scholars Press, 1985), 3–48; repr. in *Relating Religion: Essays in the Study of Religion* (Chicago, IL: University of Chicago Press, 2004), 251–302; Smith, "Close Encounters of Diverse Kinds," in *Religion and Cultural Studies* (ed. Susan L. Mizruchi; Princeton, NJ: Princeton University Press, 2001), 3–21; repr. in *Relating Religion*, 303–322; Smith, "Differential Equations: On Constructing the Other," in *Relating Religion*, 230–250; and note the remarks in Smith, "When the Chips are Down," in *Relating Religion*, 25, 28, 37–38 n. 28, 56 n. 95.

6 Jonathan Z. Smith, "A Matter of Class: Taxonomies of Religion," *HTR* 89 (1996): 387; repr. in *Relating Religion*, 160.

7 Arthur Conan Doyle, *The Sign of the Four* (1890; ed. Christopher Roden; The Oxford Sherlock Holmes; Oxford and New York: Oxford University Press, 1993), 6.

8 Smith, "A Matter of Class," 388; repr. in *Relating Religion*, 161.

9 Jonathan Z. Smith, ed., *The HarperCollins Dictionary of Religion* (San Francisco, CA: HarperSanFrancisco, 1995).

10 Smith, "A Matter of Class," 401; repr. in *Relating Religion*, 173, citing F. Max Müller, *Introduction to the Science of Religion: Four Lectures Delivered at the Royal Institution; With Two Essays, On False Analogies and The Philosophy of Mythology* (London: Longmans, Green, 1873), 123. Smith's essay represents the published version of the 1996 William James Lecture at Harvard Divinity School. Commenting on James's classic work, *The Varieties of Religious Experience: A Study in Human Nature* (1902; repr., New York: Penguin, 1982), Smith notes that "at one level James's work coincides with my own interests here. After all, the term 'varieties' is itself a relentlessly taxonomic one"—though taxonomy "is scarcely his interest" ("A Matter of Class," 388–389; cf. 402; repr. in *Relating Religion*, 161–162; cf. 174). Acknowledging that he has "always viewed comparison and classification as inseparable" (Smith, "When the Chips are Down," 20), Smith observes in his 2008 Presidential Address to the Society of Biblical Literature that "the study of religion has been conceived from the outset as one that entails comparison, and

biblical scholars ought not avoid that requirement ... For Müller, the biblical scholar is a practitioner of what he termed the science of religion to the degree she sees her work as comparative. I would argue the same" (Smith, "Religion and Bible," *JBL* 128 [2009]: 19; cf. 21).

11 Jonathan Z. Smith, "The Devil in Mr. Jones," in *Imagining Religion: From Babylon to Jonestown* (CSHJ; Chicago, IL: University of Chicago Press, 1982), 117, 118, citing Charles A. Krause, *Guyana Massacre: The Eyewitness Account* (New York: Berkley, 1978), 132.

12 Smith, "The Devil in Mr. Jones," 104, emphasis original.

13 Ibid., 105, 104, 120, adding: "[The] recognition of the ordinary humanness of the participants in Jonestown's White Night must certainly be the starting point of interpretation. For, 'nothing human is foreign to me'" (111).

14 Jonathan Z. Smith, "The Bare Facts of Ritual," *HR* 20 (1980–1981): 112; repr. in *Imagining Religion*, 53, adding: "The discovery that two events, symbols, thoughts, or texts, while so utterly separated by time and space that they could not 'really' be connected, seem, nevertheless, to be the same or to be speaking directly to one another raises the possibility of a secret interconnection of things that is the scholar's most cherished article of faith. The thought that the patterns and interrelationships that he has patiently and laboriously teased out of his data might, in fact, exist is the claim he makes when his work is completed as well as the claim that appears to be denied by the fact that he has had to labor so long. The scholar lives in the world that the poet Borges has described. And this is why coincidence is, at one and the same time, so exhilarating and so stunning. It is as if, unbidden and unearned by work and interpretation, a connection simply 'chose' to make itself manifest, to display its presence on our conceptual wall with a clear round hand." By invoking the name of Borges as "the mythographer of scholarship," Smith says, he takes his clue from the short story, "Death and the Compass," in which Borges has his police commissioner declare, "Reality may avoid the obligation to be interesting, but ... hypotheses may not" (112, 117; repr. in *Imagining Religion*, 53, 57, citing Jorge Luis Borges, "Death and the Compass," in *Ficciones* [trans. Anthony Kerrigan; New York: Grove Press, 1962], 130). In a subsequent lecture on the aims of education, Smith cites this sentence from Borges and argues: "To translate Borges into a more prosaic terminology, this difference [between reality and hypotheses] is caused by the fact that we do not argue with the world, but with each other. We argue with one another's hypotheses, proposals, and interpretations, with the way each construes the world and its parts ... [For] the world is not given, it is not simply 'there.' We constitute it by acts of interpretation. We constitute it by activities of speech and memory and judgment. It is by an act of human will, through projects of language and history, through words and memory, that we fabricate the world and ourselves" (Smith, "Puzzlement," in *Interpreting the Humanities*, vol. 2 [Princeton, NJ: The Woodrow Wilson National Fellowship Foundation, 1986], 58; repr. in *On Teaching Religion: Essays by Jonathan Z. Smith* [ed. Christopher I. Lehrich; New York: Oxford University Press, 2013], 125; repr. as "Playful Acts of Imagination," *Liberal Education* 73, no. 5 [1987]: 16).

15 Jonathan Z. Smith, "Manna, Mana Everywhere and /◡/◡/◡," in *Radical Interpretation in Religion* (ed. Nancy K. Frankenberry; Cambridge: Cambridge University Press, 2002), 188; repr. in *Relating Religion*, 117, adding: "The label 'historian' is the one I am most comfortable with; [the fact] that the focus of my interest is the history of religious representations and the history of the academic conceptualizations of religion does not alter this basic self-identification." Compare the earlier remarks on the task and stance of the historian in Smith, "The Influence of Symbols upon Social Change: A Place

on Which to Stand," *Worship* 44 (1970): 457–458; repr. in *Map Is Not Territory: Studies in the History of Religions* (SJLA 23; Leiden: Brill, 1978; repr., Chicago, IL: University of Chicago Press, 1993), 129–130; Smith, "Map Is Not Territory," in *Map Is Not Territory*, 289–290, adding: "The work of the professional scholar of religions does not consist primarily of reading our colleagues' works but in reading texts, in questioning, challenging, interpreting and valuing the tales men tell and the tales others have told about them. We are, at the very least, true anthropologists in the original Greek sense of the word— gossips, persons who delight in talking about other men" (298).

16 Smith, "Manna, Mana Everywhere," 188, 189; repr. in *Relating Religion*, 118, citing G. Zuntz, *An Inquiry into the Transmission of the Plays of Euripides* (Cambridge: Cambridge University Press, 1965), 14–15. What Smith provides in this study is a critical examination of "two instances of evidence that suggest different modes of significance and evaluation. The first concerns an episode in biblical narrative; the second is an Oceanic word/concept that has played a leading role in some anthropological theories of religion ... In the biblical case, the evidence's 'being-there' is largely uninteresting; in the anthropological case, the evidence's not 'being-there' has, for some, not diminished in the least the theory's interest ... In the case of the biblical manna narratives, too much scholarly energy has been expended on getting 'behind' the word to some natural phenomenon as if that endeavor guaranteed its being of interest ... In the case of the argumentative use of the Oceanic mana, too much scholarly energy has been expended on getting 'beneath' the word to either some supernatural 'reality' ... or some powerful social 'reality' ... as if such an endeavor guaranteed its being of interest" ("Manna, Mana Everywhere," 189, 190, 211; repr. in *Relating Religion*, 118, 133–134). Note that the citation Smith gives from Zuntz, "the piece of straw is kept in a tiny box in the safe at the Laurentian Library as the decisive piece of evidence" (189 with n. 1; repr. in *Relating Religion*, 118, 134–135 n. 1), is taken from the account given in H. Don Cameron, "The Upside-down Cladogram: Problems in Manuscript Affiliation," in *Biological Metaphor and Cladistic Classification: An Interdisciplinary Perspective* (ed. Henry M. Hoenigswald and Linda F. Wiener; Philadelphia, PA: University of Pennsylvania Press, 1987), 233.

17 In two recently published conversations, Smith mentions three basic matters he finds particularly interesting about religion. "One of the things that's interesting about religion," he says, is that "it has a drive to elaborate itself with respect to everything." Then, in response to the question, "What religious issue most interests you?" Smith replied, "I think the thing I've been interested in for thirty-odd years, though it's taken different forms, comes down to religion and its way of dealing with differences" (Jonathan Z. Smith, "The American Scholars of Religion Video Project: Interview with Jonathan Z. Smith [1999]," in *Reading J. Z. Smith: Interviews and Essay* [ed. Willi Braun and Russell T. McCutcheon; New York: Oxford University Press, 2018], 36, 38–39). And in a seminar on the craft of teaching, Smith states, "To me, the most interesting part of religion is studying data and the reinterpretation of it" (Smith, "The Dean's Craft of Teaching Seminar [2013]," in *Reading J. Z. Smith*, 100, adding: "The updating of tradition, the working of tradition, the absorption of novelty, the saying you're saying the same thing when you're never saying the same thing"—that's "the fakery of tradition and the genius of tradition ... One of the things that keeps religion alive" is "lying about it ... That's the lifeblood of religion ... It changes all the time, and it would die rather than admit it changes" [100, 101]).

18 Smith, "When the Chips are Down," 2; Smith, "The Topography of the Sacred," in *Relating Religion*, 102; Smith, "The Chicago Maroon: Interview with Jonathan Z. Smith

(2008)," in *Reading J. Z. Smith*, 5, 7; and note the remarks in Smith, "Map Is Not Territory," 291–292.

19 Smith, "Differential Equations," 230; Smith, "*Asdiwal: Revue genevoise d'anthropologie et d'histoire des religions*: Interview with Jonathan Z. Smith (2010)," in *Reading J. Z. Smith*, 47; and note the remarks in Smith, "What a Difference a Difference Makes," 17–19; repr. in *Relating Religion*, 260–261, citing Claude Lévi-Strauss, "The Work of the Bureau of American Ethnology and Its Lessons," in *Structural Anthropology* (trans. Monique Layton; 2 vols.; New York: Basic Books, 1963–1976), 2:55: "Anthropology is the science of culture as seen from the outside ... Anthropology, whenever it is practiced by members of the culture it endeavors to study, loses its specific nature [as anthropology] and becomes rather akin to archaeology, history, and philology."

20 Jonathan Z. Smith, "Discussion" of "The Domestication of Sacrifice," in *Violent Origins: Walter Burkert, René Girard, and Jonathan Z. Smith on Ritual Killing and Cultural Formation* (ed. Robert G. Hamerton-Kelly; Stanford: Stanford University Press, 1987), 207, 209; and see the discussion of application in Smith, "A Pearl of Great Price and a Cargo of Yams: A Study in Situational Incongruity," *HR* 16 (1976–1977): 18–19; repr. in *Imagining Religion*, 100–101; Smith, "Map Is Not Territory," 299–300, 304, 307–308; Smith, "Sacred Persistence: Toward a Redescription of Canon," in *Approaches to Ancient Judaism: Theory and Practice* (ed. William Scott Green; BJS 1; Missoula, MT: Scholars Press, 1978), 16–18; repr. in *Imagining Religion*, 42–44; Smith, "No Need to Travel to the Indies: Judaism and the Study of Religion," in *Take Judaism, for Example: Studies toward the Comparison of Religions* (ed. Jacob Neusner; CSHJ; Chicago, IL: University of Chicago Press, 1983), 223–224; Smith, "A Slip in Time Saves Nine: Prestigious Origins Again," in *Chronotypes: The Construction of Time* (ed. John Bender and David E. Wellbery; Stanford: Stanford University Press, 1991), 72; Smith, "When the Chips are Down," 47–48 n. 62; Smith, "Conjectures on Conjunctures and Other Matters: Three Essays," in *Redescribing the Gospel of Mark* (ed. Barry S. Crawford and Merrill P. Miller; SBLECL 22; Atlanta, GA: SBL Press, 2017), 54, 70–72 n. 119.

21 Jonathan Z. Smith, "Fences and Neighbors: Some Contours of Early Judaism," in *Approaches to Ancient Judaism*, vol. 2 (ed. William Scott Green; BJS 9; Chico, CA: Scholars Press, 1980), 1; repr. in *Imagining Religion*, 1; Smith, "Animals and Plants in Myth and Legend," *The New Encyclopaedia Britannica*, 15th ed. (1986), 24:725; Smith, "A Matter of Class," 388–389; repr. in *Relating Religion*, 161–162; Smith, "Classification," in *Guide to the Study of Religion* (ed. Willi Braun and Russell T. McCutcheon; New York: Cassell, 2000), 36, 43; Smith, "The Topography of the Sacred," 102; Smith, "When the Chips are Down," 2, 19–20.

22 Jonathan Z. Smith, "In Comparison a Magic Dwells," in *Imagining Religion*, 20–21, 35; cf. 22–26, 29, 30–32; Smith, *To Take Place: Toward Theory in Ritual* (CSHJ; Chicago, IL: University of Chicago Press, 1987), 13–14; Smith, *Drudgery Divine: On the Comparison of Early Christianities and the Religions of Late Antiquity* (Jordan Lectures in Comparative Religion 14; London: School of Oriental and African Studies, University of London; Chicago, IL: University of Chicago Press, 1990), vii–viii, 47, 50–53, 106–107, 115, 143; Smith, "The 'End' of Comparison: Redescription and Rectification," in *A Magic Still Dwells: Comparative Religion in the Postmodern Age* (ed. Kimberley C. Patton and Benjamin C. Ray; Berkeley and Los Angeles: University of California Press, 2000), 237–239; Smith, "Bible and Religion," *BCSSR* 29, no. 4 (2000): 87; repr. in *Relating Religion*, 197–198; Smith, "*Asdiwal*: Interview," 47; and note the remarks in Smith, "When the Chips are Down," 8–9, 19–25, 29, 31.

23 Smith, "Discussion" of "The Domestication of Sacrifice," 207.

24 Smith, "Fences and Neighbors," 1; repr. in *Imagining Religion*, 1; Smith, "In Comparison a Magic Dwells," 35; Smith, "What a Difference a Difference Makes," 4–9; cf. 13–21, 44–48; repr. in *Relating Religion*, 252–255; cf. 257–262, 274–276; Smith, *To Take Place*, 13–14; Smith, *Drudgery Divine*, 43, 47; Smith, "The American Scholars of Religion Video Project: Interview," 38–39; Smith, "Religion Up and Down, Out and In," in *Sacred Time, Sacred Place: Archaeology and the Religion of Israel* (ed. Barry M. Gittlen; Winona Lake, IN: Eisenbrauns, 2002), 4–5; Smith, "Differential Equations," 241–242; cf. 241–247; Smith, "Conjectures on Conjunctures," 57–58; and note the remarks in Smith, "When the Chips are Down," 25–28.

25 Smith, "Map Is Not Territory," 298–299; cf. 293–294, 296–297, 299–309; Smith, "The Bare Facts of Ritual," 122–123; repr. in *Imagining Religion*, 60–62; Smith, "Introduction," in *Imagining Religion*, xii; Smith, "In Comparison a Magic Dwells," 35; Smith, "The American Scholars of Religion Video Project: Interview," 38–39; Smith, "The Chicago Maroon: Interview," 4; Smith, "Great Scott! Thought and Action One More Time," in *Magic and Ritual in the Ancient World* (ed. Paul Mirecki and Marvin Meyer; Religions in the Graeco-Roman World 141; Leiden: Brill, 2002), 90; Smith, "Conjectures on Conjunctures," 57–58 with n. 101, 60 with n. 105, 69 with n. 118; and note the remarks in Smith, "When the Chips are Down," 16–19, 49 n. 68.

26 Smith, "Sacred Persistence," 14–18; repr. in *Imagining Religion*, 39–43; Smith, "Discussion" of "The Domestication of Sacrifice," 207, 211; and note the remarks in Smith, "When the Chips are Down," 25–28.

27 Jonathan Z. Smith, "A Twice-told Tale: The History of the History of Religions' History," *Numen* 48 (2001): 141–142; repr. in *Relating Religion*, 369; Smith, "When the Chips are Down," 11, 31.

28 Jonathan Z. Smith, preface in *Map Is Not Territory*, xi; Smith, *Drudgery Divine*, vii–viii; cf. 106–107, 143; Smith, "Here, There, and Anywhere," in *Prayer, Magic, and the Stars in the Ancient and Late Antique World* (ed. Scott Noegel, Joel Walker, and Brannon Wheeler; Magic in History Series; University Park, PA: Pennsylvania State University Press, 2003), 30; repr. in *Relating Religion*, 330; and see the discussion in Smith, "Native Cults in the Hellenistic Period," *HR* 11 (1971–1972): 236–239; Smith, "Hellenistic Religions," *The New Encyclopaedia Britannica*, 15th ed. (1986), 18:925–927, 929.

29 Smith, "What a Difference a Difference Makes," 13–14; repr. in *Relating Religion*, 257–258; Smith, "The Markan Site," in *Redescribing the Gospel of Mark*, 110–111 with n. 18, 118–119 with n. 31, 124–125.

30 Smith, "Manna, Mana Everywhere," 188; repr. in *Relating Religion*, 117; Smith, "When the Chips are Down," 2; Smith, "The Chicago Maroon: Interview," 5.

31 Smith, "Sacred Persistence," 11; repr. in *Imagining Religion*, 36; Smith, "Fences and Neighbors," 1, 6; repr. in *Imagining Religion*, 1, 5; Smith, "Introduction," in *Imagining Religion*, xi–xii; Smith, "In Comparison a Magic Dwells," 19–20, 29–35; Smith, "No Need to Travel to the Indies," 215–225; Smith, "Here and Now: Prospects for Graduate Education," in *New Humanities and Academic Disciplines: The Case of Jewish Studies* (ed. Jacob Neusner; Madison: University of Wisconsin Press, 1984), 43–44; repr. in *On Teaching Religion*, 46–47.

32 Smith, "When the Chips are Down," 20.

33 Smith, "A Twice-told Tale," 136; repr. in *Relating Religion*, 366; Smith, "When the Chips are Down," 8; cf. 3–4, 32; and see the discussion of language, representation, and experience in Smith, "Social Formations of Early Christianities: A Response to Ron Cameron and Burton Mack," *MTSR* 8 (1996): 274; Smith, "Bible and Religion," 90–91; repr. in *Relating Religion*, 206–9; Smith, "A Twice-told Tale," 131–132, 136–137, 141–146;

repr. in *Relating Religion*, 362–363, 366, 369–372; Smith, "The Topography of the Sacred," 103; Smith, "Manna, Mana Everywhere," 210; repr. in *Relating Religion*, 133; Smith, "*Asdiwal*: Interview," 54; Smith, "Conjectures on Conjunctures," 57.

34   Jonathan Z. Smith, "Trading Places," in *Ancient Magic and Ritual Power* (ed. Marvin Meyer and Paul Mirecki; Religions in the Graeco-Roman World 129; Leiden: Brill, 1995), 21; repr. in *Relating Religion*, 222; Smith, "Great Scott," 90; and note the remarks in Smith, "The Temple and the Magician," in *God's Christ and His People: Studies in Honour of Nils Alstrup Dahl* (ed. Jacob Jervell and Wayne A. Meeks; Oslo: Universitetsforlaget, 1977), 237–239; repr. in *Map Is Not Territory*, 185–189.

35   Smith, "Fences and Neighbors," 1; repr. in *Imagining Religion*, 1; Smith, *Drudgery Divine*, vii–viii, 51, 53, 99; Smith, "Social Formations of Early Christianities," 271; Smith, "A Matter of Class," 387–389; repr. in *Relating Religion*, 160–162; Smith, "The Necessary Lie: Duplicity in the Disciplines," in *Studying Religion: An Introduction* (ed. Russell T. McCutcheon; London: Equinox, 2007), 76–77.

36   Smith, "The American Scholars of Religion Video Project: Interview," 29; Smith, "When the Chips are Down," 6–7; Smith, "The Chicago Maroon: Interview," 6; Smith, "*Asdiwal*: Interview," 46.

37   Smith, "When the Chips are Down," 1–2, 19; Smith, "*Asdiwal*: Interview," 46.

38   Smith, "Discussion" of "The Domestication of Sacrifice," 224; and note the remarks in Smith, "The Bare Facts of Ritual," 126–127; repr. in *Imagining Religion*, 64.

39   Smith, "Differential Equations," 230; Smith, "The American Scholars of Religion Video Project: Interview," 29; Smith, "When the Chips are Down," 2, 8; Smith, "The Chicago Maroon: Interview," 5–6; Smith, "*Asdiwal*: Interview," 46.

40   Smith, preface in *Map Is Not Territory*, xii; Smith, "Map Is Not Territory," 292–293; Smith, *To Take Place*, xii, 27, 45–46, 86, 103, 110, 112; cf. 24–35; Smith, "Trading Places," 21; repr. in *Relating Religion*, 222; Smith, "Great Scott," 90; Smith, "When the Chips are Down," 49–50 nn. 70–71; and note the remarks in Smith, "The Influence of Symbols upon Social Change," 469; repr. in *Map Is Not Territory*, 141; Smith, "The Wobbling Pivot," *JR* 52 (1972): 148; repr. in *Map Is Not Territory*, 103.

41   Smith, "Introduction," in *Imagining Religion*, xi–xii; Smith, "No Need to Travel to the Indies," 217–218; Smith, "Discussion" of "The Domestication of Sacrifice," 206; Smith, *To Take Place*, xi–xii; Smith, "'Religion' and 'Religious Studies': No Difference at All," *Soundings* 71 (1988): 233–235, 237; repr. in *On Teaching Religion*, 79–80, 82–83; Smith, "Social Formations of Early Christianities," 271; Smith, "A Matter of Class," 392–393; repr. in *Relating Religion*, 165–166; Smith, "Religion, Religions, Religious," in *Critical Terms for Religious Studies* (ed. Mark C. Taylor; Chicago, IL: University of Chicago Press, 1998), 269, 271, 275, 281–282; repr. in *Relating Religion*, 179–180, 182, 186, 193–194; Smith, "The American Scholars of Religion Video Project: Interview," 31–32; Smith, "Classification," 39; Smith, "Bible and Religion," 90–91; repr. in *Relating Religion*, 207; Smith, "A Twice-told Tale," 132, 142; repr. in *Relating Religion*, 363, 369; Smith, "When the Chips are Down," 8; Smith, "*Asdiwal*: Interview," 52; Smith, "Reading Religion: A Life in Learning (2010)," in *Reading J. Z. Smith*, 126, citing Smith, "Connections," *JAAR* 58 (1990): 1; repr. in *On Teaching Religion*, 49.

42   Smith, "Discussion" of "The Domestication of Sacrifice," 206–207, 208–209, 214–215; Smith, "Jerusalem: The City as Place," in *Civitas: Religious Interpretations of the City* (ed. Peter S. Hawkins; Scholars Press Studies in the Humanities; Atlanta, GA: Scholars Press, 1986), 31; cf. 28–33; Smith, *To Take Place*, 62, 66; cf. 47–73, 103, 111.

43   Smith, "Discussion" of "The Domestication of Sacrifice," 209, 210.

44   Smith, "Puzzlement," 57, 59–60; repr. in *On Teaching Religion*, 124, 126–127; repr. as "Playful Acts of Imagination," 15, 16–17; Smith, "'Narratives into Problems': The

College Introductory Course and the Study of Religion," *JAAR* 56 (1988): 734–735, 738; Smith, "The Introductory Course: Less is Better," in *Teaching the Introductory Course in Religious Studies: A Sourcebook* (ed. Mark Juergensmeyer; Scholars Press Studies in the Humanities 15; Atlanta, GA: Scholars Press, 1991), 185, 187; repr. in *On Teaching Religion*, 11, 13; Smith, "The American Scholars of Religion Video Project: Interview," 39–44; Smith, "When the Chips are Down," 12; cf. 9–13, 39–41 n. 33, 42–43 n. 38, 43–44 n. 40; Smith, "The Chicago Maroon: Interview," 26–27; Smith, "The Dean's Craft of Teaching Seminar," 99.

45 Smith, "Fences and Neighbors," 1; repr. in *Imagining Religion*, 1; Smith, "Discussion" of "The Domestication of Sacrifice," 206; Smith, *Drudgery Divine*, vii-viii, 89, 99; Smith, "Social Formations of Early Christianities," 271; Smith, "The 'End' of Comparison," 237; Smith, "Bible and Religion," 90; repr. in *Relating Religion*, 206; Smith, "Religion Up and Down, Out and In," 5, 8, 9.

46 Smith, "A Twice-told Tale," 136–137; repr. in *Relating Religion*, 366; Smith, "Conjectures on Conjunctures," 57, 69; and note the remarks in Smith, "Map Is Not Territory," 297, 301–302, 307–308, 309; Smith, "When the Chips are Down," 17–19, 26, 31–32.

47 Jonathan Z. Smith, "Introducing Durkheim," in *Teaching Durkheim* (ed. Terry F. Godlove, Jr.; AARTRSS; Oxford and New York: Oxford University Press, 2005), 3–4; and see the discussion of Durkheim's work in Smith, *To Take Place*, 35–40, 105–107; Smith, "Manna, Mana Everywhere," 200–212; repr. in *Relating Religion*, 127–134; Smith, "The Topography of the Sacred," 102–111; Smith, "God Save This Honourable Court: Religion and Civic Discourse," in *Relating Religion*, 383, 385–389; Smith, "Conjectures on Conjunctures," 55–57.

48 Jonathan Z. Smith, "Acknowledgments: Morphology and History in Mircea Eliade's *Patterns in Comparative Religion* (1949–1999), Part 2: The Texture of the Work," *HR* 39 (1999–2000): 343; repr. in *Relating Religion*, 90–91; and see the discussion of Eliade's work in Smith, "Birth Upside Down or Right Side Up?" *HR* 9 (1969–1970): 284–285; repr. in *Map Is Not Territory*, 150–151; Smith, "The Wobbling Pivot," 134–149; repr. in *Map Is Not Territory*, 88–103; Smith, "Mythos und Geschichte," in *Alcheringa, oder die beginnende Zeit: Studien zu Mythologie, Schamanismus und Religion* (ed. Hans Peter Duerr; Frankfurt am Main and Paris: Qumran, 1983), 29–31, 35, 40–42; Smith, *To Take Place*, 1–23; Smith, "Acknowledgments: Morphology and History in Mircea Eliade's *Patterns in Comparative Religion* (1949–1999), Part 1: The Work and Its Contexts," *HR* 39 (1999–2000): 315–331; repr. in *Relating Religion*, 61–79; Smith, "Acknowledgments: Morphology and History in Mircea Eliade's *Patterns in Comparative Religion* (1949–1999), Part 2," 332–351; repr. in *Relating Religion*, 80–100; Smith, "When the Chips are Down," 13–17; Smith, "Introduction to the 2005 Edition" of Mircea Eliade, *The Myth of the Eternal Return: Cosmos and History* (1954; trans. Willard R. Trask; Bollingen Series 46; Princeton, NJ: Princeton University Press, 2005), ix-xxi.

49 Jonathan Z. Smith, "When the Bough Breaks," in *Map Is Not Territory*, 239; Smith, *Drudgery Divine*, 92; Smith, "*Asdiwal*: Interview," 48; and see the discussion of Frazer's work in Smith, "*Adde Parvum Parvo Magnus Acervus Erit*," *HR* 11 (1971–1972): 78–80; repr. in *Map Is Not Territory*, 251–253; Smith, "When the Bough Breaks," *HR* 12 (1972–1973): 342–371; repr. in *Map Is Not Territory*, 208–239; Smith, *Drudgery Divine*, 89–93, 103 n. 33; Smith, "When the Chips are Down," 9.

50 Smith, *To Take Place*, 26–28, 31–34, 39; Smith, "When the Chips are Down," 2–4; cf. 5; and see the discussion of Kant and Neo-Kantianism in Smith, "Acknowledgments: Morphology and History in Mircea Eliade's *Patterns in Comparative Religion* (1949–1999), Part 1," 328–330; repr. in *Relating Religion*, 71–73; Smith, "Conjectures on Conjunctures," 50, 55–57 with n. 99, 96 n. 214.

51 Smith, *To Take Place*, 111–112; Smith, "When the Chips are Down," 20; cf. 7, 32; Smith, "Conjectures on Conjunctures," 66, 94 n. 203, 96; and see the discussion of Lévi-Strauss's work in Smith, "The Domestication of Sacrifice," in *Violent Origins*, 192–195, 202; repr. in *Relating Religion*, 146–148, 153; Smith, "Discussion" of "The Domestication of Sacrifice," 224; Smith, *To Take Place*, xii, 42–45, 85–86, 98–99, 107–108, 111–112, 114; Smith, "Manna, Mana Everywhere," 209–211; repr. in *Relating Religion*, 132–134; Smith, "Conjectures on Conjunctures," 25–30, 34–35, 38–40, 46, 61–64, 66–69, 92–98.

52 Smith, "When the Chips are Down," 2–4; and see the discussion of Marx and Marxism in Smith, "In Comparison a Magic Dwells," 25; Smith, "Conjectures on Conjunctures," 55–56 with n. 99, 64–66 with nn. 111–112; cf. 76–82, 85–90, 92.

53 Jonathan Z. Smith, *"Dayyeinu,"* in *Redescribing Christian Origins* (ed. Ron Cameron and Merrill P. Miller; SBLSymS 28; Atlanta, GA: Society of Biblical Literature; Leiden: Brill, 2004), 486 with nn. 9–10; Smith, "Conjectures on Conjunctures," 47, 59, 63 n. 108, 81; and see the discussion of Sahlins's work in Smith, "Re: Corinthians," in *Relating Religion*, 347; repr. in *Redescribing Paul and the Corinthians* (ed. Ron Cameron and Merrill P. Miller; SBLECL 5; Atlanta, GA: Society of Biblical Literature; Leiden: Brill, 2011), 28; Smith, "Conjectures on Conjunctures," 17–54, 55–73; cf. 73–98; Smith, "The Markan Site," 99–101, 120.

54 Smith, "Puzzlement," 58–59; repr. in *On Teaching Religion*, 126; repr. as "Playful Acts of Imagination," 16.

55 Smith, *Drudgery Divine*, vii.

56 Smith, "Fences and Neighbors," 1; repr. in *Imagining Religion*, 1.

57 Smith introduces his 1988 Jordan Lectures in Comparative Religion at the School of Oriental and African Studies, University of London, by appealing to the urgent "task of rethinking the comparative enterprise in modes appropriate to the academy's self-understanding as well as to its perception of the processes and goals of disciplined inquiry," stating: "In what follows, I shall be reflecting on the comparative endeavour by means of a classic and privileged example: the comparison of early Christianities and the religions of Late Antiquity, especially the so-called mystery cults. I have chosen this example for reasons having little to do with its possible intrinsic interest. Rather, I have selected it because there is an unusually thick dossier of the history of the enterprise ... so that one is able to compare the comparisons and undertake archaeological work in the learned literature in such a way as to highlight both theoretical and methodological issues as well as matters of 'interest,' queries as to what is 'at stake,' in the various comparative proposals. I have selected this privileged example as well because, for the almost four centuries of this enterprise here passed in review, the data brought to the comparison, both from early Christianities and from the religions of Late Antiquity, have remained remarkably constant. This is an area of scholarly inquiry, not unlike others within the human sciences, where progress is made not so much by the uncovering of new facts or documents as by looking again with new perspectives on familiar materials. For this reason, matters of methods and models ought to be central. In the pages which follow, 'what interests us here is not so much the connections between phenomena as the connections between problems'" (Smith, *Drudgery Divine*, vii–viii; cf. 99, quoting V. N. Voloshinov, *Marxism and the Philosophy of Language* [trans. Ladislav Matejka and I. R. Titunik; Cambridge, MA: Harvard University Press, 1986], xv).

58 Commenting on "the nineteenth-century distinction between the ideal of explanation, held to be characteristic of the natural sciences, and understanding or interpretation, characteristic of the human sciences," Smith writes: "The ideal of explanation is

occasioned by surprise and seeks to reduce surprise. That is to say, explanation has as its goal the reduction of that which at first appears unknown to an instance of that which is already known. The ideal of interpretation, on the other hand, is to provoke surprise, to offer a new reading, a new understanding of that which was previously known ... The interpretative labors of the human sciences are an exercise in defamiliarization, itself often a double movement of making the familiar strange and the strange familiar. The prime decision one must make is whether or not the interpretation is worth 'seeing'; whether it is of interest in the old sense preserved by banks, that is, whether it is something in which one has a stake, something for which one is prepared to undertake risk. This can only be decided through negotiations with other interpretations, through judgments as to what other interpretations entail" (Jonathan Z. Smith, "Double Play," in *Engaging the Humanities at the University of Chicago* [ed. Philippe Desan; rev. ed.; Chicago, IL: Garamond, 1997], 57–58).

59 Addressing "the theory of the other," and seeking to discern "several senses in which the 'other' can be framed as a theoretical issue," Smith asks: "What difference does difference make? ... How different does difference have to be to constitute 'otherness'? Under what circumstances, and to whom, are such distinctions of interest?" Commenting on "the original sense of 'interest' as continued in legal and economic usage," Smith observes that "difference is rarely something simply to be noted; it is, most often, something in which one has a stake. Above all, it is a political matter ... Difference is seldom a comparison between entities judged to be equivalent. Difference most frequently entails a hierarchy of prestige and the concomitant political ranking of superordinate and subordinate ... The radically 'other' is merely 'other'; the proximate 'other' is problematic, and hence, of supreme interest" (Smith, "What a Difference a Difference Makes," 3, 4, 5; cf. 14–16, 44–48; repr. in *Relating Religion*, 251, 252, 253; cf. 258–259, 274–276). For Smith, therefore, "When we confront difference we do not encounter irrationality or bad faith but rather the very essence of thought. Meaning is made possible by difference" (Smith, "Differential Equations," 246).

60 In the introduction to his second collection of essays, Smith argued: "If we have understood the archeological and textual record correctly, man has had his entire history in which to imagine deities and modes of interaction with them. But man, more precisely western man, has had only the last few centuries in which to imagine religion. It is this act of second order, reflective imagination which must be the central preoccupation of any student of religion ... The student of religion, and most particularly the historian of religion, must be relentlessly self-conscious. Indeed, this self-consciousness constitutes his primary expertise, his foremost object of study. For the self-conscious student of religion, no datum possesses intrinsic interest. It is of value only insofar as it can serve as exempli gratia of some fundamental issue in the [scholarly] imagination of religion. The student of religion must be able to articulate clearly why 'this' rather than 'that' was chosen as an exemplum. His primary skill is concentrated [strategically] in this choice. This effort at articulate choice is all the more difficult, and hence all the more necessary, for the historian of religion who accepts neither the boundaries of canon nor of community in constituting his intellectual domain, in providing his range of exempla. Implicit in this effort at articulate choice are three conditions. First, that the exemplum has been well and fully understood. This requires a mastery of both the relevant primary material and the history and tradition of its interpretation. Second, that the exemplum be displayed in the service of some important theory, some paradigm, some fundamental question, some central element in the academic imagination of religion. Third, that there be some method

for explicitly relating the exemplum to the theory, paradigm, or question and some method for evaluating each in terms of the other" (Smith, "Introduction," in *Imagining Religion*, xi-xii). This programmatic agenda is also cited in Smith, "No Need to Travel to the Indies," 217-218; Smith, "'Religion' and 'Religious Studies,'" 234-235, 237; repr. in *On Teaching Religion*, 80, 82-83; see also Smith, *To Take Place*, xi-xii.

61 Discussing his year-long introductory course, "Religion in Western Civilization," and noting the stake students have in answering what "tradition" or "civilization" is, and how both are contested and constructed by acts of reinterpretation, Smith writes: "the notion of a stake [is] the proper sense in which a matter is 'interesting'" (Smith, "'Narratives into Problems,'" 734; see also Smith, "Scriptures and Histories," *MTSR* 4 [1992]: 98; repr. in *On Teaching Religion*, 29).

62 Smith, "Puzzlement," 59-60; repr. in *On Teaching Religion*, 126-127; repr. as "Playful Acts of Imagination," 16-17, emphasis original.

63 Smith, "Discussion" of "The Domestication of Sacrifice," 206, adding: "Ritual offers a good example and testing ground for the construction of such a theory. In my terms, it's an 'e.g.' Sacrifice then becomes an 'e.g.' of ritual. And in many ways, it's not a very interesting 'e.g.'"; cf. 206-212.

64 Ibid., 221, 222, adding: "There are moments when I am willing to venture, occasionally, an observation about adequacies and inadequacies, when I'm at least prepared to note that here possibilities do not seem to have been culturally developed. But I don't know that I'd draw any deep conclusions from this. 'Normative' is a very big word, and I don't know whether I quite want to do that. I'm much more inclined to frame it as an observation: 'Isn't it curious?' Isn't it curious, for example, that some religions have polite ways of exiting, some religions have no ways of exiting, and other religions have odd ways of exiting?" (222).

65 Smith, "Social Formations of Early Christianities," 271.

66 I have taken the following paragraphs on theory and method, with revisions, from Ron Cameron and Merrill P. Miller, "Introduction: Ancient Myths and Modern Theories of Christian Origins," in *Redescribing Christian Origins*, 8-15. See, in addition, Ron Cameron, "An Occasion for Thought," in *Introducing Religion: Essays in Honor of Jonathan Z. Smith* (ed. Willi Braun and Russell T. McCutcheon; London: Equinox, 2008), 100-104.

67 Smith, "The Devil in Mr. Jones," 104, 105.

68 Translation, Smith says, is "a key notion in relation to that most challenging goal of the study of religion: explanation" (Smith, "When the Chips are Down," 30). For "explanation is, at heart, an act of translation, of redescription" (Smith, "The Topography of the Sacred," 105-106). Translation is "our way of explaining. After all, an explanation does nothing else than say ... 'this is an example of that' and a translation makes it possible to talk about something in other terms. What [cognitive scientists] call 'explanation' I call 'comparison' and what they call 'interpretation' I call 'translation'" (Smith, "*Asdiwal*: Interview," 50, adding: "for someone in the human sciences, comparison is our form of experimentation" [49]; see also Smith, "Bible and Religion," 90; repr. in *Relating Religion*, 206-207; Smith, "Manna, Mana Everywhere," 211-212; repr. in *Relating Religion*, 134; Smith, "Conjectures on Conjunctures," 58).

69 Jonathan Z. Smith, "Teaching the Bible in the Context of General Education," *Teaching Theology and Religion* 1 (1998): 77.

70 Smith, "A Twice-told Tale," 143-144; repr. in *Relating Religion*, 371; see also Smith, "Social Formations of Early Christianities," 273; Smith, "A Matter of Class," 393; repr. in *Relating Religion*, 166; Smith, "Bible and Religion," 91; repr. in *Relating Religion*, 208; Smith, "The Topography of the Sacred," 105-106.

71 Smith, "Close Encounters of Diverse Kinds," 15; repr. in *Relating Religion*, 316.

72 Smith, "Bible and Religion," 91; repr. in *Relating Religion*, 208.

73 Smith, "Social Formations of Early Christianities," 274, alluding to Emile Durkheim, *The Elementary Forms of Religious Life* (1912; trans. Karen E. Fields; New York: Free Press, 1995). "For those of us who study religion," Smith argues, "as is characteristic of the human sciences in general, the little prefix *re-* is perhaps the most important signal we can deploy. It guarantees that we understand both the second-order nature of our enterprise as well as the relentlessly social character of the objects of our study. We re-present those re-peated re-presentations embedded in the cultures and cultural formations that comprise our subject matter ... The history of the history of religions is not best conceived as a liberation from the hegemony of theology ... A more fundamental issue that yet divides us ... is the debate between an understanding of religion based on *presence* and one based on *representation* ... Language ... is not posterior to experience, rather, it is the very way in which we think and experience. The human sciences become conceptually possible largely through the acceptance of the ... argument that [one's] objects of study are holistic linguistic and language-like systems, and that, therefore, they are the study of 'eminently social' human projects ... The central debates within the study of religion revolve around the relations of language and experience" (Smith, "A Twice-told Tale," 131, 132, 137–138; repr. in *Relating Religion*, 362, 363, 366, emphasis original; see also Smith, "Are Theological and Religious Studies Compatible?" *BCSSR* 26, no. 3 [1997]: 61; repr. in *On Teaching Religion*, 75–76; Smith, "Bible and Religion," 90; repr. in *Relating Religion*, 207; Smith, "Asdiwal: Interview," 54).

74 Smith, "Social Formations of Early Christianities," 273; see also Smith, "A Twice-told Tale," 144–146; repr. in *Relating Religion*, 371–372.

75 Smith, "Bible and Religion," 91; repr. in *Relating Religion*, 209, emphasis original.

76 Jorge Luis Borges, "On Exactitude in Science," in *Collected Fictions* (trans. Andrew Hurley; New York: Viking, 1998), 325. As Claude Lévi-Strauss has argued, "the intrinsic value of a small-scale model is that it compensates for the renunciation of sensible dimensions by the acquisition of intelligible dimensions" (*The Savage Mind* [The Nature of Human Society Series; Chicago, IL: University of Chicago Press, 1966], 24).

77 Smith, "Bible and Religion," 91; repr. in *Relating Religion*, 209.

78 Smith, "*Adde Parvum Parvo Magnus Acervus Erit*," 67, 68; repr. in *Map Is Not Territory*, 240, 241, emphasis original.

79 Smith, "*Adde Parvum Parvo Magnus Acervus Erit*," 71–89; repr. in *Map Is Not Territory*, 244–263; Smith, "In Comparison a Magic Dwells," 21–26.

80 Smith, "The 'End' of Comparison," 237.

81 Smith, "In Comparison a Magic Dwells," 29; and note the remarks in Smith, "Acknowledgments: Morphology and History in Mircea Eliade's *Patterns in Comparative Religion* (1949–1999), Part 1," 329–330; repr. in *Relating Religion*, 72–73; Smith, "When the Chips are Down," 9; Smith, "Conjectures on Conjunctures," 58.

82 Smith, "In Comparison a Magic Dwells," 20.

83 Smith, "The 'End' of Comparison," 240 n. 3, adding: "Similarity and contiguity have proved incapable of generating interesting theory" (237). The roles that similarity and contiguity play in memory had already been identified by Plato (*Phaedo* 73D–74A). Aristotle's contribution was to describe how, in memory, we start "from something similar (*homoios*), or different (*enantios*), or contiguous (*synengys*)" (*Mem.* 451b19–20).

84 Smith, "Social Formations of Early Christianities," 273, 274.

85 Smith, *Drudgery Divine*, 46–47.

86 Smith, *To Take Place*, 13–14, who makes this argument as part of his critique of Mircea Eliade's interpretation of the Australian aboriginal myth of the sacred pole of the Tjilpa, writing: "what is at stake, finally, is a question of the comparative enterprise itself" (13; cf. 1–23, citing Mircea Eliade, *The Sacred and the Profane: The Nature of Religion* [trans. Willard R. Trask; New York: Harcourt Brace Jovanovich, 1959], 32–33). This programmatic statement is also cited in Smith, *Drudgery Divine*, 47; compare the remarks in Smith, "In Comparison a Magic Dwells," 35.

87 Smith, *Drudgery Divine*, 52, 51, 53; cf. 115, emphasis original. See Max Black, "Models and Archetypes," in *Models and Metaphors: Studies in Language and Philosophy* (Ithaca: Cornell University Press, 1962), 219–243, esp. 236–238; Fitz John Porter Poole, "Metaphors and Maps: Towards Comparison in the Anthropology of Religion," *JAAR* 54 (1986): 411–457. The term "redescription" appears to be borrowed from Mary B. Hesse, "The Explanatory Function of Metaphor," in *Models and Analogies in Science* (Notre Dame: University of Notre Dame Press, 1966), 157–177; see Smith, "Sacred Persistence," 11, 27 n. 2; repr. in *Imagining Religion*, 36, 141 n. 2.

88 Smith, "Bible and Religion," 87; repr. in *Relating Religion*, 197, adding: "[All] of these processes have in common that they are varying modes of redescription."

89 Smith, "The 'End' of Comparison," 239, emphasis original. The description of Smith's method as "the performance of four operations, not necessarily in separate, sequential stages: description, comparison, redescription, and the rectification of categories," was first given by Burton L. Mack, "On Redescribing Christian Origins," *MTSR* 8 (1996): 256; cf. 256–259; repr. in *The Christian Myth: Origins, Logic, and Legacy* (New York: Continuum, 2001), 70; cf. 70–74. Smith accepts Mack's formulation (Smith, "Social Formations of Early Christianities," 275) and, elaborating on this description of his own work, as quoted above, also cites it in Smith, "Bible and Religion," 87; repr. in *Relating Religion*, 197–198; Smith, "When the Chips are Down," 29.

90 Smith, "The Introductory Course: Less is Better," 188; repr. in *On Teaching Religion*, 14, emphasis original.

91 Smith, "'Narratives into Problems,'" 729, 733, emphasis original.

92 Smith, "The Introductory Course: Less is Better," 188; repr. in *On Teaching Religion*, 14.

93 Smith, 'Puzzlement,' 56–57; repr. in *On Teaching Religion*, 123; repr. as "Playful Acts of Imagination," 15, slightly adapted.

94 Smith, "Puzzlement," 57; repr. in *On Teaching Religion*, 123–124; repr. as "Playful Acts of Imagination," 15.

95 Jonathan Z. Smith, "Basic Problems in the Study of Religion," in *On Teaching Religion*, 20; cf. 24, emphasis original, adding: "The aim of an undergraduate program of studies in religion should be the understanding of religion as one of man's primary responses to and expressions of the human condition. Religion is one of the major means man possesses for constructing a significant world and for establishing his existence by expressing the truth of what it is to be human" (21). Compare the remarks on the study of religion, in relation to history, the humanities, and the human sciences, in Smith, "Map Is Not Territory," 290–291.

96 Smith, "Basic Problems in the Study of Religion," 27. But, as Smith remarks in a subsequent conversation about teaching, "my aim is that [my students] not be defeated by that. I want it to be a spur to more thought, not a blockage or impediment" (Smith, "The Devil in Mr. Smith: A Conversation with Jonathan Z. Smith [2012]," in *Reading J. Z. Smith*, 69, adding: "'Wrinkles on the brow' is the most basic definition I have of the teaching enterprise"; and note the reference in the critique by Smith, "Commentary" on "William J. Bennett's *To Reclaim a Legacy: A Report on the Humanities*

in Higher Education," *American Journal of Education* 93 [1985]: 544). "Above all," Smith says, "what ... I want the students to know is that matters are always more complex than they first appear, and that this is liberating rather than paralyzing. I want them to know that this complexity requires them to make decisions which have consequences" (Smith, "Introduction: Approaching the College Classroom," in *On Teaching Religion*, 3).

97 Smith, "The Dean's Craft of Teaching Seminar," 99, adding: "I'm not interested in majors ... I don't want to train anybody for something. I really don't like that role—I play it, but I don't like it."

98 Smith, "The Introductory Course: Less is Better," 185; repr. in *On Teaching Religion*, 11, adding: "The least interesting term in the [course] title is 'religion' ... *An introductory course serves the primary function of introducing the student to college-level work,* to work in the liberal arts. Its particular subject matter is of secondary interest" (185, 186–187; cf. 190–191; repr. in *On Teaching Religion*, 11, 12; cf. 16–17, emphasis original). For a discussion of introductory and core courses in religion, together with syllabi, see Smith, "Basic Problems in the Study of Religion," 21–23, 24–26; Smith, "When the Chips are Down," 10, 12, 39–41 nn. 33–34, 42–44 nn. 38, 40; Smith, "Introduction: Approaching the College Classroom," 2, 6–8; Smith, "The Dean's Craft of Teaching Seminar," 86–89, stating: "In my judgment, the syllabus is the most important piece of academic writing anyone does in the academic field. It's both a descriptive map of an area ... and an implicit, at least, argument" (87).

99 Smith, "The Introductory Course: Less is Better," 186–187; repr. in *On Teaching Religion*, 13, emphasis original; see also Smith, "The Devil in Mr. Jones," 113; Smith, "No Need to Travel to the Indies," 216; Smith, "Why the College Major? Questioning the Great, Unexplained Aspect of Undergraduate Education," in *On Teaching Religion*, 115.

100 Smith, "Puzzlement," 60, 62, 66; repr. in *On Teaching Religion*, 128, 130, 134; repr. as "Playful Acts of Imagination," 18, 20, citing Wallace Stevens, "Imagination as Value," in *The Necessary Angel: Essays on Reality and the Imagination* (New York: Vintage Books, 1951), 136.

101 Smith, "Puzzlement," 62–63; cf. 64; repr. in *On Teaching Religion*, 130; cf. 132; repr. as "Playful Acts of Imagination," 18; cf. 19.

102 Smith, "'Religion' and 'Religious Studies,'" 242–243; repr. in *On Teaching Religion*, 88.

103 Smith, "Conjectures on Conjunctures," 55, 57–58.

104 Smith, "In Comparison a Magic Dwells," 35, citing Ludwig Wittgenstein, *Philosophical Investigations* (trans. G. E. M. Anscombe; 3rd ed.; Oxford: Blackwell, 1967), 84e (no. 215), emphasis original.

NORTH AMERICAN ASSOCIATION FOR THE STUDY OF RELIGION PANEL

This section, containing Chapters 9–12, is composed of papers presented at the 2018 North American Association for the Study of Religion Annual Meeting in Denver, Colorado. The panel was entitled "Remembering Jonathan Z. Smith."

Chapter 9

Introduction: Remembering J. Z. Smith

Willi Braun and Russell T. McCutcheon

Jonathan Z. Smith of the University of Chicago passed away in the final days of 2017, nearly a year ago, and just weeks after NAASR had held its annual meeting in Boston. There is of course much to say about Jonathan, his career, and his countless contributions to the academic study of religion. Indeed, it is difficult to think of anyone who has had a comparable influence on the study of religion during the past fifty years. To use some key terms from Jonathan's own lexicon, he introduced "religion" to the study of religion. Both "introduced" and "religion" are important. We all know that he constantly insisted that the word "religion" is a second-order term, a critical concept for scholars who study culture and those cultural practices that by some stipulation we call religious. And he once said "our primary expertise" as religion scholars and teachers "is introducing." By this he didn't mean some colloquial sense of the term; rather, he was talking about the very heart of our intellectual and pedagogical practice: to set up occasions for thought by fore-fronting conceptualizations that have constituted religion as a field of studies, by challenging our familiarity with our cultural practices by introducing comparisons with the unfamiliar, to juxtapose the "here" with the "out there," and so forth. Drawing on the biological sciences, as he was wont to do, he thought of "introducing" in the sense of the invasion of a foreign species that would have perturbing effects on the familiar habitat of the study of religion, and mess with—in intellectual ways—the habitual practices of scholars of religion. Surely, it is the introducing, this incisive perturbing, this profound messing around that we will miss most about Jonathan. Our speakers will soon tell us more about Jonathan's remarkable influence on them and the field.

Many of you know that Jonathan was the President of this organization, from 1996–2002, serving two terms in that role. In fact, he was a member of NAASR from its very start. Conceived by Donald Wiebe, Tom Lawson, and Luther Martin at the 1985 Congress of the International Association for the History of Religions (held that year in Sydney, Australia), and holding its first organizational meeting in 1985 at that year's AAR conference in Anaheim, California, NAASR was looking for members. When Don and Luther—as Don tells the story—came across Jack Neusner at the AAR that year, they convinced him to pay the $10 membership fee and join. And he did just that. When Jack got home after the conference, he paid the fee to sign up several friends of his own without their knowing—one of whom was Jonathan, a friend since their days at Dartmouth College in the early 1960s, and of whom Neusner once said (as quoted by Aaron Hughes in his biography of Jack), "he was able to teach us things we didn't know possible in the field of religion." Not one to see such a good deed go unpunished, the story is that Jonathan then joined Jack up, unannounced and without his permission, for membership in the American Communist Party. And then, a few years later, with NAASR having already been denied affiliated status within the AAR (for a variety of reasons, one of which was that "[a]ll three of the AAR initials appear in the NAASR letters" [quoting Jim Wiggins, then Executive Director of the AAR, in his letter to NAASR]), Tom and Luther had the idea that the organization needed some credibility. What better way than to invite Jonathan to stand for President, which he did in 1996. In May of 1998 the AAR granted NAASR the "related scholarly organization" status that it had been denied back in 1987 and which it still holds today.

Whether in its formal leadership or not, his presence at these panels over the years was always unmistakable, whether or not seated up at the podium, and by his mere presence challenging us to do our work better, or as a member of the audience, often peering downward, his head and hands perched on the top of that cane, pensive and listening carefully and, more than likely, striking varying amounts of fear into the presenters who could imagine what he might say when they were done their paper. But that was not all that there was to him, and to know him only as an intellectually intimidating figure was to have missed the kind and even playful person that he was as well—as the two anecdotes above make clear.

Like some others present here on the occasion of this panel devoted to remembering Jonathan Z. Smith, we had the good fortune of getting to know him a bit, of visiting him at his house in Chicago and and being invited upstairs to see his home office and his library stacks. This brought with it the delight of also getting to know his wife, Elaine, who, along with their daughter Siobhan, has made the trip to Denver to join us for this session today. We are so pleased to have both of them here.

The speakers will tell us a little bit about the man whom they knew. The order in which they will speak they are: Stephanie Frank, of Columbia College, Chicago; Sam Gill, of the University of Colorado Boulder; and James Tabor, of the University of North Carolina in Charlotte. All three, we should note, earned their Ph.D.s at the University of Chicago, ranging from Sam in 1974, James in 1981, and Stephanie in 2015—thereby covering many of the years when Jonathan was a faculty member there, whether within or outside the Divinity School.

Willi Braun is a Professor Emeritus in the Department of History and Classics and the Program in Religious Studies at the University of Alberta. Although a specialist in earliest Christianities in the Roman Empire, his work also focuses on the methods and theories of the study of religion.

Russell T. McCutcheon is University Research Professor and longtime Chair of the Department of Religious Studies at the University of Alabama; he has published widely on a variety of topics in the history of the field and on the tools that scholars use when going about their work.

Chapter 10

Transformed Agendas: Generalism in the Work of J. Z. Smith and the Study of Religion

Stephanie Frank

Jonathan Z. Smith—the most cited scholar in the study of religion of his generation—is perhaps most often cited for his insistence that part of what we must study, when we study religion, is the study of religion. This is because, as he famously put it, "Religion is solely the creation of the scholar's study. It is created for the scholar's analytic purposes by his imaginative acts of comparison and generalization. Religion has no existence apart from the academy."

This passage is usually cited to draw attention to the way in which our field constructs its object of study; without minimizing the importance of that point, I instead want to focus here on the part of this passage that is often elided. Smith's claim is not just that scholars create religion—it is that they create it by *the imaginative acts of comparison and generalization*. It follows that to do this work, scholars of religion need to be, to some extent, comparativists and generalists. Smith's career made this point both implicitly and explicitly, and it is one that has been increasingly overlooked by both scholars in the field and the institutional structures of the field.

I was first exposed to Smith's work, as an undergraduate, through his essay in *Imagining Religion* "A Pearl of Great Price and A Cargo of Yams." The piece approaches the question of the relationship between Melanesian cargo cults and Jewish and early Christian apocalyptic and messianic movements. This is not (and was not ever) a debate in which I am equipped to take a position. Rather, I want to use a method to which Smith himself was partial—the selection and examination of an exemplum. I want to analyze the essay's argument as an entrée to thinking about Smith's contributions to the field of religious studies.

"A Pearl of Great Price" juxtaposes the ritual text of the Babylonian New Year Festival (the Akitu Festival) with the Ceramese myth of Hainuwele. The portion of the Akitu text that interests Smith is the ritual humiliation of the king, on the fifth day of Nisannu. Smith provides this translation of the king's script: " I did [not] sin, lord of the countries. I was not neglectful of your godship. [I did not] destroy Babylon. I did not command its overthrow ... I did not humiliate [the Babylonians]. I watched out for Babylon. I did not smash its walls" (Smith 1976: 2). Smith goes on to detail actions of the priest in response, which involve providing reassurances to the king that the god Bel will heed his prayers and "magnify [his] lordship" even as he ritually strikes the king. "If the tears flow, (it means that) the god Bel is friendly; if no tears appear, the god Bel is angry" (ibid.: 3).

Before Smith's contribution, this peculiar text had been understood in the general framework established by Frazer's The Golden Bough: the humiliation and redemption of the king is just a version of the dying and rising of the king. Smith, however, suggests a radically different contextualization of the Akitu ritual text, juxtaposing it instead with the Ceramese myth of Hainuwele. In that myth, an ancestor was instructed to plant a coconut he found, and when his blood dripped on the palm that resulted, a girl grew from the tree. She was called Hainuwele ("coconut girl"). What was distinctive about Hainuwele, according to the myth, was her excrement, which "consisted of all sorts of valuable articles, such as Chinese dishes and gongs" (quoted in Smith 1976: 12). Eventually the people were envious of Hainuwele's wealth-generating capacities and murdered her. From her dismembered corpse sprung previously unknown tuberous plants, which became a staple of Ceramese food.

In venturing an interpretation of the Hainuwele myth, Smith once again strikes out against scholarly consensus, which (following Adolf Jensen) famously considered the myth as one of a class of myths about the origins of death, reproduction, and agriculture. But as Smith points out, the text, in referring to another Oceanic myth about the emergence of humans from bananas, presupposes mortality and sexuality—it does not give an account of their origins. Similarly with the cultivation of plants. Smith instead focuses on the element of the myth that strikes him (as it does the characters who encounter Hainuwele) as incongruous: her excretion of manufactured goods.

What I want to draw attention to, here, is not just Smith's juxtaposition of two radically dissimilar texts: I take it that does not require highlighting. It is the fact that he juxtaposes two radically dissimilar texts, pulling them out of the frameworks in which they had been placed by scholarly consensus, in order to highlight something new about them. This is in line with another oft-quoted point of Smith's: that a comparison involves not two entities but (at least) three, and one of these is (sometimes invisibly) provided by the comparator.

This point is, I think, often too quickly assimilated to a more general poststructuralist point about the politics of knowledge production—selecting and categorizing our data changes what it tells us, and we make these choices according to a variety of factors, conscious and unconscious. Of course that point is worth making. But I think it elides the parallel point that selecting and categorizing our data changes the questions we ask of it. This is what I consider Smith's strength to be as a generalist and a comparativist: transforming questions.

In juxtaposing the Akitu text and the Hainuwele story, "Pearl of Great Price" suggests that scholarly consensus had misclassified both: the former was not about a dying-rising king, nor was the latter about mortality or sexuality or even agriculture. By putting them together Smith constructs a category of religious texts centrally pertinent to rectification. The Akitu text, he argues, is a response to the "apocalyptic situation" of an occupying foreign king; the Ceramese myth is a response to the "cargo situation" of the colonial encounter between the native Oceanic economy and the European economy.

In both cases, Smith suggests, the texts represent the outcome of people reckoning with what he calls "incongruous situations" via a repurposing of an earlier paradigm. In the Akitu case, Smith speculates, the first slapping of the king (for the symbolic punishment of an external aggressor) is a repurposing of an archaic ritual meant to produce tears as an index for rain (the second slapping). In the Hainuwele myth, Smith thinks, a Wemale "mythic precedent" involving the killing and eating of mysterious figures who introduced new foodstuffs in order to properly acculturate them was repurposed to project the incorporation of Chinese manufactured goods into the Ceramese economy.

If Smith is right, we have learned quite a lot from his classification of these two texts together. We have learned something about both the Akitu text and the Hainuwele text—Smith's recontextualization of these texts involve datings much later than had been conjectured before in both cases. We have a sketch for a new class of religious texts that serve purposes not of prophecy or of validation but of "rectification," as Smith describes it. And we have the suggestion of a new paradigm for understanding the way texts are generated to address "situational incongruity."

None of these insights—preliminary though they be—would have been available to us without Smith's first step to construct the field of his inquiry—ritual and mythic texts drawn from across time and space but which both address "situational congruity." The Ceramese text and Babylonian text, read together, make something visible about each other that would not otherwise be. This extends not just to generalities about the way religion functions in certain kinds of situations but even at the level of granularity of the dating of the particular texts in question—generally thought to be the sort of thing reserved exclusively for the province of specialists. Smith's work reminds us not only that it is possible for generalists to "contribute to the literature" on specific questions, but that there are contributions that *only* generalists can make.

Generalism has a currency that I am not sure is fully recognized in today's academic landscape. Religious studies departments, like most humanities departments, are shrinking. Most of us teach at universities that are not research universities, which typically means there are not even enough faculty positions to cover the so-called "major" religions, let alone all the religions in all of the time periods. A significant number of us are the only person who teaches religious studies at our institutions.

Considering this reality, it is peculiar and perturbing that subdisciplines—and in some cases, subsubdisciplines—continue to organize academic labor markets. In religious studies as in other fields, it is common to see job ads constrained to a narrow specialization. At the same time, in religious studies as in other fields, it is common for the person hired as a scholar of Hebrew Bible or medieval Islam to be asked also to teach Religions of East Asia—or vice versa. Perhaps the department's Buddhologist is on family leave, perhaps there is no qualified adjunct available in the small town where the college is located, or perhaps declining enrollments means that fewer religious studies courses can be offered and the department wants to attempt to preserve the diversity of its course offerings. In all of these cases, a faculty member ends up teaching a course that they would never be hired to teach if the department were hiring someone to teach the course in question. And if we take the idea of specialization seriously, it is hard to imagine who could possibly be qualified to teach the "world religions" course that is the bread and butter of many departments.

It is common to couch criticisms like this in terms of the working conditions of faculty. And it bears acknowledging that it is disproportionately contingent and untenured faculty who are asked to teach so far afield of the specialties in which they are credentialed, and that this adds a great deal of work to the load of scholars of whom the system already takes advantage.

But the problem is not merely that the current situation involves unrecognized labor for faculty members asked to teach outside their "specialty." The point is that even in spite of the teaching requirements of today's university, the study of religion continues to sink deeper into the comfortable and comforting pillow of "expertise"—and the study of religion as Smith understood it and practiced it seems further and further away, as though a dream. As horrific as it has been and is, the current crisis of the university puts us in its debt in at least this one way: its vicissitudes have highlighted the divergence between the premise of the field of religious studies and the way the field is organized at present.

And thus it has reminded us of the lesson Smith taught us in both word and deed. For if we are going to take seriously the premise of the field of religious studies—if we're going to teach our students that religion, the object of "religious studies," is a scholarly construction—we must acknowledge the generalizations that go into constructing it. And that means we must encourage, rather than belittle or dismiss, generalism as a facet of our thought. For surely we need to think as generalists even to begin to assess the generalizations that undergird any given deployment of "religion" or related concepts. And, at least some of the time, so we must. If we are not willing to take Smith's lead and commit to at least this, religious studies might as well be dissolved into the constellation of fields rather incommodiously called "area studies."

I of course would not suggest that there is no place for "specialization." Obviously there is a great deal that specialization has taught us, and our understanding of religion (and everything else) would be deeply impoverished were it not, for instance, for the years of language learning that specialists have invested. But I still believe we have much to learn from both Smith's pronouncements and his practice—not only because of the constructed nature of our field, but also because of the particular situation the university finds itself in, at the moment. That is, like Smith's work, generalism is important not just for our research, but also for our teaching.

The argument for generalism can also be posed from the opposite angle. If one theme of Smith's corpus is that the study of religion is always at the same time the study of the study of religion, another is the way the study of religion can collapse into religion. In his essay "A Twice-Told Tale," subtitled "the history of the history of religions," Smith riffs on Jane Harrison's epithet that ritual and myth are "representation represented." He argues that to shy away from generalization, as a student of a given religion—to fail to take up the task of translation that he finds at its heart—is basically to involve oneself in the enterprise of the *practice* of the religion. It is merely a scholarly form of repetition of the same. He writes,

> Too much work by scholars of religion takes the form of a paraphrase, our style of ritual repetition, which is a particularly weak mode of translation, insufficiently different from its subject matter for purposes of thought. To summarize: a theory, a model, a conceptual category, a generalization cannot be simply the data writ large. The alternative would be to persist... in denying that science depends on the construction of its theoretical object of study, insisting rather that it is founded on the discovery of a unique reality that eludes any translation other than paraphrase. (Smith 2004: 372)

This passage encapsulates that the outlook characteristic of Smith's scholarship: namely, its theoretically coherent path avoiding both, on the one hand, assigning a *sui generis* reality to religion and, on the other, dissolving religion into an infinite number of phenomena that cannot be related in any way. But though he warns against allowing the study of religion to collapse into a bloodless form of the practice of religion, Smith is always quick to point out the affinities between the two. The example of this that occurs most commonly, in Smith's work, is the analogue between the close reading of the philologist and that of the Talmudist.

But in "Pearl of Great Price," Smith is at pains to point out the way in which his own enterprise, like those of the Babylonians and the Ceramese, centers around situational incongruity. The Ceramese are confronted with goods that are, essentially, untranslatable in their exchange economy; the Babylonians are faced with accepting as their king someone who was yesterday the conquering enemy. They use myth and ritual, respectively, to try to make things right. And the things that rankle them also rankle Smith, as they are recounted in the texts (the proclamation that the anointed king did not hurt the free citizens of Babylon, Hainuwele's defecation of china and gongs).

Smith, though, doesn't want to use the texts to make things "right"—he wants to make the texts themselves intelligible. For Smith, the text's incongruities are the crack in the façade that allows the text to be split open, in order for its problems and questions to be seen more fully. This is, of course, the conviction motivating much of Smith's work: no matter how inexplicable or mystifying seems some datum in the human endeavors we group together under the mantle of "religion," it is, in fact, intelligible, if we do our work properly—which is to say, if we choose the right generalizations and comparisons to construct our data.

I began to think about generalism in Smith's work when I came across his claim in his autobiographical essay "When The Chips Are Down" that working in the mode of the self-reflective scholar of religion means working within others' paradigms: "I understand the role of one who identifies himself as a generalist and comparativist to be that of interacting with the agenda and data of others" (Smith 2004: x). The assessment is accurate, to an extent. Smith arrived to the fields of the Akitu ritual and the Hainuwele myth with certain problems already constituted, problems about which he (always a thorough researcher) read the extant literature and opined on.

But I think Smith—always humble, if never meek—was not being wholly fair to himself. It is true that the fields of Akkadian philology and Ceramese anthropology had already organized themselves around certain problems, decades before he ventured into them. And surely Jonathan suggested provocative new answers to these existing questions—why is the king of Babylon ritually struck? What should we make of the strange story of the murder of the coconut girl? From which historical periods did these stories emerge?

However interesting, though, these answers are not ultimately the interest of "Pearl of Great Price." What is interesting about Smith's essay is precisely the way that, by making of Babylonian ritual and Ceramese myth unlikely bedfellows, it *transforms* the agendas which he inherited. It does this. Smith's question is not why the Babylonian king was struck, but why he was struck twice; his question is not why Hainuwele's dismembered corpse generated tubers, but why she defecated manufactured goods. And by juxtaposing these two data points—by populating the category of texts dealing with situational incongruity—Smith changes the question. By changing the question, Smith begins to develop his important idea of rectification in myth and ritual, as well as gestures toward the mechanism (repurposing of older mythic/ritual themes) through which rectification is attempted.

Because my career has, for the last several years, been dominated by the concern of designing a religious studies curriculum for my institution, my first thought, when I was invited to speak about Smith's contribution, was to talk about Smith's contribution to questions surrounding pedagogy—a contribution that was both substantial and close to his heart. But my mind continuously wandered back to Smith's line about generalists serving the agendas of others—both for its insights and for its limitations in describing his work.

As I thought more about this question, though, it occurred to me that if Smith's work, in serving the agendas of others, transforms these agendas, what we do when we teach is much the same. The most basic thing we do as pedagogues is to answer students' questions; but arguably the most powerful thing we do is to change the questions students ask. Often we do this by recontextualizing whatever the datum under consideration is and asking students to consider it anew; or again, by demonstrating to students that the same event, the same text, the same phenomenon, takes on an entirely different countenance depending on with what we classify it. That is, the generalism of teaching is not just a function of the situation of the humanities in our particular historical moment but a function of teaching properly understood.

I of course understand the risks involved in generalization, and in being a generalist. They are real. Smith's point was that these risks make the study of religion the study of *religion*. Smith's work implicitly reminds us that in being so self-conscious about this fact—and in making these risks and their rewards so explicit—the study of religion constitutes a powerful argument for the power of the humanities and of humanistic education.

Stephanie Frank is Associate Professor of Instruction in the Humanities, History, and Social Sciences Department at Columbia College, Chicago; she teaches a variety of courses in religious studies, philosophy, and history at Columbia.

Reference

Smith, Jonathan Z. (1976). "A Pearl of Great Price and a Cargo of Yams," *History of Religions* 16: 1–19. https://doi.org/10.1086/462753

——. (2004). *Relating Religion: Essays in the Study of Religion.* Chicago, IL: University of Chicago Press.

Chapter 11

J. Z. Smith and the Necessary Double-Face

Sam D. Gill

The University of Chicago. Fifty years ago. Jonathan arrived from the University of California at Santa Barbara; I from Wichita Kansas.[1] As new faculty, Jonathan was a bright young star widely recognized among religion scholars. As a new student, I had been a corporate research analyst with degrees in mathematics and business with virtually no understanding of religion or its academic study.[2] Given my choice to study Native Americans and, eventually, dancing and technology, it may seem odd that Jonathan would be the most important person to my studies over these fifty years, yet that has been my great fortune.

Smith's Frazer Studies

The year I finished my Ph.D., 1973, I read Jonathan's article "When the Bough Breaks" published that year in the *History of Religions* (Smith 1973, reprinted in Smith 1978). I had taken many a course from Jonathan, including one that required reading much of Erwin Goodenough's ten-volume *Jewish Symbols*; yet Jonathan had, in my memory, referred only infrequently to Frazer. I'm not sure that I was aware that Smith had written his Yale dissertation on Frazer, titled *The Glory Jest and Riddle: James George Frazer and The Golden Bough*, finished in 1969. Reading "When the Bough Breaks" I was amazed by Smith's Frazer studies, as I came also to appreciate the scale of Frazer's work; the third edition, comprised of a dozen green volumes, cites five thousand sources and includes some one hundred thousand cultural examples. Smith's article suggested that he had done the impossible work of critically checking the bulk of Frazer's examples against Frazer's own sources; a work that should have taken a lifetime.

Most curious to me was Smith's conclusion:

> Frazer appears to have answered his two questions,[3] although we may judge his answers to be failures ... The original purpose of the book[4] was not accomplished ... There have been no answers because there have been no questions ... The *Bough* has been broken and all that it cradled has fallen. It has been broken not only by subsequent scholars, but also by the deliberate action of its author. (Smith 1978: 238–239)

Jonathan leaves his readers with a multi-layered riddle. Why would Frazer spend more than twenty-five years on a project intending it to fail? Why would Jonathan spend six years source-checking and analyzing Frazer to confirm the scale of his failure? What is broken? Is it specifically Frazer's scholarship, the comparative enterprise, the academic study of religion, or the whole academy?

Two years later, in 1975, at the national meeting of the American Academy of Religion (AAR), I ran across Jonathan at a social gathering in the Chicago Hilton. When I asked him about his Frazer riddle, he launched a rant about the world having seen enough of his Frazer work. He told me that he had liberated the copies of his dissertation from the library at Yale and that he had instructed the dissertation reprint folks not to make any reprints. Then the conversation shifted to other topics.[5]

Happily, I soon acquired a copy of Jonathan's dissertation and, should you be curious, it is still available. I read the work and, comparing it with his article, "When the Bough Breaks," discovered that the article was an abridged presentation of Part I *"Homo Ludens,* Frazer as Play" with emphasis on chapter 4, "No Answers, No Questions."[6]

When Smith published his first collection of essays in 1978 (completed in 1976), *Map is Not Territory: Studies in the History of Religion,* he included "When the Bough Breaks" but added an Afterword. The riddle of the 1973 publication was compounded, perhaps turned into a joke, by the following statement in this Afterword.

> I had originally intended a companion piece to this essay[7] accounting for the reasons that Frazer chose to make his central work a joke. It was to argue that Frazer, in his researches, encountered the Savage which put the axe to his Victorian confidence in Progress and, in his studies of dying gods and kings, was brought up short before the absurdity of death. The history transcended—namely death, "no figurative or allegorical death, no poetical embroidery thrown over the skeleton, but the real death, the naked skeleton" (GB[3], Vol. VII, p. vi). And, in the face of this "real death," one can only act absurdly, or, to put it another way, all action is joke. (Smith 1978: 239)

The joke that is the deliberate failure is linked with Frazer's existential concern about death, the real death, his death, death as an aspect of being human. *The Golden Bough* was, Jonathan showed, no merely academic objective exercise; it was also a sustained effort by Frazer to come to terms with his personal existential concerns.

And then Jonathan concludes his provocative Afterword with this:

> I would not wish "When the Bough Breaks" to be misunderstood. Frazer, for me, becomes the more interesting and valuable precisely because he deliberately fails. (Smith 1978: 239)

Over the decades I have often reflected on Jonathan's Frazer writings and, as my own work has developed almost always in conversation with Smith's work, I increasingly came to believe that what is deeply important in the accumulated body of his work has its origins in his study of Frazer.

Smith and a Proper Academic Study of Religion

As I look at Jonathan's work today it seems that he regularly presented examples and principles aimed at establishing a proper[8] academic study of religion, yet I believe his work has yet to be adequately understood or engaged; and the field has yet to appropriately establish itself in the secular academy. In 2010, referring to the founding events of the field in the early 1960s, which saw the US field grow from 25 to 173 departments in just half a dozen years, Smith said,

> The groundwork, it seemed to me, *then* was there laid for the development of a generic study of *religion*, but that expectation has largely remained unrealized. We seem still committed to the priority of species over genera, apparently confident that a focus on the former is the route to a responsible consideration of the latter without, however, much reflection on how one sort of expertise might, in fact, lead to the other. (Braun and McCutcheon 2018: 126; italics in the original).

Smith refers to the field's trending development towards area studies (species) accompanied by a decline in interest in religion (genus) understood as a human phenomenon.[9]

In Willi Braun's and Russell McCutcheon's 2008 collection of essays, *Introducing Religion: Essays in Honor of Jonathan Z. Smith*, many of their authors do little more than an obligatory mention of Smith. Other than the editors, it was Smith's lifelong colleague Burton Mack who engaged Jonathan's work in some depth. Consider this statement by Mack describing the first time he heard Jonathan speak; we should also recognize it as a list of key criteria for the proper study yet to be established. Mack writes,

> The effect was stunning. No ontologized Sacred. No divine agency. No dramatic breakthrough events, whether primordial or personal. No romanticism. No mysticism. No otherworldly symbolism. Instead, human ingenuity, taking note of situations, crafting languages, constructing grammars, working with symbol systems, manipulating displacements, marking icons, attending to collective ratiocination, deciding upon strategies of application, rules of exegesis, classification, comparison, structural social and imaginary world-building. (Mack 2008: 299)

Among the areas where Smith's technical legacy has yet to be adequately appreciated, surely comparison, which he referred to as a "persistent pre-occupation,"[10] is the most important and pervasively applicable. Any proper academic study of religion must be located in an environment shaped by comparison engaged as an essential powerful method of negotiating the vast exempla tentatively identified by scholars as relevant to a study of religion. While clearly few scholars should, or even could, engage principally in global comparative studies, I believe that all religion scholars must be aware of what is at stake in comparison and how it shapes, although often tacitly, all religion studies.

Smith on Comparison

In my preparation for this talk I wrote a long essay on Smith's rich understanding of comparison; to honor Jonathan's style its footnotes comprise as much real estate as does the body of the text.[11] Because of its extent, I cannot even summarize that essay, so I must simply cut to the chase and adumbrate what I find to be the core dynamic of comparison which was evident in Jonathan's Frazer study. In concluding his dissertation, the following statement echoes what he wrote in the Afterword to "When the Bough Breaks":

> What Frazer has sensed in *The Golden Bough* is what later philosophers have termed the absurdity of the human condition ... Striving to conquer death by means of death, man asserts the reality of death, its omni-presence and omnipotence, all the more strongly. It is tragic, it is comic, it is absurd ...
> Frazer, as the chronicler of "these efforts, vain and pitiful, yet pathetic" [*Golden Bough*, vol. IX, p. 241], adopts the necessary double-face. (Smith 1969: 376, 378)

The necessary double-face—this, to me, is the core dynamic of comparison and much else that persistently occupied Jonathan. In other contexts, Smith used alternative terms such as "gap," "difference" or "incongruity;" also "riddle," "joke," and "play."

The immediate reference made by the phrase "the necessary double-face" is the inseparable pairing of comedy and tragedy illustrated by the classical "sock and buskin" masks of ancient Greek theater.[12] Through our evolution, humans have come to be distinguished by our *capability to hold together without resolution two things declaring them to be the same, even identical, while at once knowing full well they are not the same at all.* This structural dynamic is at the core of most things human: metaphor, art, language, fiction, myth, and ritual. Riddle and jest are pure playings at this impossible copresence. I call this structurality an *aesthetic of impossibles.*[13] It is also the forte of what we recognize as religion. Comparison, the interplay of things that are at once alike yet different, is the dynamic that transduces all these objects and artifacts into the actions and awarenesses felt as life, as vitality.

In practical terms, a proper academic study of religion cannot avoid comparison. Classification, definition, typology, terminology, data identification, discourse, perception, and advancements to knowledge are shot through with applications of comparison, if often implicit. While comparison, as it operates in metaphor and art, for example, will always be mostly tacit, there must be an explicit understanding of the technical requirements for comparison when used as an academic method. Smith's many writings show that comparison is not a simple linear method that leads from one point to another, from knowing nothing to knowing something. Nor is comparison a fundamentally rational objective method that assures definitive conclusions. Comparison is at the heart of the processes we know as both religion and religions; comparison conjoins things that are at once the same and different in an aesthetic of impossibles.

Smith gave full expression to his sense of the importance of comparison to a proper academic study of religion in the closing paragraphs of his chapter "On Comparison" in *Drudgery Divine*, where he wrote,

> Comparison, as seen from such a view, is an active, at times even a playful, enterprise of deconstruction and reconstitution which, kaleidoscope-like, gives the scholar a shifting set of characteristics with which to negotiate the relations between his or her theoretical interests and data stipulated as exemplary. The comparative enterprise provides a set of perspectives which "serve different analytic purposes by emphasizing varied aspects" of the object of study.[14]

He continues:

> It is the scholar's intellectual purpose—whether explanatory or interpretative, whether generic or specific—which highlights that principled postulation of similarity which is the ground of the methodical comparison of difference being interesting. Lacking a clear articulation of purpose, one may derive arresting anecdotal juxtapositions or self-serving differentiations, but the disciplined constructive work of the academy will not have been advanced, nor will the study of religion have come of age. (Smith 1990: 53)

Rooted in Smith's studies of Frazer, we must appreciate that comparison has the necessary double-face of being powered by the distinctly human capacity to say that one thing is another, yet what is important, what is essential, what is interesting, is that the one thing is not the other, and that we know it all along.[15] Such a structurality—one of play and joke and riddle—applies remarkably not only to comparison, but, writ large, to *religion* as we make the effort to invent it and *religions* as we endeavor to observe and find ourselves abducted by them. Comparison, like religion, has an abductive quality. Abduction, as Charles Sanders Peirce spent a lifetime studying, is that feeling-kind of knowing, often described as initiated by the surprise of incongruity; it gives rise to hypothesis.[16] Comparison is an oscillating structurality that engenders fascination and obsession. It is the structurality of vitality itself, an exercise of life that fueled Frazer to spend over twenty-five years copying and arranging ethnographic data from five thousand sources into ever-evolving patterns that tended, over time, to be a repetitive gestural practice, each iteration an enactment of his life practice. It is the structurality that drove Smith to spend six years checking thousands of exempla presented by Frazer knowing all along that Frazer had deliberately failed; with each iteration of comparison attesting to the glory of Frazer's, and Smith's, jests and riddles.[17] Comparison, as understood by Jonathan Smith, is the magic of the necessary double-face, the impossible co-presence that might impassion an entire field of study to broadly offer insights and values to human cultures.

Sam Gill is Professor Emeritus University of Colorado at Boulder. J. Z Smith was his most important influence and mentor for nearly fifty years. He works on indigenous religions, dancing and religion, religion theory, and religion and technology.

Notes

1 My memory of the date was somewhat fuzzy about my first meeting with Jonathan. I'd initially thought that it was likely in the Winter or Spring terms 1968. My first term at Chicago was Fall, 1967. Pete Grieve's biographical memorial, "Jonathan Z. Smith (1938–2017): The College's Iconoclastic, Beloved, Chainsmoking Dean" (2018), provides evidence in the form of a letter from Jonathan to Mircea Eliade dated June 4, 1968, informing him that he would be joining the University of Chicago faculty in the Fall term. This paper, presented in November 2018, would then bear out that it was precisely 50 years ago that I first met Jonathan.

2 Given my background in math and business, for years my admission to the Divinity School would be an unexplained mystery. I frankly knew nothing of the University of Chicago, its Divinity School, the study of religion, or much of anything beyond math and business. Many years later it finally dawned on me that I was surely accepted only because Justice Clark's opinion in the US Supreme Court case *Abington v Schempp* (in 1963) had initiated a vast expansion of departments of religion; the growth was from only 25 departments in 1960 to 173 by 1966 (see Smith 2004b: 55). I finally realized that most any warm body with a Ph.D. could find a position in one of these new departments. I was a warm body; nothing more. Yet I now also recognize that one of the long term advantages I might have had with my strange background is that I wasn't seminary-trained or even religious. I was as close as one might find to *tabula rasa* for an academic study of religion. And, while I've spent my life in the study of religion, I've never felt I fit. My advantage, as I now might attempt to see it, if desperately so, accidentally coincided with Jonathan's lifelong effort to chart a proper academic study of religion. Such a study, distinctive to the modern secular academy, had to be independent of seminary preparations, religious beliefs, or even necessarily by the scholars in the field being religious. These criteria, plus knowing almost nothing, described me.

3 The first extended section of Smith's "When the Bough Breaks" is devoted to what Frazer indicated in each of the editions of *The Golden Bough* as his core concerns. While Smith shows that Frazer's concerns grew, shifted, and radically changed from edition to edition, he nonetheless continued to state his purpose as answering the two questions "Why had the priest of Nemi (Aricia) to slay his predecessor? And why, before doing so, had he to pluck the Golden Bough?" (Smith 1978: 208–212).

4 Smith's reading of the first edition of *The Golden Bough* found that Frazer stated his purpose as answering the question of "the meaning and origin of an ancient Italian priesthood" (Smith 1978: 208) and to "explain a single rule of an ancient Italian priesthood" (ibid.: 211–212).

5 Jonathan sometimes gave me a rundown on what treasures of connection he'd found in the local Yellow Pages in his hotel room. Such things endlessly fascinated him. The near disappearance of Yellow Pages is something likely few other than Smith lamented.

6 Smith indicated (2004a: 38 n. 29) that he understood it to be an abridged version of Part I.

7 It would have been based on the fifth and final chapter, "The Pattern of Divine Kingship," of his dissertation's Part II, "*Rex Sacrorum* [Sacred King]," dealing largely with the African evidence related to the killing of the sacred or divine king.

8 I've found myself using this term "proper" to indicate an academic study of religion fully suitable to a secular environment. Certainly, academic studies of religion may occur in religious settings for religious purposes; this surely marks the long history

of religion studies. I feel the need to include the term "proper" in reference to studies of religion in non-religious environments, like publicly funded colleges and universities, because I believe that most studies of religion that presently occurs in those environments either remains more appropriate to a religious setting with specific religious motivations or these studies are not adequately self-conscious of the importance of engaging the field-marking concerns, that is, what distinguishes and is essential to a study of religion as a human comparative intellectual endeavor. The distinction I'm making here is not new to me; I addressed it in "The Academic Study of Religion" (Gill 1994). Notably, Willi Braun and Russell McCutcheon use the term "a properly academic comparison" in their introductory essay to their edited volume, *Reading J. Z. Smith* (2018: viii).

9 Clarifying and amplifying Smith's statement in 2018, his editors wrote: "Another way to phrase Smith's point might be to cite the general lack of interest among the majority of current scholars with studies of religion (in the singular), understood as a human phenomenon, especially with studies that apply explanatory tools from the social and natural sciences, in order to account for the tendency to be religious, while also noting the obvious wealth of so-called area studies in the field, devoted to studying the history or features of the religions in the plural" (Braun and McCutcheon 2018: 126, n. 24).

10 In "When the Chips are Down" (2004b) Smith identifies and provides an overview discussion of "Taxonomy and Comparison" as one among five "persistent preoccupations" (see 19–25).

11 It includes these minimal concerns:

Four Modes/Styles: Smith's historical studies revealed for him four great classes of comparison: ethnographic, encyclopedic, morphological, evolutionary.

Four Great Classes: cultural comparison; historical comparison; assimilation, diffusion, or borrowing; and comparison as hermeneutic device.

Technical Requirements: Smith took pains to articulate the rigorous requirements for comparison to be a legitimate and useful technique or method. "Comparison is never dyadic, but always triadic; there is always an implicit 'more than,' and there is always a 'with respect to'. In the case of an academic comparison, the 'with respect to' is most frequently the scholar's interest" (Smith 1990: 51).

Naturalness: Jonathan frequently argued that comparison is a fundamental characteristic of human intelligence; thus, comparison is of the nature of the human intellect. Yet, he also held that there is nothing natural about the comparative enterprise as method; that is, in engaging the technique of comparison the scholar creates the terms and selects the exempla compared.

Uniqueness: Jonathan critically discussed the common use of the term "unique," which he disliked, in the context of comparison; technically it means "one of a kind" or simply "incomparable"; a discussion that he often paired with the claims for religion as special, *sui generis*, and requiring some special acumen, religious in character, to be even studied.

Ends: Smith was concerned with the ends to which comparison is directed. While his technique is often reduced to the linear sequence—description, comparison, redescription, reconciliation—I think this the least interesting of his views on comparison (Smith 2000: 239). Smith was far more interested in jokes and riddles which have the character of persistence; they exemplify the necessary double-face.

And it is the quality of jest and riddle—this necessary double-face, that, I believe, to be central to the most profound of Smith's imaginings on comparison—that has the most importance not only for a proper study of religion, but also for the most existential of human concerns: our facing death. I can here but sketch this notion focusing on Smith's Frazer studies. I cannot emphasize enough that I believe that the future existence of religion as a proper academic study depends on us paying very careful attention to what Smith offered.

12 The sock and buskin are two ancient symbols of comedy and tragedy. In Greek theatre, actors in tragic roles wore a boot called a buskin (Latin, *cothurnus*) that elevated them above the other actors. The actors with comedic roles only wore a thin-soled shoe called a sock (Latin, *soccus*). Melpomene, the muse of tragedy, is often depicted holding the tragic mask and wearing buskins. Thalia, the muse of comedy, is similarly associated with the mask of comedy and comic's socks. Some people refer to the masks themselves as "Sock and Buskin."

13 Notably the word aesthetic comes from Greek *aisthētikos*, from *aisthēta* 'perceptible things,' from *aisthesthai* 'perceive.' The connection with beauty didn't occur until mid-eighteenth century, a connection that remained controversial until late nineteenth century. I like the idea that the impossible things are perceptible as in given some concrete perceivable forms; for example, gods as wise old men in the sky or blue many-armed figures.

14 His quotation in this paragraph is from F. J. P. Poole's "Metaphors and Maps" (1986: 432).

15 Elsewhere I refer to this as the Ultimate Turing Test (see chapter 5, "Ava and the Ultimate Turing Test," in Gill 2018b).

16 See my "Religion by Abduction" (Gill 1987) and "To Risk Meaning Nothing: Charles Sanders Peirce & the Logic of Discovery" (Gill 2018a). Pierce held that the methods of argumentation we refer to as induction and deduction add little if anything to our knowledge; both tend to re-arrange what is already known. Yet abduction, the experience of incongruity, gives rise to new hypotheses. Hypothesis, best guess, once formulated, takes us to induction and deduction and the application of these methods eventually takes us back to abduction. Back and forth.

17 It is the structurality that inspired me to go to Australia to track the sources of each and every word in the principal example my teacher, Mircea Eliade, used to establish his theory of religion and which Jonathan later would carefully criticize. It was a multi-year storytracking project (Gill 1998) in which I attempted to trace sources back to an actual person place and time; knowing all along that the story was concocted.

References

Braun, Willi and Russell T. McCutcheon (eds.) (2008). *Introducing Religion: Essays in Honor of Jonathan Z. Smith.* New York: Routledge.

——. (eds.) (2018). *Reading J. Z. Smith: Interviews and Essay.* New York: Oxford University Press.

Gill, Sam D. (1987). "Religion by Abduction," in *Native American Religious Action: A Performance Approach to Religion,* 3–16. Columbia, SC: University of South Carolina Press.

——. (1994). "The Academic Study of Religion," *Journal of the American Academy of Religion,* 62 (4): 201–11.

——. (1998). *Storytracking: Texts, Stories, and Histories in Central Australia.* New York: Oxford University Press.

——. (2018a). "To Risk Meaning Nothing: Charles Sanders Peirce & the Logic of Discovery," in *Creative Encounters, Appreciating Difference: Perspectives and Strategies,* 197–226. Lanham, MD: Lexington Books.

——. (2018b). *Religion and Technology into the Future: From Adam to Tomorrow's Eve*. Lanham, MD: Lexington Books.

Grieve, Pete (2018). "Jonathan Z. Smith (1938–2017): The College's Iconoclastic, Beloved, Chainsmoking Dean" *The Chicago Maroon* (March 23); www.chicagomaroon.com/article/2018/3/23/jonathan-z-smith-dean-of-college-university-of-chicago (accessed December 18, 2018).

Mack, Burton (2008). "Sacred Persistence" in Willi Braun and Russell T. McCutcheon (eds.), *Introducing Religion: Essays in Honor of Jonathan Z. Smith*, 296–310. New York: Routledge.

Poole, F. J. P. (1986). "Metaphors and Maps: Towards Comparison in the Anthropology of Religion," *Journal of the American Academy of Religion* 54: 411–457. https://doi.org/10.1093/jaarel/LIV.3.411

Smith, Jonathan Z. (1969). *The Glory, Jest and Riddle: James George Frazer and The Golden Bough*. Ph.D. dissertation, Yale University.

——. (1973). "When the Bough Breaks," *History of Religions* 12: 342–371. https://doi.org/10.1086/462686

——. (1978). *Map is Not Territory: Studies in the History of Religions*. Leiden: Brill.

——. (1990). *Drudgery Divine: On the Comparison of Early Christianities and the Religions of Late Antiquity*. Chicago, IL: University of Chicago Press.

——. (2000). "The 'End' of Comparison" in Kimberley Patton and Benjamin Ray (eds.), *A Magic Still Dwells: Comparative Religion in the Postmodern Age*. Berkeley, CA: University of California Press.

——. (2004a). *Relating Religion: Essays in the Study of Religion*. Chicago, IL: University of Chicago Press.

——. (2004b). "When the Chips Are Down," in *Relating Religion: Essays in the Study of Religion*, 1–60. Chicago, IL: University of Chicago Press.

Chapter 12

Remembering J. Z. Smith: Some Personal Reflections

James D. Tabor

I want to thank Brad Stoddard and all the others responsible for putting together this panel focused on remembering our teacher and colleague Jonathan Z. Smith. I am honored to be a part of it and want to express my personal sympathies to Elaine Smith, Jonathan's wife, and his daughter Siobhan Smith, who are with us this morning, just three days shy of what would have been his 80th birthday (November 21, 1938–December 30, 2017). Today I want to relate a few personal memories of Mr. Smith, as we students always called him, as well as an account of how he has so profoundly shaped or, as I will explain, "impressed" my scholarship.

In the neglected book Qohelet, which many known by the awkward name Ecclesiastes (not to be confused with Ecclesiasticus)—appellations that deserve etymological and historical exposition for another occasion—we encounter a two word admonition in Hebrew: *uzkór et-bor'ékah* (וזכר אֹת־בֹראיך): "Remember your creators..." Mr. Smith might well have pointed out that the verb *zakar*, quite literally "to press, or thrust," was the noun for "male" in Hebrew (lit. "the thrusting one), in contrast to the word "female," that is quite literally "a hole or cavity" (Genesis 1:27). Accordingly, to remember is quite literally based on "impression," or formation, as opposed to recollection in the Platonic sense. Further, the form "creators" (Qal masc plural participle in the Masoretic text), *Creatorum tuorum* in the Vulgate, but "corrected" to the singular κτίσαντος in the LXX, only occurs in the plural here in the entire Hebrew Bible. This, of course, led to all sorts of theological machinations about an allusion to the Trinity in eighteenth- and nineteenth-century commentaries (Matthew Henry, Adam Clarke, Albert Barnes, et al.). In context, the admonition is to a youth who is to look back upon those who contributed one's formation, whether parents, teachers, or mentors, before the incompetence of older age takes its toll. I hope to do that today, and thus fulfill this ancient prescription of the Jewish Scriptures.

I had never heard of Jonathan Z. Smith, when I arrived at the University of Chicago in October 1972 to begin working on my Ph.D. in New Testament and Early Christianity in the Humanities Division. I had come to study with the late Robert M. Grant (History of Christianity) and Norman Perrin (New Testament). Grant urged me to sign up for Smith's course in "Hellenistic Religions" the Fall quarter, which I did. I still have the mimeographed handouts from that class; usually a primary text, often done by Smith himself for the class meeting, with extensive bibliographical notes. One of the beginning texts we covered was the 3rd millennium BCE Sumerian "Ode to the Pickax":

The hoe (*al*) makes everything prosper, the hoe makes everything flourish. The hoe (*al*) is good barley, the hoe (*al*) is a hunting net (*one ms. has instead:* an overseer). The hoe (*al*) is brick moulds, the hoe (*al*) has made people exist (*jal*). It is the hoe (*al*) that is the strength of young manhood. The hoe (*al*) and the basket are the tools for building cities. It builds (*aldue*) the right kind of house, it cultivates (*aljaja*) the right kind of fields. It is you, hoe, that extend (*dajal*) the good agricultural land! The hoe (*al*) subdues for its owner (*lugal*) any agricultural lands that have been recalcitrant (*bal*) against their owner (*lugal*), any agricultural lands that have not submitted to their owner (*lugal*). It chops the heads off the vile esparto grasses, yanks them out at their roots, and tears at their stalks. The hoe (*al*) also subdues (*aljaja*) the *hirin* weeds. The hoe (*al*), the implement whose destiny was fixed by father Enlil—the renowned hoe (*al*)!

I remember as Smith began to work through that text, line-by-line, I found myself wondering, what could any of this possibly have to do with Hellenistic Religions much less my interest in the history of early Christianity. I was soon to find out. It took a semester, but I gradually began to realize that Smith was slowly taking us through texts that illustrated the profound differences in the shifts in cosmology from the ancient Near East to the new world of Hellenism. Little could I understand at the time that various forms of ancient Judaism and early Christianity were fully integrated into this "brave new world" of Hellenistic dualism.

Over the course the that quarter I was exposed to a host of names and texts of which I had never heard, even though I arrived at the University of Chicago with what I thought was a solid M.A. from Pepperdine University in Biblical studies—with my Hebrew, Greek, Latin, French, and German in good shape. The names flew by me: Reitzenstein, Priezendanz, Widegren, Wendland, Prümm, Bieler, Festugière, Nilsson, Nock, Goodenough, Colpe, "Poimandes," "The Mithras Liturgy," "The Golden Ass," "The Prayer of Joseph"—some of which I recognized, most of which I had never heard, and none of which I had read. But more important than assembling a bibliographic reading list to prepare for exams, I slowly began to realize that Smith was up to something far different. This is the Jonathan Z. Smith that famously said he could teach an entire Humanities introduction course from the latest issue of *Time* magazine or the Yellow Pages of any local phonebook.

I begin to read Smith intensely that year. He had never published a book, but many of the articles that later appeared in his *Map is Not Territory* (1978) were available. Over the next couple of years several of us who began to gravitate toward Smith's courses and his ideas, collected these articles together, including: "The Garments of Shame" (1966), "The Prayer of Joseph" (1968), "Earth and Gods" (1969), "Birth Upside Down or Right Side Up?" (1970a), "Symbols on Social Change: A Place on Which to Stand" (1970b), "*Adde Parvum Parvo magnus Acervus Erit*" (1971), "I am a Parrot (Red)" (1972a), "The Wobbling Pivot (1972b), "When the Bough Breaks" (1973). In those days photocopying (called "Xeroxing") was beginning to catch on—mostly in the business world, but in a more limited way in universities. One of our group just happened to work for a company that allowed him unlimited personal photocopies done after hours so long as he supplied the paper and ink cartridges. We came up with the idea of putting together a kind of J. Z. Smith "Festschrift," bringing together all of Smith's articles into a nicely bound volume with a short introduction we composed, inspired by his 1974 William Benton Professorship lecture at Chicago "Map is Not Territory"—which we found utterly ground-breaking.

I will never forget the day a few of us took a copy to Smith's office in the Humanities building, and unceremoniously presented it to him. He was completely surprised, taken aback, but pleased, by the gesture, remarking that he did not realize he had written that much!

I ended up taking half a dozen more courses from Smith as I continued my coursework with Grant, Perrin, McGinn, Ahlstrom, Eliade, Colpe, and several others. My interest in early Christianity continued, but in a way that had been fundamentally transformed by my in-depth exposure to Smith's lectures and published articles.

By 1975 I begin to think about asking Smith if he would agree to direct my dissertation. I planned to deal with Paul's first-person account of his "ascent to Paradise" in 2 Corinthians 12:1–10, and thus the broader phenomenon of "heavenly ascent" in the ancient Mediterranean world. So far as I knew he had only had one other Ph.D. student dealing with early Christianity. I was later to learn that Smith wrote an entire Ph.D. dissertation on the Gospel of John at Yale, influenced by E. R. Goodenough, but it was stolen out of the back of his parked car and never recovered. In those days we sometimes had only a single typed copy of our work, as working with carbon paper was so tedious. Rather than reproduce it from handwritten notes and drafts, he changed his entire topic and ended up writing on Frazer's *Golden Bough*, as we all know.

Smith agreed to work with me. I was as terrified as I was thrilled. As fate would have it, all of my handwritten notes and research were stolen in 1977 at the Hyde Park post office while I was waiting in line—not for their value but for the Samsonite briefcase I carried them around in and the hope it would contain money or something of market value.

I almost gave up at that point, but Smith related to me the story of his stolen dissertation and encouraged me to go on. Over the next two years, we spent hours going through the chapter drafts of my dissertation one by one—he with his English Ovals and me rolling Drum tobacco. I would send him a draft, he would mark it up with his characteristic blue ink, and we would then go through section by section. I have saved all those drafts with the hundreds of markings and they are of incalculable value to me. He was the same way in returning course papers. His marginal notes were always insightful, both correcting and pointing one to other possible ideas and sources.

These dissertation meetings were cordial, but I can't say they were pleasant. There is nothing I have ever experienced that can compare to a one-on-one with Jonathan Z. Smith going through one's written work! I would go away from those meetings inspired to give things a better try, but with my head spinning with new ideas and insights. Smith was kind but demanding. At the same time, he was incredibly encouraging. He connected me with Morton Smith, Jacob Neusner,

Alan Segal, and other scholars, who assisted in dealing with Jewish mystical and rabbinic texts. He let me know that he thought what I was doing with Paul had never been done before—and was of immense value. I will always remember the day he approved the final draft—and shortly after that wrote a recommendation letter in my behalf for a position at University of Notre Dame—which I got.

Based on all I had learned from Jonathan Z. Smith, my challenge was to present Paul in light of our understanding of Hellenistic Religions. There were five fundamental insights Smith summarizes in his masterful article on "Hellenistic Religion" in the *Encyclopedia Britannica* that were foremost in my thinking. I sought to incorporate these into my treatment of Paul in a way that only Jonathan Z. Smith could guide me through. Here is a summary of those principles using his words:

1 The study of Hellenistic religions is a study of the dynamics of religious persistence and change in this vast and culturally varied area. Almost every religion in this period occurred in both its homeland and in diasporic centers—the foreign cities in which its adherents lived as minority groups.

2 Rather than a god who dwelt in his temple, the diasporic traditions evolved complicated techniques for achieving visions, epiphanies (manifestations of a god), or heavenly journeys to a transcendent god. This led to a change from concern for a religion of national prosperity to one for individual salvation, from focus on a particular ethnic group to concern for every human. The prophet or savior replaced the priest and king as the chief religious figure.

3 The history of Hellenistic religions is rarely the history of genuinely new religions. Rather it is best understood as the study of archaic Mediterranean religions in their Hellenistic phase within both their native and diasporic settings. It is usually by concentrating on the diaspora that the Hellenistic character of a cult has been described.

4 The archaic religions of the Mediterranean world were primarily religions of etiquette. At the center of these religions were complex systems governing the interrelationships between gods and humans, individuals and the state, and living people and their ancestors. The entire cosmos was conceived as a vast network of relationships, each component of which, whether divine or human, must know its place and fulfill its appointed role.

5 The old religions of conformity and place no longer spoke to this new religious situation and its questions. Rather than the archaic structures of celebration and conformity to place, the new religious mood spoke of escape and liberation from place and of salvation from an evil, imprisoned world. The characteristic religion of the Hellenistic period was dualistic. People sought to escape from the

despotism of this world and its rulers (exemplified by the seven planetary spheres) and to ascend to another world of freedom.

Toward the end of the 1970s, as most of us were finishing up our Ph.D. degrees, we began regular after-hours informal gatherings with Smith in Hyde Park, either at his house or one of ours. We would put drinks out on the table and discuss a given paper or topic. This practice continued years after we graduated, into the 1980s, 1990s, and 2000s, after AAR annual meetings for dinner, as well as special gatherings at UC Davis for several years. We sometimes jokingly referred to ourselves as "The Chicago Seven." In 2007 we published a set of papers from one of these conferences in a special issue of *History of Religions* 47/2–3 (November 2007/ February 2008), dedicated to Smith.

I will close with two personal anecdotes and a quotation. In 1995 Eugene Gallagher and I published the book *Why Waco: Cults and the Battle for Religious Freedom in America* (1995). We dedicated the book to Jonathan Z. Smith, noting his work on Jonestown that had so influenced us. As we all know, Jonathan detested using the telephone and never used email. We all knew never to try calling him, although over the years we would sometimes call Elaine to work out this or that dinner arrangement. Sometime after Jonathan received the book, he *called* me on my home phone and left a message thanking me: "Jim, I got the book and read it. Thanks a hell of a lot for the dedication. You and Gene have done a great service with this book. I am proud of you both."

Then in 2009, as chair of the Department of Religious Studies at UNC Charlotte, I invited the Smiths to Charlotte, for a lovely spring visit. We had invited Jonathan to give the 25th Anniversary Loy H. Witherspoon lecture—our oldest and most distinguished lecture series at the university. That lecture, "Things Said/Things Done: The Relations of Myth and Ritual," was published by our department and is now online.[1] The lecture hall filled to capacity with university and community folk. That afternoon Jonathan had held a special open seminar with our undergraduate and graduate students, so many of whom had read his works in the course of their studies. Jonathan showed such devotion to the students, giving them extended time as he leaned on his magnificent cane and demonstrated his classic form of gesturing and facial expressions. Smith had a way of pulling students in and letting them know they were full participants in the sacred space of academic discourse.

Lori Woodall and I, with Jorunn Jacobsen Buckley who joined us on the visit, were able to spend a couple of days of personal time with Jonathan and Elaine. This included several lingering meals and a visit to our UNC Charlotte Botanical Gardens, which Jonathan so immensely enjoyed. After a long lunch I read to him from my latest publication, a collection of poetry by James Whitehead titled *The Panther*, and presented him with a signed copy. He wrote to me two days after his return to Chicago—one of his beautiful handwritten letters in blue ink on notebook paper: "I have spent some time reading and rereading the Panther poems. They are quite wonderful (especially orally), and this resolved quickly my taxonomic question as to whether to shelve them on the 3rd floor with Christian apocrypha or on the second floor with modern and contemporary poetry in clear favor of the latter. I'm grateful for the gift."

Finally, I will close with a quotation from Plato that several of us exchanged upon hearing of Smith's death. It is so quintessentially, "Smith," I can't imagine anything better:

> "Well, Socrates, do you wish to leave any directions with us about your children or anything else—anything we can do to serve you?"
>
> "What I always say, Crito," he replied, "nothing new. If you take care of yourselves you will serve me and mine and yourselves, whatever you do, even if you make no promises now ..."
>
> "We will certainly try hard to do as you say," he replied. "But how shall we bury you?"
>
> "However you please," he replied, "if you can catch me and I do not get away from you."
>
> And he laughed gently ... Such was the end, Echecrates, of our friend, who was, as we may say, of all those of his time whom we have known, the best and wisest and most righteous man.

James Tabor is a Professor in the Department of Religious Studies at the University of North Carolina at Charlotte, where he studies Christian origins and ancient Judaism. His work combines the study of ancient texts with extensive field work in archaeology in Israel and Jordan.

Note

1   See https://goldmine.uncc.edu/islandora/object/uncc%3A597#page/1/mode/1up (accessed June 7, 2019).

References

Gallagher, Eugene and James Tabor (1995). *Why Waco: Cults and the Battle for Religious Freedom in America.* Berkeley, CA: University of California Press.

Smith, Jonathan Z. (1966). "The Garments of Shame," *History of Religions* 5: 217–238. https://doi.org/10.1086/462523

——. (1968). "The Prayer of Joseph," in J. Neusner (ed.), *Religions in Antiquity: Essays in Honor of E. R. Goodenough*, 253–294. Leiden: Brill.

——. (1969). "Earth and Gods," *Journal of Religion* 49: 103–127. https://doi.org/10.1086/486164

——. (1970a). "Birth Upside Down or Right Side Up?" *History of Religions* 9: 281–303. https://doi.org/10.1086/462610

——. (1970b). "Symbols on Social Change: A Place on Which to Stand" *Worship* 44: 457–474.

——. (1971). "*Adde Parvum Parvo magnus Acervus Erit*" *History of Religions* 11: 67–90. https://doi.org/10.1086/462642

——. (1972a). "I am a Parrot (Red)" *History of Religions* 11: 391–413. https://doi.org/10.1086/462661

——. (1972b). "The Wobbling Pivot," *Journal of Religion* 52: 134–149. https://doi.org/10.1086/486294

——. (1973). "When the Bough Breaks," *History of Religions* 12: 342–371. https://doi.org/10.1086/462686

——. (1978). *Map Is Not Territory: Studies in the History of Religions.* Leiden: E. J. Brill.

Part II

Blogs

Chapter 13

J. Z. Smith: The College's Iconoclastic, Beloved, Chain-Smoking Dean

Pete Grieve

An eager yet unimpressive Tutorial Studies student managed to convince a dean to let him have one more read on his senior paper after his two assigned faculty reviewers chose not to recommend it for honors. "He was trying to write about the Holocaust, and I just think he had no real ideas," said Classics professor James Redfield (Ph.D. '61), who taught at the University of Chicago for 50 years, retiring in 2016. He's telling a story from the 1970s. Redfield was the master of the New Collegiate Division, which runs Tutorial Studies (the College's design-your-own-curriculum program), and he was fed up with having to accommodate this student. But he knew just the man for the job: Jonathan Z. Smith, a historian of religion at the University of Chicago who is remembered by colleagues and students as an honest intellectual and an unshy critic.

Redfield will never forget how Smith, who was born Jewish but secular, responded to the paper. "This is the first time I have ever felt sympathetic to anti-Semitism," he said. That was Smith's style as a scholar. He was a brutal critic who pushed academia to join him in raw, deliberate analysis. "He did not suffer fools gladly, either on the page or in person. He was critical in every sense of the word," said Wendy Doniger, the Mircea Eliade Distinguished Service Professor of the History of Religions at the Divinity School, and a longtime colleague. "His critique of the way religion was studied is that it was not critical enough. Paradigms were not closely enough examined. He had a sharp mind, and he rightly wanted scholars to be more cold-blooded, more analytical in their treatment of religious phenomenon."

Scholars throughout Europe and America listened to Smith and changed the way they studied religion, Doniger said.

On campus, Smith was a beloved teacher. He taught prolifically at the university from 1968 until he retired in 2013, serving as dean of the College from 1977 to 1982. He was a sharp writer, a mesmerizing lecturer, and an intriguing character. A lifelong smoker, he died suffering from lung cancer at age 79 on December 30. Dean of the College John Boyer, who went to Smith for advice when he was offered the deanship in the early '90s, said Smith was a wonderful man, loved by students, and an excellent colleague. Boyer, an expert on the university's history, said his conversation with Smith when he was offered the deanship inspired him to write his book, *The University of Chicago: A History*. "He told me he thought it would be very important for whoever took the deanship to try to give more of a public voice to the university's and the college's history," he said, adding that Smith was always an interesting person for him to debate:

> The thing about Jonathan is that you never quite knew which side of an argument he was on because he was able to see not only what emerged as his own point of view, but to understand and to give legitimate representations of other people's points of view. You never quite knew where he was coming from, or where he was going until the end of the argument.

Hanna Gray, whose 15-year term as university president from 1978 to 1993 overlapped with Smith's deanship, said he was a remarkable teacher and colleague. She remembers the hard conversations they had about whether the College could be expanded from 2,700 to 3,200 students without losing its character:

> The important things about him were an extraordinary commitment to teaching—a wonderful commitment to teaching; a person of the highest kinds of standards; a person who taught really quite selflessly, that is, he didn't think about how many courses a person was obliged to give. He gave more courses than anyone I know because he really loved it. He was an extraordinary colleague and an extraordinary *presence* at the university, and that was in a way the most important thing about Jonathan Smith.

"An Extraordinary Presence"

Even in elementary school it was clear Smith was a bit different. "There was something sort of extra-worldly about him as a youngster," his childhood friend, attorney David Simpson, said. "He was interested in things that were beyond the usual purview of children—he marched to his own drum a little bit." They went to Hunter College Elementary, an experimental school for gifted students on the Upper East Side of Manhattan. Simpson lived just a few blocks away from Smith's home at 86th Street and Riverside Drive, and Simpson went over there quite often. He remembers that Smith was obsessed with animals and with learning about different cultures, Native American culture in particular. Smith's parents were a fairly ordinary Jewish couple: "They weren't anything like what Johnny became," he said. They lost touch around age 12 when Smith went to Horace Mann School and Simpson stayed in public school.

As a junior Smith worked on a farm for an agriculture program that Cornell offered to high schoolers. "I started off originally in grass breeding. That was what I wanted to do with my life," he once said in a *Maroon* interview:

> I went to a farm, because since if you're a city boy going [to] an agricultural school which is free, you have to prove that you can stand in cow shit, so they send you to a barn for a while ... It still remains to this day the best thing I ever did in my life. But it was a bad time in Cornell's history. They would let you take no liberal arts courses.

Smith was frustrated that they wouldn't let him study history or philosophy, so he protested to his headmaster who said, "That's good, you'll go to Haverford; they'll figure you out there." He made a phone call and got Smith into college.

On his first day at Haverford Smith scoped out the one spot in the library where it looked like you could smoke. "Turns out it was a shrine where Quaker philosophers would study. And if there was one place where no one had ever smoked before, that was it. So there I was, happy as could be ... Then [philosophy professor Martin Foss] came in. Then some other students came in, and there was supposed to be a senior philosophy seminar on Hegel's Phenomenology of Mind," he said in the interview. "I was absolutely enthralled by [Foss's] way of talking. So that afternoon I became a philosophy major." From there Smith went to Yale to study religion, finishing a 574-page dissertation on James George Frazer in 1969.

But the story of Smith and the University of Chicago begins before that, around 1968 with Hans Penner (Ph.D. '65), a leading scholar in comparative religion at Dartmouth.

Penner died in 2012, but Charles Long (Ph.D. '62), a professor emeritus of religious studies at UC Santa Barbara, remembers the story. At the time, Smith was a young and promising scholar on the faculty in the just-established religious studies department at Santa Barbara.

Penner had gotten to know him at Dartmouth when Smith was an instructor there for a year from 1965–66, and he thought he would be a good fit at the University of Chicago. Penner excitedly told Long: "I met this person who thought like we thought at Chicago."

Long was co-teaching a class called World History of Religions, one of the first courses in Chicago's nascent New Collegiate Division, which was conceived as an interdisciplinary fifth division on top of the physical sciences, the biological sciences, the social sciences, and the humanities. "It was clear that it had legs," Long said, remembering that the classes would overflow into the Swift Hall common room. He knew that the founding master of the division, professor Redfield, was still recruiting, and Smith seemed to him like a perfect candidate.

Upon Long's recommendation, Redfield visited Smith in California, and he was immediately impressed. Mircea Eliade, then the most prominent professor at University of Chicago's Divinity School, also met Smith out in Santa Barbara, on the evening of February 14, 1968, which was the day after Smith's interview in Chicago and the day when Eliade arrived at UC Santa Barbara for a visiting professorship.

That summer, in a June 4, 1968 letter, Smith reported to Eliade that he had accepted the New Collegiate Division position and would be moving to Chicago. "Dear Professor Eliade, I have delayed in writing to you until I could have definite news to report. I have just written to Dean [Wayne] Booth accepting the position," Smith wrote. "Both Elaine and I are looking forward to seeing both you and your wife when we arrive in Chicago in the Fall. Your stay in Santa Barbara gave both of us much happiness and a foretaste of what we hope to continue after we move."

On July 1, 1971, Eliade wrote to Dean of the Divinity School Joseph Kitagawa, recommending Smith be promoted to the rank of Associate Professor. "I firmly believe that Jonathan Smith will become one of the most important historians of religions in the United States," he predicted. "Of course, we must help him to realize his vocation, and I think that his promotion to Associate Professor is not only imperative, but overdue."

At Chicago Smith lived up to Eliade's high expectations: colleagues said they place Smith among a group of renowned University of Chicago scholars that includes Charles Wegener, Wayne Booth, and Jock Weintraub. "I always think of Jonathan as being part of that old-school Chicago, which is extremely erudite, an intellectual polymath," said history and law professor Dennis Hutchinson (J.D. '70). "Not afraid to challenge any conventional wisdom, and also stylized: They never called each other 'professor.' It was always 'Mr.' and no honorifics, as there should be no hierarchy of learning or intelligence." College students were not to be called "undergraduates," for Smith believed that would imply they were beginners, waiting to become *real* students when they went to graduate school. "Smith thought this was all wrong and that college education was where it was at," said Christopher Lehrich (Ph.D. '00), a professor of religion at Boston University and a former mentee of Smith's. Lehrich later edited a collection of Smith's writings about teaching, titled *On Teaching Religion*. Smith came to be known as one of the most influential historians of religion of his generation, but Lehrich was inspired to put together the book when he discovered that there was a whole other side to Smith's scholarly output: essays about teaching that were often "very radical." Lehrich remembers sitting in Smith's office, talking to him about changes to the College and the Core. University president Hugo Sonnenschein was trying to expand the College—this time from 3,500 to 4,500 students. Too few students were applying to Chicago to allow for such an expansion, so the College had to move toward, as Sonnenschein said, "a curriculum more appealing to 17–year-olds." The "Chicago plan" reduced the size of the Core from 21 to 15 classes.

Smith rejected this curricular trend away from a rigid core and toward "electivity," which he took to mean the offering of more pre-professional tracks. "I think that College students should be able to major in Undecided. It would be a wonderful thing if you didn't have to major," Smith proclaimed to Lehrich between drags on his cigarette. "From Jonathan's point of view, he loved the place, and he loved the students, and he loved what in his mind Chicago was devoted to and all about," Lehrich said. "And so he was sickened to see what was happening to it. He could be a little bit sort of 'the sky is falling!' about everything, but I think he was horrified by things like the Chicago plan." Lehrich said Smith was so "greatly beloved by the students in part because he just didn't seem to have any respect for anything, *except*, he loved the students and he loved the College."

In 2000, item #265 on the University of Chicago Scav list was "J. Z. Smith in a lawn chair on the quads, drinking MGD; what else? [20 points]." Smith was approached by one of the Scav teams, eager to collect points. "Oh yes. Absolutely," he told them, as Lehrich remembers. And he lounged in a lawn chair and threw back a beer in front of the administration building.

"He was not pandering to the students. It's like: The students want him to do something, and he can see why it's funny. 'Sure, I'll be happy to do that.' I don't think he had any sense that this was beneath his dignity, or an inappropriate thing to do. *No, it's part of the College life,"* Lehrich said.

Smith was a private person; he organized his life to maximize time for reading and thinking. At the same time, however, he was a very human presence on campus. He ate lunch in Cobb Hall before class and had coffee in Swift Hall after class, and he welcomed his students to join him. Doniger remembered that Smith always commanded the attention of a room when he talked. "He smoked; he was a chain smoker. And he would let the ash on his cigarette roll longer, and longer, and longer, and longer. And everyone in the room was mesmerized watching the ash on the end of his cigarette, waiting for it to fall. You could've heard a pin drop," she said.

If his character and presence brought people in, it was his ideas that kept them engaged. "That crazy stick he walked with in recent years and so forth—that kind of made him a beloved character around campus. But the reason you listened to him when he talked was because he was a brilliant and arresting speaker," Doniger said. "He was just smarter than anybody else."

As Smith aged, he grew out his beard, carried a hand-carved cane, and wore huge glasses. "I'm going to invent myself as this old guy!" Long remembers Smith saying to him, around the time he started losing his curly black hair. "The giant rhododendron cane, the beard down to his navel—He was a character, and he knew it. And he took advantage of it," Hutchinson said:

> It made him more engaging: *What's this guy on about? What's his intellectual agenda?* And it turned out his intellectual agenda would get people to think. And I think one of his accomplishments of being in the College—and something John Boyer has carried on—is he viewed himself as a spokesman for liberal education: What are we trying to do here? How do we do it? Is the Core such a good idea, or is the Core authoritarian?

The College Was His Home

Unusual for a scholar of his stature, Smith almost exclusively taught College students. "He *did not* teach doctoral students," said Harvard Divinity School professor Kimberley Patton. "I mean, that is unheard of. He could have taught them, and he could have easily been chair of the department for years and years and established a doctoral dynasty." Colleagues and academics have different theories for why this was. It's clear that Smith wasn't interested in teaching students who were highly specialized or pursuing a preprofessional track. He did not like that graduate students already had their minds made up; to Smith, college students tend to be more intellectually honest because they are more open to being influenced. That was the theory, at least.

"I think his view was that doctoral students were so far socialized into repeating what they thought their professors wanted to hear that you often didn't hear what *they* really thought," Patton said. Lehrich, one of only a handful of Divinity students whose dissertations were supervised by Smith, said he probably felt graduate students were in it for the wrong reasons: Most of them "wanted to say,

'Oh, I worked with J. Z., so I'm a strong candidate.' He wasn't interested in that kind of thing."

But this is probably not the full story of why Smith distanced himself from the Divinity School. Smith held very strong and particular views about teaching that made it challenging to find the right place for him at the university. A year or two into Smith's three-year appointment in the College, he came to Redfield's office and explained that he wanted to go to the Divinity School full time. "I can't believe I can't make something that works for everybody," Redfield remembers telling Smith, referring to the New Collegiate Division he founded. "You may remember that the Creator had the same problem," Smith quipped back.

Smith didn't last long at the Divinity School. By 1973 he had designed his own undergraduate program in the College—Religion and the Humanities. He officially resigned his Divinity School affiliation in 1977. "The religious studies program coming out of the Divinity School was seen as a direct counterpoint to Jonathan's own religion program, so there's some intellectual tension involved in how he developed and applied his field within the university," said professor Hutchinson, now the master of the New Collegiate Division:

> He saw religion, as far as I understand his views, as more of a conversation—an act of creation—whereas so many in the Divinity School, at least when he was kind of railing against them, were much more academic in the sense of specialized key areas and more of the graduate taxonomy of specific knowledge—he saw no use for that.

Professor and former Divinity School Dean Margaret Mitchell explained that Smith is perhaps most famous for his argument that scholars produce religion: "Religion is solely the creation of the scholar's study," he wrote in a 1982 book of essays, *Imagining Religion*. "It is created for the scholar's analytic purposes by his imaginative acts of comparison and generalization. Religion has no independent existence apart from the academy." She notes that the co-director of Religion and the Humanities was Divinity School professor Anne Carr, but she still said that "to some degree Smith thought of the major as an alternative to the Divinity School." Mitchell said that Smith had a remarkable ability to talk across ideological divides. She said he is "*the* figure who has most left his mark on the American Academy of Religion, and yet he was also the president of the Society of Biblical Literature." (The two groups had a divorce about a decade ago.) She said there's no other scholar who could speak across the field of the study of religion like Smith:

> He is the person who almost everybody in the study of religion has read, and thought with, and interacted with. His mode of exposition was the essay. Most of his oeuvre—his scholarly work—is really brilliant collections of essays. And what he's known for is both theorizing about the nature of comparing religions, and setting up himself really interesting pairings of artifacts and texts from very different contexts, and bringing them into conversation.

His mode of teaching was the lecture. He typically wrote out his lectures by hand before each class. It took him at least three or four hours of preparation to give one hour of lecture, and until near the end of his career he would throw out his notes on the last day of the quarter to force himself to design his next course from scratch. Mitchell, who sat in on some of Smith's classes, described how his lectures set up comparisons of unlike things that always seemed out-there at first, but Smith would bring them together in a way that was masterful and compelling.

Ideological Differences

While Smith seems to have had real disagreements with the Divinity School at times, nearly everyone who spoke to *The Maroon* for this story pointed out that he had a remarkable ability to separate intellectual disputes from personal relationships.

Smith used Friedrich Nietzsche's note to readers in *Ecce Homo*, "I am one thing, my writings are another," as an epigraph to his 2010 address at the annual meeting of the American Academy of Religion in Atlanta, Georgia. Smith was invoking the Nietzsche line in a different context—he was modestly resisting the concept that there is that much to learn from a scholar lecturing about his own life—but the choice of that epigraph speaks to his belief that there was an important distinction between scholars and ideas. He was in the business of taking down the latter.

Patton and Doniger both remembered that Smith played a significant role in organizing the university's 100th anniversary conference for Eliade in 2007, despite Smith's frequent criticism of Eliade. Patton co-edited a book that collected responses to Smith's 1982 essay *In Comparison a Magic Dwells*. Smith argued in that influential essay that comparison in the human sciences was practiced in a way that was problematically unscientific, with a lack of objective and agreed-upon rules (i.e., "magic"). It was a devastating critique of comparative religion, and it had a profound impact on the field. Mitchell credits Smith for the establishment of models and criteria for responsible comparison.

The essay was not a critique of him specifically, but Patton said that Eliade, who was in the field of comparative religion, "typified for Smith much of what was problematic about the field." At the university's commemorative conference, Eliade's work faced significant criticism, and Smith certainly could have piled on. But he didn't, and instead chose to present a defense of Eliade. He wrote a "wonderful article" defending Eliade as a scholar of religion, Doniger said, which was presented as a lecture at the conference and then published as an article in the book that came out of the conference. "Most people would not do that for someone whom they had critiqued so powerfully, with whom they had disagreed so much. And yet he did. Why? Well, he liked Eliade, and he felt he was just a really important—and he was—scholar in the field of the history of religions," Patton said.

It's clear in Eliade's archived papers and correspondences that he and Smith were good friends, but the last letter from Smith in Eliade's collection, dated November 21, 1980, takes a sad turn. Smith writes that he is pained that Eliade was touched by his rage, explaining he wanted to have no formal relationship with the Divinity School. To that end, he planned to resign and leave for a different university in 1982, when his five-year term as Dean of the College would end. Smith wrote:

> I had the naive hope that you and I could continue as if nothing had happened. Without rehearsing details, problems that persisted for two years came to such a pass by last December that I determined that I did not wish the slightest formal suggestion of any relationship between myself and what was being called 'History of Religions' in the Divinity School. I still persist in my naive hope that, for us, none of this has happened.

Smith did not leave the university, but *The Maroon* was not able to put together a complete account of what changed his mind. "I didn't know about the letter, but he did consider leaving the university and they wooed him back and he stayed," Doniger said.

Smith's Legacy as Dean of the College

Professor Hutchinson met Smith in 1981, the first month he joined the faculty, when there was a holdup with his appointment. "That's a bureaucratic snafu! I can take care of that. What a stupid rule!" Smith told him animatedly. "He had just no pretense, no decanal affect. And I immediately warmed to him," Hutchinson said.

Smith could navigate university bureaucracy and get things done.

Katherine Karvunis, who was Smith's assistant for the nine years he was an administrator (1973–1982), spoke in awe about his productivity. He dutifully followed through on all tasks, he made every meeting, and he was very easy to work with, she said. President Gray was disliked by a lot of students because she was seen as too focused on fundraising. Smith, however, wasn't thought of as a money-grabber; he was regarded as someone who cared about academic standards, multiple alums from that era told *The Maroon*, remembering that Smith was dean at a time when the university was more apathetic toward College students. "He was very well liked by a student body that didn't like many administrators," said Abbe Fletman (A.B. '80), a judge in Philadelphia, who was editor-in-chief of *The Maroon* from 1978 to 1979.

But not everyone remembers Smith as the outlier in a cold administration. Wendy Oliver (A.B. '81), now a business attorney in Portland, Oregon, described the administration during this time period as "indifferent at best to students. It was kind of like an English boarding school, where they felt they needed to toughen you up," she said, adding that Smith was at least partially responsible. Oliver recalls being brushed off by Smith after going to his office to request a sexual misconduct investigation. According to Oliver, a professor had told her to come to his apartment to pick up an assignment, offered her a drink, and then tried to proposition her sexually in exchange for a grade, asking: "What's it going to be: an A or a B?"

A January 22, 1982 *Maroon* story about the administration's mishandling of her complaint explained that Smith had told her he would investigate the allegations fully. During their meeting, however, Smith treated her report lightly: "He went on to tell me little anecdotes about other cases of female harassment where professors met their students at the door in a bathrobe or something ... He thought it was funny," Oliver was quoted saying. "It was certainly another time. The college was just not very responsive to students. It was just not a very friendly place to be. And I don't think anyone I knew considered the administration to be friendly or helpful," she said.

When Smith informed then-Divinity School Dean Joseph Kitagawa of his intent to leave the university at the end of his term as Dean, he would have been in the process of overseeing a major review of the university's curriculum. Even during that process he indicated he didn't want to continue as Dean for another term. In the May 4, 1979 issue of the *Maroon*, Smith was interviewed about his three-year curriculum review. "I want it done before I go out," he said, also describing the review as "huge, the most significant report in the history of the College."

Karvunis said Smith wanted to do a complete reevaluation of the Core, but he was somewhat constrained by Gray, who Karvunis said didn't want to make sweeping changes to the degree Smith wanted. Gray, however, insists she agreed with Smith completely:

> We both agreed entirely on the opposition to pre-professional education, and believed that it was in the tradition of the College and a distinctive strength of the College that half of its program was devoted to that kind of broad education ... And we believed in the importance of the commonness, that is of students all sharing at least some important portion of their education so they could really learn from each other as well.

Smith articulated his views on the Core in an epic two-hour 2008 interview with Supriya Sinhababu (A.B. '10) for the inaugural issue of *The Maroon*'s revived long-form publication *Grey City*. Sinhababu reflected on that conversation a decade later for this story. "He's this guy with the giant glasses and the beard and a walking stick. I mean, he looks like a wizard. He died at 79, but in my head he's at least like a thousand. He really feels like a legendary figure." Smith never used a computer and despised the telephone, so it wasn't always easy to contact him.

His aversion to technology stemmed from his desire to maintain uninterrupted time when he could focus on thinking and writing, said chair of the religious studies department at Yale, Kathryn Lofton (A.B. '00), who majored in Smith's Religion and the Humanities program. Lofton regularly went to Smith's office hours, and she said she would always have headphones in her ears. "He would ask me whether I could hear anything over the noise of my music. And I would say, 'I want the noise,' and he would say, 'I don't know if you can hear anything that way.' We probably had exchanges along these lines ten different times," she wrote in an e-mail. "I never gave up the Walkman, and he never gave up his sense that listening to a Walkman while walking defeated the point of music and walking. Yes, it was a Walkman. This was 1996–2000!"

All Sinhababu had to get her interview was Smith's address, so she went and knocked on the door of the Greystone house where he lived, just up the street from Salonica, the corner diner where he was a regular:

> Which I felt like a creep about, but in the absence of any other choice I decided to knock on his door. And when I did so, his wife answered kind of through the glass screen door. And by answering, I mean she looked through the glass at me. And kind of stared at me for a couple seconds and left. Like, "*Who is this person?* I don't know you." But his door had a mail slot, and so I dug a little piece of paper out of my backpack, wrote the interview request on it, and slid it through. Apparently he got it.

She said her interview with Smith was—by far—the most-read article she ever wrote. Obviously that was due entirely to my subject," she said:

> We tried to put the whole thing on the website but it actually broke the character limit for an article at the time. I kept getting e-mails for years afterwards, like, "This is a great interview, but why does it cut off at the end?" It speaks to just how interesting he is and how much people want to know about him. Even after reading thousands and thousands of words they want more.

There's one more memorable story about Smith and the *Maroon*. The front page of the paper on May 4, 1979 had two photo slots, each one column in width: One was Jonathan Z. Smith; one was a police sketch of a rapist in Hyde Park. Smith's picture should have appeared under a headline about the College's ongoing review of the Core, but you can guess the mistake when the printer went to line up the photo negatives with the corresponding picture slots. Fletman, the editor at the time, said she called the Dean immediately so he would not have found out about it another way. Chris Isidore, a senior business writer at CNN, who was editor-in-chief of *The Maroon* in 1982, remembers that Smith was easy-going, answering the phone as "the friendly neighborhood rapist." "I of course had great trepidation about making this phone call, but he was very good humored about it," Fletman said. "It's a good story because it does really reflect what an accepting guy he was." The joke at *The Maroon* was that the rapist was furious because he didn't want to look like Smith.

The papers were picked up from newsstands, and the corrected version made it to the library's microforms collection.

"An After-Dinner Speaker"

Smith's status in the administration and his membership on two national commissions that issued major reports on liberal education drew "attention to the continued musings of a college teacher," he said in his self-written preface to Lehrich's collection of his essays. Smith came to be regarded as somewhat of a thought leader in higher education, giving 150 addresses at universities, professional associations, and conferences over the years. He started calling himself "an after-dinner speaker," Lehrich said.

While advancing his beliefs about education Smith tried to hold the university to its own word, and he was an excellent spokesperson for principles he saw as fundamental to the university. His talks would get published, but often in remote, out-of-the-way journals.

"Some of these essays really challenged the whole notion of how collegiate education ought to be done," Lehrich said. "I felt that this stuff shouldn't be forgotten." He worked with Smith to find copies of his lectures and to select which ones to include. "It's the kind of thing a graduate student does for an old mentor."

Central to Smith's education philosophy was what colleagues came to refer to as "Smith's iron law": *A student may not be asked to integrate what the faculty will not.* This law manifests itself in Smith's first three rules for teaching (as printed in Lehrich's collection, *On Teaching Religion*):

1   Students should gain some sense of mastery. Among other things, this means read less rather than more. In principle, the students should have time to read each assignment twice.

2   Always begin with the question of definition, and return to it.

3   Make arguments explicit. Both those found in the readings and those made in class.

An application of this law is found in the 2008 interview. Sinhababu asks about his criticisms of the Core:

> I think the Core, if it were a Core, is terrific. Now, the thing about a Core is it really has to represent a hard-won faculty consensus ... It has to be that of all the books we could possibly inflict on you—only in 10 weeks, and you waste the first week, you waste the last week, so you've got eight weeks. If they're not crazy, they're going to take two weeks to read a book. So you're down to four books. Now what that Core really ought to be doing is saying that out of all the books in the world, these are the four books you should read. If they're not prepared to say that, they should shut up shop. That's my first comment... The second issue is I really think that if it's a Core, there shouldn't be so many of them. How can you say "we hold these truths to be self-evident, and by the way we've got eight sets of truths. You can choose which one you'd like to take." I'm not a fan of the fantasy of the Core in the days when on Wednesday, April 8, every student was reading exactly the same page of Plato. It's the automaton theory of uniformity. I mean, stick with one or two, but then it's five, six, seven, eight. The word fundamental means something or it doesn't mean something.

So what made something "fundamental" to Smith? What would a proper, "hard-won faculty consensus" look like?

In line with rule #2, Smith's talks usually involved creating definitions, as did his writing. "His notion of the argument always had to do with a discussion about language ... He thought universities were special arenas for the clarifications of language and therefore the argument," Long said. Mitchell calls him their field's "great definer," like a "modern-day Aristotle" because his work was obsessed with the question of classification and organization of material

The 1982 Aims of Education address challenged Smith because it forced him to define *two* words. Referencing a dictionary definition of "aim," Smith said in his speech to first-years:

> If "aim implies a clear definition of something that one hopes to effect," then my assigned title puts me in double jeopardy. For it requires a "clear definition" of education (no small task), a clarity, even if attainable, that seems to be placed at risk by the pluralism of "aims." If education, in the context in which we gather this evening, means baccalaureate education or liberal education, the problem is intensified. What, then, to do? I was about to give up and hunt for another title, when my eye was caught by the etymology of "aim."

The word "aim," he explained, is derived from the old French verb for "to guess," giving Smith some solace because there is confusion and uncertainty built into it. He declared that he was retitling his address, "A Guess About Education."

> Regardless of the academic calendar employed, there is almost always less than one hundred hours of class-time in a *year-long* course ... We do not reflect often enough together on the delicious yet terrifying freedom undergraduate education offers by these rigid temporal constraints ... A college curriculum, whether represented by a particular course, a program, or a four-year course of study, thus becomes an occasion for deliberate, collegial institutionalized choice. This, then, is what our common discourse needs to be about.
>
> The talk continues, and Smith pauses to wrestle with defining the word "interesting." He says that when we use the word interesting, we often use it to mean *"tres amusant,"* French for "very amusing."

But the "very amusing" is not fundamental, and it shouldn't be the basis of a curriculum.

"Translated into the world of collegiate education, such a gossipy, inconsequential understanding of 'interesting' is what often governs the elective curriculum, and, all too often, the survey course."

What Smith wanted was "quality," Redfield said. "He was always looking for it." Smith, in the Aims address, moves on to another understanding of the word "interesting": the one that his iron law says ought to ground a college curriculum. "In this understanding, things that are 'interesting,' things that become objects of interest, are things in which you have a stake, things which place you at risk, things which are important to you, things which made a difference," he said. "Courses must be designed to be 'interesting.' For, students cannot be asked to be consequential while the faculty abstains. Students cannot be asked to integrate what the faculty will not. Students will not be critical if the faculty is not."

Pete Grieve is a Political Science graduate of the University of Chicago. He worked as editor-in-chief of the student newspaper, *The Chicago Maroon*, where he also wrote in-depth pieces for *Grey City*, the publication's long-form supplement. He has completed internships at the *San Francisco Chronicle*, the *Chicago Sun-Times*, and *CNN Politics*.

Acknowledgments

This was originally posted online at the *Chicago Maroon* on March 23, 2018; see www.chicagomaroon.com/article/2018/3/23/jonathan-z-smith-dean-of-college-university-of-chicago (accessed June 26, 2019). Reproduction of the archival letters quoted are posted there.

Chapter 14

How I Failed J. Z. Smith

Brett Colasacco

I first heard about Jonathan Z. Smith on the second day of my second quarter as an undergraduate at the University of Chicago. A dormmate had rushed back to Snell Hall to tell my friends and me about his new Self, Culture, and Society professor: a tall old man in a vintage suit, with shoulder-length white hair, a beard, and an ancient-looking walking stick. Gandalf the wizard, only with large glasses and a less pointy hat. More striking even than his appearance, it seemed, were his wit and erudition—about such texts as Durkheim's *Elementary Forms of Religious Life* or Lévi-Strauss's *The Savage Mind* and virtually any topic tangential to them—and for the next ten weeks the same friend would frequently regale us with retellings of J. Z.'s latest anecdotes, bon mots, and other recent happenings from class.

Needless to say, I knew that I had to take a course with this professor.

The following autumn, I enrolled in Introduction to Religious Studies. It was Smith's first time teaching that course, which he would go on to do several more times before his retirement in 2011. On the first day he asked each of us to write down, on a sheet of paper, our best attempt at definitions of (a) "religion" and (b) "the study of religion." Then we handed in our sheets. On the second day he presented an incredibly detailed typology of the definitions we had submitted, which would go on to play a crucial role in the final paper assignment for the course. Immediately, I gained through first-hand experience what countless students of religion have acquired from Smith's many classic essays: an intense admiration for his rigorous commitment to problems of definition, classification, theorization, and comparison, and his understanding that these "second-order" problematics are the very essence of a scholar's work.

The first time I failed J. Z. Smith was in a course he offered in spring 2005 on Mircea Eliade's *Patterns in Comparative Religion*. As Smith observes in his extraordinary "bio-bibliographical" essay, "When the Chips Are Down" (from his 2004 collection *Relating Religion*), his reading of *Patterns*—and subsequent exploration of Eliade's exhaustively footnoted sources—constituted his education in the field of the study of religion. Suffice to say that my study of Smith's analysis and interpretation of *Patterns* constituted my own true introduction to the field. He began each class by filling the chalkboard with a remarkably comprehensive bibliography of texts relevant to the day's assigned chapter from *Patterns*. He then commented at considerable length on these texts, and instructed us—if we were moved to seek out any of these materials in the library—to read not only those books, but also the five books to the left and five books to the right of every one. It's a goal I have often aspired to, but rarely met. But that's not how I failed J. Z. Smith.

Integral to the course was the role of "discussant." Each student had signed up to be responsible for a particular chapter of *Patterns*, and on the day for which that chapter was assigned, Smith engaged in a brief, Socratic exchange with the discussant, which led into a broader class discussion. I was responsible for the very last chapter, "The Structure of Symbols." That day, Smith initiated the exchange with a question I will never forget: "What's special about Jacob's stone?"

I said nothing.

Seconds passed. Maybe a minute. It felt like hours. In college, I sometimes struggled with speaking up in class. Yet never to this extent of total paralysis. I knew the answer. Eliade stated it explicitly in the first sentence of the second paragraph. I had read and reread the chapter, annotated it. I had underlined that sentence. Still, in that moment, I couldn't muster up the courage to say it. Eventually, another student chimed in with the awaited response. The discussion proceeded as I sunk into my chair.

Graciously, Smith allowed all of this to transpire without comment or intervention. He had been looking me straight in the eyes the whole time; not in judgment or in anger, but in what appeared to be curiosity. He never once confronted me about it. When I went to his office hours he quickly took control of the conversation and steered it such that I never had the opportunity to apologize or try to explain myself. We just talked. He talked mostly, while I listened and laughed. Later on, after many more memorable visits to Smith's office, I became one of the last two students to graduate with a concentration in Religion and the Humanities, the now defunct undergraduate program Smith had created and coordinated since 1973.

The second time I failed Smith was when I asked him for letters of recommendation for graduate school. Nervously, I took the elevator up to his office in the west tower of Harper and told him I intended to pursue a career as a scholar of religion. As anyone who knew Smith knows well, he claimed never to want his undergraduate students to follow so closely in his footsteps. He approached college teaching and mentorship as the impartation of essential skills—good reading, good writing, good thinking—which would be and should be transferrable to any and all walks of life. The specific subject matter (e.g., religion) mattered not. He professed especially to take pleasure and pride in those of his students who absorbed his lessons on classification and comparison and applied these in entirely different contexts. More than once I heard him refer to those of his students who went on to become religion scholars as his "failures."

Of course, I was never good at getting Smith's jokes. An example: Once, in the Eliade class, he brought up Charles de Brosses's *Du culte des dieux fétiches* [*The Cult of the Fetishistic Gods*], a 1760 text which Smith argued was the most important of the early, foundational works in the discipline of the academic study of religion. He said he kept a copy of it above his desk, so he could take it down from time to time, just to stroke its cover. The joke was lost on me. I went directly from class to the library, searching the stacks for a copy of the book that I could touch myself.

So I suspect that Smith's periodic swipes at those of us who went on from his college courses to do graduate work in religion may have been, at least a little bit, tongue-in-cheek. I needn't have been apprehensive to come forth as one of his "failures," and he had nothing but encouragement for me in my chosen path. The point of it all, I now believe, was that the study of religion is no different, fundamentally, than any other intentional human activity. It is an opportunity to examine the astonishing fecundity of the human imagination in its interactions with its variegated cultural and (culturally postulated) superhuman environments. It is an occasion for thought, and for play. For having fun—while undertaking intellectual labor of the utmost seriousness. Religions, and the study of religions, can be mysterious, terrifying, and fascinating. They are also thoroughly, confoundingly human.

There are others who can attest, better than I can, to Smith's influence on our field. I can attest to how he changed my life. Today, in addition to the grief and sadness I feel at the news of his death, I feel grateful beyond words for being able to count myself among the failures of Jonathan Z. Smith.

Brett Colasacco has a Ph.D. in religion, literature, and visual culture from the University of Chicago, where he now works as a writer.

Acknowledgments

This essay originally appeared in Sightings on January 4, 2018, a publication of the Martin Marty Center for the Public Understanding of Religion at the University of Chicago Divinity School; see https://divinity.uchicago.edu/sightings/how-i-failed-j-z-smith (accessed June 26, 2019).

Chapter 15

The Positive Genealogy of J. Z. Smith

Tenzan Eaghll

I never had the honor of meeting Jonathan Z. Smith, and to be honest, I haven't even had the opportunity to read all of his works yet. However, the publications of his that I have had the pleasure of reading immensely influenced my teaching and writing style, and I am grateful for the critical contribution he made to the academic study of religion. The pedagogical usefulness of his work is quite remarkable. He had the ability to write about extremely difficult ideas in an accessible and fun manner. Whenever I use his work in my classroom, I find students grasp the underlying point very easily and tend to appreciate the candor with which he addresses deep questions and problems in the field.

Without a doubt, the essay of Smith's that I have used the most in class has been "Religion, Religions, Religious." Originally published in *Critical Terms for Religious Studies*, this essay provides a brief genealogy and history of the category of religion, summarizing the various uses, etymologies, taxonomies, and morphologies that have been associated with it since the sixteenth century.

It is written in a way that introduces students to the general history of the category of religion and to the fundamental problematic that underlies the study of religion; namely, 'what is it we are talking about when we are talking about religion'? The essay is also a bit ahead of its time, for although other attempts to trace the history of the category religion were written before it, Smith's broad sweeping summary of its naturalization and permutation into the "world religions" paradigm, prefigures recent full-length studies on the subject.[1]

In particular, Smith begins this seminal article with four general observations about religion that have gone on to tremendously influence subsequent critical studies and histories in the field. These are, respectively: (1) Religion is not a native category in the world; (2) in most of its early theoretical formulations it was presented as a universal human phenomenon; (3) it tends to be treated as a distinct natural occurring entity in the world that can be used to account for cultural difference; (4) religion is an anthropological, not a theological category (Smith 1998: 296).

By stating that religion is not a native category in the world, Smith was arguing that religion is a second order colonialist and scholarly term—it was originally used to categorize and characterize native cultures by Western missionaries and explorers. As he notes, the earliest accounts of the "New World" by Europeans in the sixteenth-century documents their attempt to determine whether or not natives in other cultures had religious dogmas, institutions, priests, etc. (Smith 1998: 296). These early explorers tended to assume that religion was a universally occurring human practice that was distinct from other aspects of social life, a sentiment that was later developed and systematized by philosophers, anthropologists, historians, and scientists between the seventeenth and twentieth centuries. What was common to the early explorers and theorists that used the category is that they all tended to naturalize religion as an objective fact or archaeological remain that could be directly studied as data in other historical periods and cultures. Though each applied and understood the term differently, they demonstrated how religion is inextricably connected to the all too human act of definition, classification, and taxonomy.

Of course, these broad sweeping observations were only broached by Smith in this relatively short essay, but they have been documented in depth by recent full-length studies on the category, such as Tomoko Masuzawa's *The Invention of World Religions* and Brent Nongbri's *Before Religion*. Masuzawa traces the intellectual origins of the world religions paradigm back to a strand of Christian theological universalism that was held by its earliest proponents. Much like in Smith's seminal essay, she finds that the universalism originally associated with religion was first expressed in different colonialist settings, but that later morphed into the world religions paradigm as it was applied to other cultures and became associated with an established taxonomy (Masuzawa 2005). Nongbri goes even further back than Masuzawa, tracing the use of the category religion all the way back to antiquity and showing that there was no clear distinction between religion and other areas of social life in the ancient world. Again, much like Smith, Nongbri points out how our modern understanding of religion has been projected across space and time by European missionaries, philosophers, and scientists, and assumed to be a natural and necessary aspect of world history (Nongbri 2013).[2]

All this being noted, I think the real influence of Smith upon the field is not in any of the specific conclusions he arrived at in any one essay, but his general methodology, which is certainly on display in "Religion, Religions, Religious." Much like Foucault, his methodology was part genealogy, part archaeology, and part mere history, and with this, he inspired a whole generation of subsequent scholars to reject the naturalization of religious discourse and history. Just as Foucault pointed out that "man is an invention of recent date" (Foucault 1989: 422), so Smith pointed out that religion (and related categories of classification) is an invention of rather recent date. Moreover, Smith engaged in what Foucault described as the "grey, meticulous, and patiently documentary" work of genealogy; he studied religion like Foucault studied the history of the "subject," as a field of "entangled and confused parchments, on documents that have been scratched over and recopied many times" (Foucault 1984: 76). In the Preface to *Map is Not Territory*, Smith put this in his own terms when he described his analysis of the history of religion as a mixture of "archaeology, history, and philology." He suggested that his work is more closely related to exegesis than most historians of religion, as what interests him is the way that data is compared and assembled into a whole (Smith 1978: ix).

As scholarly approaches, genealogy and archaeology are typically connected because the genealogical analysis of the 'history of systems of thought' tends to lead to a more detailed analysis of the archives of society (recorded philosophical debates, official records, chronicles, diaries, journals, logbooks, grand theories, popular knowledge, subjugated knowledge, and so on; Crowley 2009: 2). In Smith's work, this is quite apparent because his philological analysis of the religion, early Christian documents, ritual, etc., always leads to a discussion of the various taxonomic assumptions that inform the present assumptions in the field. As Aaron Hughes recently noted, it was this "higher" type of comparison that interested Smith, he was not interested in comparing for the sake of accumulating more and more data, but analyzing why scholars compare "x" with "y" as opposed to with "z," and to expose the hidden terms and ideological agendas that underlie these decisions (Hughes 2019: 3).[3] In this manner, Smith used both genealogy and archaeology to reveal how definition and classification establish the boundaries of knowledge and how these acts take shape in scholarship. In particular, in "Religion, Religions, Religious" Smith demonstrates this by isolating religion as a category and deconstructing our accepted knowledge of it by exposing the randomness of its interpretation, application, as well as the various taxonomic orderings that have become normative for it. Moreover, by showing how a certain unity and naturalness has been granted to the category—a fact that tends to disqualify local beliefs, understandings, and knowledge of the cultures and historical periods it is applied to—he exposes the violence implicit in its everyday application.

However, I must say that my favorite thing about Smith's work is that he uses these methodological tools to derive something positive for the study of religion. One never gets the impression from Smith's work that he is deconstructing the categories in the field for some negative end. He never makes the claim, for instance, that because the study of religion is founded upon colonialist categories and its boundaries are constantly being contested and reinvented by scholars the study of religion is hopeless, or that there shouldn't be religious studies departments. Rather, he uses his work to derive positive lessons about the creative act of definition, classification, and taxonomy, and to use this as an instructive lesson for his readers. This is valuable because sometimes critical scholars of religion are criticized for being valueless and nihilistic, yet Smith eschews this by presenting the human act of classification as a fascinating object of study in itself.[4]

Personally, this is what most stood out to me the first time I read "Religion, Religions, Religious" as a graduate student in a Method and Theory class. The teacher of the class used Smith's essay as a primer before we read *The Invention of World Religions*, and it influenced how I understood the latter. What I learned from Smith's essay upon this first reading was that it is possible to understand the invention, construction, and naturalization of religion as a positive pedagogical lesson. Though it is possible to see the lack of categorical stability in religious studies as a negative fact about our field—not to mention the nihilistic plight of the religion scholar—Smith encourages us to see it as evidence for what aligns religious studies with other academic fields, and as evidence for the various ways in which humans organize their world. At the end of the essay, after detailing many of the permutations and interpretations of religion since the sixteenth century, Smith writes,

> It was once a tactic of students of religion to cite the appendix of James H. Leuba's *Psychological Study of Religion* (1912), which lists more than fifty definitions of religion, to demonstrate that "the effort clearly to define religion in short compass is a hopeless task" (King 1954). Not at all! The moral of Leuba is not that religion cannot be defined, but that it can be defined, with greater or lesser success, more than fifty ways. (Smith 1998: 281)

When confronted with the reality that religion is not a native category to the world, but is in fact a second order anthropological term used to organize data, one could throw their arms up in frustration and conclude that it is best to abandon the study of religion and switch to history, or even anthropology itself, but Smith encourages us to see this terminological diversity *as the very object* of the academic study of religion. What do people say about religion? How do they use it to carve up the world and create maps for the terrain before them? This positive pedagogical lesson influenced my reading of *The Invention of World Religions* and other genealogical accounts because it led me to see these works not as refutations of the central category of our field, but evidence for its diversity and importance. According to this perspective, what makes religious studies important is not that religion is "sacred" or "special" in some regard, but that humans use it in various social ways to shape the world around them. Moreover, what makes our field fascinating is that what gets to count as religion in the world is always an open and contested possibility.

There is something almost Deleuzian about this latter subtle point that Smith makes which I really love, as it affirms the creative play at the heart of discourses about religion. Recall that in *What is Philosophy?*, Deleuze argues that "philosophy is the art of forming, inventing, and fabricating concepts" (Deleuze and Guattari 1994: 2). Moreover, he suggests that the role of the philosopher is different from that of the mystic or the sage because the philosopher must be treated as one who thinks and invents concepts through his relation with the objective world. As Deleuze writes, "concepts are not waiting for us ready-made, like heavenly bodies. There is no heaven for concepts. They must be invented, fabricated, or rather created and would be nothing without their creator's signature" (ibid.: 5). I find this somewhat similar to Smith's above cited claims, such as his point that religion is an anthropological not a theological category, as well as his statement in the opening of *Imagining Religion: From Babylon to Jonestown*, where he writes that religion is an analytical category that is created by imaginative acts of scholarly comparison and generalization (Smith 1982: xi). Like Deleuze, Smith calls attention to the creative work involved in the construction of discursive worlds of meaning and suggests that we must pay attention to these creative acts. Of course, the parallels between Deleuze and Smith may stop there, as Deleuze is advocating for the continued creation of philosophical concepts and Smith is merely interested in pointing out that religion exists in the imaginative work of the scholar, but I think this parallel is interesting nonetheless.

Last year I was given the opportunity to teach a graduate Method and Theory class and I had the honor of introducing the students to "Religion, Religions, Religious" and the positive pedagogical lesson it contains. Much like how the essay was used in the class I took as a graduate student, I used it to prime students for more complex genealogical material. At one point during the seminar, a student asked me what I thought all this material implied about the study of religion: "If 'religion' is a modern invention with no singular definition to encapsulate its meaning," the student questioned, "what are we studying in this class and in this college of religious studies." I replied that we study how people use and think about religion, and that this is an exciting thing because there are an infinite variety of ways this has been done, not just in the past, but right now in our contemporary world. Acknowledging the invention, construction, and naturalization of religion does not mean it cannot be studied, but simply that what we study are these creative acts and their affects.

I look forward to reading more of J. Z. Smith's work in the future and learning other lessons from him, but so far, this positive pedagogical point about genealogy and the construction of our world is my favorite.

Tenzan Eaghll is a Lecturer and Chair of the International M.A. program at the College of Religious Studies, Mahidol University, Bangkok. His research focuses on continental philosophy, religion and film, and method and theory in the study of religion.

Acknowledgments

This originally appeared on the *Bulletin for the Study of Religion* blog on January 2, 2018; see http://bulletin.equinoxpub.com/2018/01/something-i-learned-from-j-z-smith (accessed June 22, 2019).

Notes

1   For another early attempt to focus on the category of religion, see McCutcheon (1997).
2   For an overview of the treatment of religion in recent publications see McCutcheon (2018), specifically chapter 1, "The Category 'Religion' in Recent Publications."
3   This short essay by Hughes is part of a recent collection of essays dedicated to the memory of J. Z. Smith published by the *Journal of the American Academy of Religion* 87/1. For this and other essays see the entire issue, "Roundtable on Jonathan Z. Smith: Whence and Whither the Study of Religion?"
4   For an interesting discussion on the role of "values" in the critical study of religion see Martin 2015, which records a conversation on the topic by Russell McCutcheon and Warren S. Goldstein.

References

Crowley, Una (2009). "Genealogy Method," in Rob Kitchin and Nigel Thrift (eds.), *International Encyclopedia of Human Geography*, 341–344. Amsterdam: Elsevier Science. https://doi.org/10.1016/B978-008044910-4.00443-0

Deleuze, Gilles and Félix Guattari (1994). *What is Philosophy?* Hugh Tomlinson and Graham Burchell (trans.). New York: Columbia University Press.

Foucault, Michel (1984). "Nietzsche, Genealogy, History," in Paul Rabinow (ed.) *The Foucault Reader*, 76–100. New York: Random House.

——. (1989). *The Order of Things*. New York: Routledge.

Hughes, Aaron W. (2019). "Introduction," *Journal of the American Academy of Religion*. 87/1: 18–21. https://doi.org/10.1093/jaarel/lfy046

King, Winston L. (1954). *Introduction to Religion*. New York: Harper and Row.

Martin, Craig (ed.) (2015). "On the Nature and Ends of Critique in the Study of Religion: Part One," *Bulletin for the Study of Religion* 3/1: 3–12.

Masuzawa, Tomoku (2005). *The Invention of World Religions: Or, How European Universalism Was Preserved in the Language of Pluralism*. Chicago, IL: University of Chicago Press. https://doi.org/10.7208/chicago/9780226922621.001.0001

McCutcheon, Russell (1997). *Manufacturing Religion: The Discourse on Sui Generis Religion and the Politics of Nostalgia*. New York: Oxford University Press.

——. (2018). *Fabricating Religion: Fanfare for the Common e.g.* Boston, MA: Walter de Gruyter.

Nongbri, Brent (2013). *Before Religion: A History of a Modern Concept*. New Haven, CT: Yale University Press. https://doi.org/10.12987/yale/9780300154160.001.0001

Smith, Jonathan Z. (1978). *Map is Not Territory*. Chicago, IL: University of Chicago Press.

——. (1982). *Imagining Religion: From Babylon to Jonestown*. Chicago, IL: University of Chicago Press.

——. (1998). "Religion, Religions, Religious," in Mark C. Taylor (ed.), *Critical Terms for Religious Studies*, 269–284. Chicago, IL: University of Chicago Press.

Chapter 16

In the Laboratory of Taxonomy and Classification
(When the Chips Were *Really* Down)

Richard D. Hecht

Jonathan's introductory essay, "When the Chips are Down" (2004), provides us with an extraordinary map of the influences that shaped arguably one of the greatest historians of religions of our times—and chronologically developed and were deployed as the central anchors of his distinctive contributions to the study of religion. In that essay he described how his early interest in botany and fascination with taxonomy led him to comparative study. Reaching back to 1952 and his small trailside museum that he called *Same, Like, Different*, in which he tried to illustrate "the issues attendant on taxonomy with examples of common wild plants. Put simply," he wrote, "taxonomy seemed a comparative enterprise which sought similarity across obvious individual variations and which asserted significant difference even in the face of apparent resemblances" (Smith 2004: 20). But perhaps there was another source for the powers he assigned to taxonomy, a source forged in the bitter conflict over the Vietnam War.

I had met Jonathan and Elaine Smith shortly after they arrived in Santa Barbara in 1966 and in one of Jonathan's first courses he taught here. The war in Vietnam was heating up. By the end of 1966, there were almost 400,000 American soldiers in Vietnam, and President Johnson was under enormous pressure to increase the number of American military personnel in the combat zone. Most of my male friends had student deferments and most of us were against the war in Southeast Asia. I knew that as soon as I graduated, my deferment would end and the chances were very high that I would be drafted into military service. I had been reading Gandhi and believed I was a conscientious objector. I had gone to my draft board in Pasadena where I had grown up and discovered very quickly the draft board prided itself in never classifying anyone as a conscientious objector. Pasadena was also the headquarters of the Quaker American Friends Service Committee that provided information and support for those who claimed conscientious objection. Robert Michaelsen, the Chair of the Department of Religious Studies and who had won his claim as a Conscientious Objector at the end of World War II, suggested I speak with Jonathan who was meeting with Conscientious Objectors in a Quaker Fellowship Church. I began going to listen to his conversations and to take notes, and I recall that I followed these meetings until Spring, 1967.

Jonathan regularly participated in a one-hour silent anti-war protest organized by faculty in the sociology department during the lunch hour. I recall that I had bumped into him a several weekend anti-war demonstrations, and I think I may have heard him speak at one or two of them. The American Friends Service Committee and the Jewish Peace Fellowship were training draft counselors to help young men make their claim to conscientious objection, to use the draft law to defend themselves against the draft, and support them within jails if they had been arrested for failing to appear for induction. But as the war escalated and more and more men were required for the draft, resistance required some legal training as well.

We discovered there was another Smith, William G. Smith, a former Air Force Captain who was training draft counselors in bookstores, churches and synagogues in Los Angeles. So we went together, I think Elaine must have driven us, because I do not think I had a car and Jonathan was not driving at that time. Bill Smith won some very important cases against the Selective Service (the Draft) and he would begin his training sessions by saying that going to jail or leaving the country were too drastic. It was much easier to use the law itself against induction. One of his best-known cases involved a young student who refused to register for the Draft. It was estimated that more than 800,000 young men failed to register, but the US Department of Justice targeted only 43 for prosecution. This disparity allowed Smith to bust the young man out of a federal prison sentence of years to six months confinement in his grandmother's home. In one case of lesser importance he mounted a successful defense for two anti-war protesters who dressed as army officers—General Hershey Bar (the Director of the Selective Service at the time was General Lewis Hershey) and General Wastemoreland (General William Westmoreland was the commander of the US military forces in Vietnam during the massive escalation to over one-half million military personnel)—who were arrested for impersonating military officers. Smith won another case involving a Navy enlisted man who was charged with assault for throwing a pie in the face of his commander. Smith brought the comedian Soupy Sales into court and he testified that he had thrown perhaps 20,000 pies and had never been prosecuted. The sailor was acquitted. After the end of the war, Smith went on to represent veterans who were not treated fairly by the Veterans' Administration. Smith died in 1999 (Woo 1999).

The US's Selective Service Act, which had its origins in the First World War, and had been revised several times, was a vast taxonomic system intended to classify every American male 18 years or older and to process them to meet monthly, national military goals in wartime and in peace. The 1948 taxonomy of the Draft had five major categories, numbered 1 through 5. And, within these five categories, there were 32 taxa, denoted by a combination of numbers and letters. So 1-A was "available for unrestricted military service" and 5-A was defined as a registrant who was over the age of 26 (however, if the individual had received a deferment, the age liability was extended to the age of 35). If you were in the 1-A taxon you could expect very soon to receive your "Greetings" letter from the President ordering you to an induction center in thirty days, and stipulating that failure to report for induction was a felony.

The Selective Service Act was a tyrannical comparative system, intended to do what every taxonomic system resolves to do: sorting the differences among similar phenomena (in this case, the young or relatively young, 18 years or older, American males). There were fourteen taxa in the 1 class, five taxa in the 2 class, two taxa in the 3 class, ten taxa in the 4 class, and only one taxon in the 5 class. Every possibility was subsumed into these five classes. Among the many taxa there were 1-A-O for a conscientious objector available for noncombatant military service, as distinct from 1-O, that was for a conscientious objector to all military service. In order to achieve this taxa, the draft eligible male had to demonstrate to the satisfaction of the local draft board that his request for this taxonomic classification and exemption from combatant and noncombatant military training was rooted in moral, ethical or religious beliefs that were described as playing a significant role in his life and his objection to participation in war was not confined to a particular conflict; this status required the taxon to serve in alternative civilian service.

Among the deferments, also taxonomic classifications, were: an individual in a military reserve unit; students completing their education in one of the service academies; students still in high school (although they had to complete their education no later than the age of 20); essential agricultural or non-agricultural workers or full-time study or training in community college or an approved apprenticeship program; a student preparing for the ministry (up to the age of 24); and one of the most highly prized deferments: 2-S, for college or university study granted until the age of 24. 2-S also included graduate professional education for medicine, dentistry, veterinary medicine, osteopathic medicine and optometry. Graduate students in their fifth year of continuous study toward the doctoral degree were deferred for one year. To retain a student deferment you had to maintain what your college or university considered a full course of study as they defined it and in good standing, i.e., not in academic trouble. If you failed either, you could expect to receive your letter of greetings from the President in a matter of days.

If you finished your education, and did not want to participate in the war you only had a few days to find an alternative to re-classify yourself and not be re-classified in the taxon 1-A. My college roommate, for example, took off the tip of his right index finger, his trigger finger, by sticking it under the family lawn mower. When he answered his greetings letter, the induction center reclassified him as 4-F, the taxon that defined you as not acceptable for military service for reasons having to do with physical, mental or moral standards. Everyone wanted to know what those moral standards might be for the 4-F and that question became the center of Arlo Guthrie's talking blues piece, "Alice's Restaurant Massacree," recorded in 1967. The narrative told about how Arlo and one of his friends took a half-ton of garbage the day before Thanksgiving to the dump that was closed. Nevertheless, they dumped the trash and were subsequently arrested by Officer Obie for public littering. They were required to surrender their wallets, so they could not buy anything in jail, their belts so that they could hang themselves, and the toilet seat in their jail cell had been removed so they could not hit themselves in the head and drown. The next morning, he and his friend were brought before the magistrate. They were fined $50 and had to pick up garbage around town, Stockbridge, Massachusetts.

But this is only the prologue to the real story of the song that is about taxonomic reclassification. Like so many other young men facing induction, Arlo spent the night before his physical getting good and drunk, so that "he would look and feel his best," hoping to be judged as 4-F. He is sent to room 604 for psychiatric evaluation. There he tells the doctor that what he really wants to do is "kill, kill, kill." And he starts to jump up and down and the psychiatrist starts jumping up and down and both are yelling, "KILL, KILL, KILL!" And the sergeant says, "You're our boy." After several additional efforts to get the 4-F classification, he is asked, "Have you ever been arrested?" When he tells the story of his arrest by Officer Obie and that he was found guilty of public littering, he is told to join the Bench W group of really mean characters. When he completed the written description of his crime, the sergeant said to him, "Kid, have you rehabilitated yourself?" Arlo responded, "'Sergeant, you got a lot of gall to ask me if I've rehabilitated myself ... I'm sittin' here on the bench, I mean, I'm sittin' here on the Group W bench, 'cause you want to know if I'm moral enough to join the army, burn women, kids, houses and villages after bein' a litterbug." He looked at me and said, "Kid, we don't like your kind, and we're gonna send your fingerprints off to Washington." And, so, Arlo Guthrie was taxonomically transformed from 1-A to 4-F.

There are only a few scattered references to the Vietnam War in the corpus of Jonathan's work. For example, in his essay "Earth and Gods" he borrowed the rubric "enclave" and "strategic hamlet" from the war to describe one of the ways that ancient Israel spoke about the land of Israel (1978: 109). "Strategic hamlet" referred to a program begun under the French and continued into the 1960s, whereby villagers were removed from the ancestral lands and resettled in larger communities that could be guarded by the South Vietnamese army forces and also, American army and marine personnel. Another, of course, was his Durkheimian interpretation (in his essay, "The Topography of the Sacred") of the Vietnam Veterans' Memorial and pilgrimage in contemporary America (2004: 108–109). Certainly, we would agree that one of the most important theoretical and interpretive structures in Jonathan's work was taxonomy and I would suggest that long before he set and anchored it in his work, he already knew its analytic power, as he worked with young men caught in one taxon and helped them transform themselves into other taxa. His work counseling conscientious objectors and others provided him with a laboratory where he worked the existential powers of taxonomy where the chips were really down.

Richard Hecht is Professor of Religious Studies at the University of California, Santa Barbara. He is also affiliated with the Jewish Studies Program. He has become increasingly interested in the deep contextualization of religion in its lived environments and most centrally the intersections of religion, politics, and culture.

Acknowledgments

A version of this chapter originally appeared on the blog of the Department of Religious Studies at the University of Alabama on October 18, 2018; see https://religion.ua.edu/blog/2018/10/18/conscientious-objection-the-war-in-vietnam-and-jonathan-z-smith (accessed May 24, 2019).

References

Smith, Jonathan Z. (1978). *Map is not Territory: Studies in the History of Religions* Leiden: E. J. Brill.

——. (2004). *Relating Religion: Essays in the Study of Religion.* Chicago, IL: University of Chicago Press.

Woo, Elaine (1999). "William G. Smith; Lawyer for Draft Resisters, Veterans," *Los Angeles Times* (August 4); www.latimes.com/archives/la-xpm-1999-aug-04-mn-62550-story.html (accessed May 27, 2019).

Chapter 17

My Preliminary Journey through the World of J. Z. Smith

Mitsutoshi Horii

I am an amateur traveler in the world of the late Jonathan Z. Smith. My encounter with J. Z. Smith's scholarship was relatively recent, and I do not claim any comprehensive understanding of the entirety of his works. To be honest, I am currently lost in J. Z. Smith's world. Nevertheless, I believe that becoming lost is often an effective way of learning about a new place you are visiting for the first time.

Though my disciplinary background is in Sociology, I have also written on some topics relating to Religious Studies, including this one. I often feel there is some distance between these two academic disciplines which I am constantly jumping across. This pales in comparison with the cross-disciplinary journey of Jonathan Z. Smith, who in an interview in 2008, said: "I started off originally in grass breeding" (Sinhababu 2008).

I often wonder about my own academic identity, constantly travelling across Sociology, Religious Studies, and Japanese Studies: Where do I belong? The story of Smith's enormous cross-disciplinary jump, however, gives me comfort.

I completed my Ph.D. in Sociology at a university in the UK towards the end of 2005. My thesis was on the de-professionalization of Buddhist priests in contemporary Japan. At that time I took for granted the conceptualization of Japanese Buddhism as a "religion," and the academic discipline of Sociology as "secular." This assumption was implicit throughout my Ph.D. thesis. Immediately after the completion of my Ph.D., I came across Timothy Fitzgerald's *The Ideology of Religious Studies* (2000). It was in my reading of Fitzgerald's other related works, that I first encountered Jonathan Z. Smith.

Fitzgerald's works shook the conceptual foundation upon which I had stood until that point, and made me realize the religious-secular distinction is an ideological construction—making such a distinction is a classificatory practice. In the process of my post-Ph.D. exploration of the critical studies of the religious-secular distinction (known as "critical religion"), Smith's famous essay "Religion, Religious, Religions" has been one of the foundational texts to which I still return. Other works I came across include *Imagining Religion* (1982) and *Map is Not Territory* (1978).

As a non-specialist in religion, whose main focus tends to be on Japan and on social theories, I have found some of Smith's texts impenetrable. However, some of his more general remarks scattered across his works have often been sources of inspiration to me. The inspiration I got from his texts may not be Smith's intention when he composed these words, and I believe Smith might not agree with my more deconstructionalist approach to the concept of "religion." Nevertheless, here are some examples.

In the opening page of *Imagining Religion*, Smith claims: "Religion is solely the creation of the scholar's study. It is created for the scholar's analytic purposes by his imaginative acts of comparison and generalization. Religion has no independent existence apart from the academy" (Smith 1982: xi). These sentences reminded me that "religion" was a scholarly construction. In other words, the category "religion" exists merely in the minds of scholars studying culture. It is merely an arbitrary grouping of cultural features created by academic scholars for the purpose of study, comparison, and generalization. This seems to echo Richard King's proposition in his *Orientalism and Religion: Postcolonial Theory, India and "The Mystic East"*: "religious studies as a discipline might better conceive of itself as a form of "cultural studies," rather than as an offshoot of theology" (King 1999: 2).

This has also made me wonder whether "religion" is actually a useful category to analyze the everyday social world of ordinary people outside academia. People outside academia generally know the word "religion," which generates a multiplicity of meanings in different discursive fields in their social world. Meanings of "religion" in this context would often differ from the one constructed in academia. Then I pose a question: Is the scholarly concept of religion useful to analyze everyday social reality?

Smith seems to provide us with an interesting answer to this question. At the very end of *Map is not Territory*, he states:

> [W]e may have to relax some of our cherished notions of significance and seriousness. We may have to become initiated by the other whom we study and undergo the ordeal of incongruity. For we have often missed what is humane in the other by the very seriousness of our quest. We need to reflect on and play with the necessary incongruity of our maps before we set out on a voyage of discovery to chart the worlds of other men. For the dictum of Alfred Korzybski is inescapable: "Map is not territory"—but maps are all we have. (Smith 1978: 309)

The scholarly notion of religion is part of the conceptual map widely shared by academics. This is all that we have. It may guide us to a destination, but it is often useless for us to explore the area of investigation. We may have to rely on local knowledge, or get a more detailed map from a local specialist. We should not hang on to the map we brought with us from the modern West. We should stop trying to understand the area with that modern Western map. If we keep using that map, our understanding of the area can be distorted, or we may get lost. What we should commit ourselves to is not the map, but the expedition.

I am originally from Japan, and I came to the UK for my university education. I went back to Japan to carry out fieldwork for my Ph.D. By that time, I carried with me the modern Western scholarly conceptual map which is embedded with the religious-secular distinction. This was all that I had at that time. However,

as Smith suggests, I gradually learnt to "reflect on and play with the necessary incongruity" caused by my own map. For example, there are discrepancies
between the sociological meaning of "religion" and what the same term means in
the Japanese colloquial discourse. My post-Ph.D. study in "critical religion" inter-
rogates the scholarly concept of religion, and now my recent book, *The Category
of "Religion" in Contemporary Japan* (2018), problematizes the serious attachment
among scholars of Japanese religions to the concept of religion as a category of
analysis. I have taken Smith's remarks as if he is telling me to "relax" my attachment to my modern Western scholarly map. It is useful to guide me up to a certain
point, but useless to go further. Of course, as Smith says, my own conceptual map
is all that I have. When one's map does not make sense, however, one has to ask
for local knowledge (e.g. learning emic classifications in their own terms). If it is
available, we should get a new more detailed and nuanced map to navigate more
effectively in a way which is more rooted to the local culture. In this process, we
may have to abandon the category "religion." I believe that this intellectual flexi-
bility is essential, most especially, for cross-cultural explorations.

If we abandon the category "religion," what would academic studies of religion
be left with? In my view, William Arnal and Russell McCutcheon (2013: 28) have
provided an answer to this question: "the academic future of religion as a concept will need focus on deconstructing the category and analyzing its function
with popular discourse ... rather than assuming that the category *has* content and
seeking to specify what that content is."

In this light, J. Z. Smith's "Religion, Religious, Religions" is extremely informative from the very beginning. It starts with quoting the occurrences of "religion"
from two sixteenth-century colonial-era travel journals. Firstly, Smith refers to an
example from *A Treatyse of the Newe India* (1553), which is Richard Eden's English
translation of part of Sebastian Müenster's *Cosmographia* (1544). The quotation
goes: "At Columbus first coming thether, the inhabitants went naked, without
shame, religion or knowledge of God." The second example is from Pedro Cieza de
León's *Crónica del Perú* (1553). In this book, Smith reports, the north Andean indigenous people were described as "observing no religion at all, as we understand it."
Given these examples, Smith notes: "both are factually incorrect" (Smith 2004:
179).

I am wondering, however, whether J. Z. Smith was right to say "both are factually incorrect." In my view, both may well be actually "factually correct." I believe
that these indigenous people did not have either "religion" or "knowledge of God,"
as understood by Europeans in the sixteenth century. In my view, we should pay
more attention to the point that these colonial-era writers were somehow deeply
struck by the absence of "religion" or "knowledge of God" in these indigenous
people's cultures. This highlights the important historical fact that "religion" is a
European native category, and the tendency in these European writers to assume
their concepts were universal.

Walter Mignolo recently argued: "It was from Eurocentered epistemic assumptions that their New World or their America was the continent inhabited, according to their beliefs, by people without knowledge of God. Which was true, but

it really did not matter at all, except for Europeans' coloniality of knowledge."
(Mignolo and Walsh 2018: 195) In my recent research, I have found that the same
colonial projection of "religion" had been carried out by the descendants of
European settlers in the United States of America almost exactly three centuries later. This time, it was done against people and cultures in East Asia. When
the American President Millard Fillmore ordered the Expedition to Japan (1853–
1854), commanded by Matthew Perry, the term "religion" in many contexts in
the United States "referred mainly to Christian Truth, especially in the form of
Our Protestant Faith" (Fitzgerald 2011: 2). Protestantism symbolized the "civility"
of the United States, and contrasted with "barbarous" Catholics and "pagans."
In this light, it was assumed in the July 1856 issue of *The North American Review*:
"the civilization of Japan lacks all the elements which it would have derived from
religion" (Hildreth 1856: 241). Japan was believed to be ignorant to the civiliz-
ing power of Protestant Truth. Even when Japan was believed to have "religion,"
it was regarded by an unknown writer in the December 1852 issue of *De Bow's
Southern and Western Review* as "the grossest paganism" (55), whose darkness was
to be eradicated by the true religion of Protestantism. The opening of Japan to
commerce was believed to be the first step to this mission.

In the colonial context, the category of "religion" was applied to non-European
cultures as if it denoted a universal aspect of human life. And the lack of it was
believed to be an indicator of inferiority of these cultures compared with that of
Europeans which had "religion." Following from the two quotes in the beginning
of his "Religion, Religious, Religions," Smith continues: "'Religion' is not a native
category," in the sense that "[i]t is a category imposed from outside on some
aspect of native culture" (Smith 2004: 179). In other words, "religion" is a native
category of European colonialists imposed upon the colonized. For me, this is an
extremely important point. In my amateur exploration of Smith's works, however, I have not yet come across his other writing in which Smith further develops
his thought on the issue of colonialism and the category "religion."

I may be wrong because my reading of J. Z. Smith has been rather sporadic.
Nevertheless, at this moment in my on-going exploration, I am feeling a slight
disappointment, especially, when Smith appears to be universalizing the concept
of religion in spite of his critical awareness. For example, while stating "Religion
is solely the creation of the scholar's study," in the same page of his *Imagining
Religion*, Smith also claims:

> If we have understood the archeological and textual record correctly, man has his
> entire history in which to imagine deities and modes of interaction with them. But
> man, more precisely western man, has had only the last few centuries in which to
> imagine religion. (Smith 1982: xi)

This is a very different notion of religion from the previous examples from the colonial contexts, which indicated the encompassing idea of Protestant (or Christian)
Truth as opposed to "pagan barbarity." This specific idea of religion above (which
is "to imagine deities and modes of interaction with them") is conceived to be
something which belongs to the inner realm of individuals, as opposed to the

imagined "secularity" of the public realm. Historically speaking, this kind of idea of "religion" had been powerfully institutionalized by the American and French Revolutions and their respective proclamations of a new world order. According to Fitzgerald, it was partly as a result of the influence of writers such as John Locke, William Penn and others on the framers of the US Constitution (1790) that "religion" and "the secular" came to be imagined as two distinct domains, and this separation was also commonly expressed as the separation of church and state (Fitzgerald 2011: 81).

From my own rather demolitionist approach to the category of "religion," I found the concluding part of Smith's "Religion, Religious, Religions" disappointing in the sense that he seems to be universalizing this specific notion of religion. Towards the end, he repeats almost the same sentence he had in the beginning of this essay: "'Religion' is not a native term" (Smith 2004: 193–194). However, the reason given to this repeated statement is different from the one in the beginning. At this point, according to Smith, this is because "it is a term created by scholars for their intellectual purposes and therefore is theirs to define" (ibid.: 194). In my view, it appears that "religion" is still a native term within a specific community called academics in the study of religion. It is not a native category for many groups of people outside the academy. Whereas Smith tacitly problematizes the imposition of "religion" upon native cultures by the colonialists, he seems to be justifying the imposition of the same category by contemporary scholars. My contestation is that I cannot see any essential differences between these two forms of imposition. It is in this light that my recent monograph critiques the scholarly imposition of "religion" upon Japan.

In spite of my brief disappointment mentioned above, J. Z. Smith seems to have shared with me a kind of deconstructionist spirit, when he claims: "we in religious studies must set about an analogous dismantling of the old theological and imperialistic impulses towards totalization, unification, and integration" (Smith 1982: 18). I believe that this spirit occupied an important place in Smith's scholarship, as he later quotes himself exactly with this sentence in his intellectual autobiography, "When the Chips are Down" (Smith 2004: 23). However, he might tell me to relax my strong demolitionist and often polemic attitude and take more easily the issue of category. He might point out that "religion" is just a category for grouping certain cultural features together. It seems that what he takes more seriously is not the category *per se*, but the actual things put together by the category. He accepts the category "religion" is arbitrary and problematic, but he is genuinely interested in the variety of subjects which are put together in this category. In his interview in 2008 (Sinhababu 2008), when J. Z. Smith was asked "What got you interested in the religions that you study?" he answered: "Because they're funny. They're interesting in and of themselves." In contrast, I am deeply fascinated with the arbitrariness and power of classificatory practices, especially the ones that employ the category "religion." I am more interested in human ingenuity in inventing such a conceptual container. As I read Smith's works more, however, I began to learn that the actual contents in the container I study are also very interesting in and of themselves.

The generic notion of "religion" which appears in Jonathan Z. Smith's writing still frustrates me, but I deeply admire the scholarly contents of this works. I have only begun to read part of J. Z. Smith's lifetime achievement, and looking forward to exploring more of his writings. Because of the profundity of Smith's writings, the more I read his works, the more I get confused. I am still lost in Smith's texts, and I am currently looking for a useful map to navigate myself through his writings. I believe that this current volume would provide the amateur travelers like myself with a useful map to explore the land and sea in the fascinating world of Jonathan Z. Smith. His death came too early for me. I wish I had known about Smith's works much earlier in my academic life. I wish I could have had a chance to meet him in person and posit my claim: "Religion" is a native category of Western academics and not a native category for me, a native Japanese. I am sure, from the depth of his wealth of knowledge, he would have given me an intriguing and witty answer.

Mitsutoshi Horii is Professor at Shumei University, Japan, working at Chaucer College, UK, as Shumei's representative. His research focuses on the function of modern categories, such as "religion," and examines the ways they authorize specific norms in a variety of contexts.

Acknowledgments

This originally appeared on the Bulletin for the Study of Religion blog on February 21, 2018; see: http://bulletin.equinoxpub.com/2018/02/something-i-learned-from-j-z-smith-mitsutoshi-horii (accessed June 26, 2019).

References

Anonymous (1852). "The Empire of Japan," *De Bow's Southern and Western Review* 13 (December): 541–563.

Arnal, William and McCutcheon, Russell (2013). *The Sacred is the Secular: The Political Nature of "Religion."* New York: Oxford University Press.

Fitzgerald, Timothy (2000). *The Ideology of Religious Studies.* New York: Oxford University Press.

——. (2011). *Religion and Politics in International Relations: The Modern Myth.* London: Continuum.

Hildreth, Richard (1856). "The American Expedition to Japan," *North American Review* 83/172 (July): 258–59

Horii, Mitsutoshi (2018). *The Category of "Religion" in Contemporary Japan.* Palgrave: Macmillan. https://doi.org/10.1007/978-3-319-73570-2

King, Richard (1999). *Orientalism and Religion: Postcolonial Theory, India and "Mystic East."* New York: Routledge.

Mignolo, Walter and Walsh, Catherine (2018). *On Decoloniality: Concepts, Analytics, Praxis.* Durham, NC: Duke University Press. https://doi.org/10.1215/9780822371779

Sinhababu, Supriya (2008). "Full J. Z. Interview," *The Chicago Maroon* (June 2); www.chicagomaroon.com/2008/06/02/full-j-z-smith-interview (accessed June 24, 2019).

Smith, Jonathan Z. (1978). *Map Is Not Territory*. Chicago, IL: University of Chicago Press.
——. (1982). *Imagining Religion: From Babylon to Jonestown*. Chicago, IL: University of Chicago Press.
——. (2004). *Relating Religion: Essays in the Study of Religion*. Chicago, IL: University of Chicago Press.

Chapter 18

On J. Z. Smith and the Remarkable

Richard Newton

In my judgment, the syllabus is the most important piece of writing one does in
the academic field.   —J. Z. Smith (2018a: 87)

A start of a new year, the ominous weather forecast, the beginning of yet another
semester ... If this moment is anything, it is one where we can signify our resolve
by any number of means. And in that unremarkable fact, we might ask how and
why such moments become remarkable.

Currently many students of religion are using this occasion to reflect on the
passing of Jonathan Z. Smith, a prolific scholar who challenged the field to ask
how and why about so much that we take for granted. Two statements of his come
to mind on this point. The first is from the introduction to *Imagining Religion:* "For
the self-conscious student of religion, no datum possesses intrinsic interest. It is
of value only insofar as it can serve as exempli gratia of some fundamental issue
in the imagination of religion" (Smith 1982: xi). The second is from his interview
with the scholar of religion and pedagogy, Alfred Benney:

> Well, I guess the biggest question would be—and it's raised as a question—but the
> biggest question would be: why we, in our sort of cultural complex, have found
> it necessary, out of the complexities of human activity, to say we can find one in
> there that we want to call religion. (Smith 2018b: 37)

I'm not going to pretend to have known the man, nor will I count myself among
those best tutored in his scholarship. On the other hand, I am astonished by the
kind of impact this stranger has had on my own career path. Given my own junior
standing, maybe the same reaction should befit any veteran scholar. But his lega-
cy--like his scholarship--is a cut above so much of the rest that we cannot be clear
on just how deep it goes.

I'm of a generation of scholars fortunate to have been introduced to his work in
the undergraduate classroom. And in 2008, Smith was the president of the Society
of Biblical Literature, which just so happened to have been my first annual meeting. His address, "Religion and Bible," called for the kind of "massive syncretism"
of theoretical tools, data sets, and conversation partners that I would seek out at
the Institute for Signifying Scriptures (the center of my doctoral training), the
Society for Comparative Research in Iconic and Performative Texts, the Society of

Religion as an Analytical Discipline, and the North American Association for the Study of Religion (Smith 2009: 6). This is in addition to my membership in larger bodies such as the Society of Biblical Literature and the American Academy of Religion.

Throughout the most recent (and concurrent) annual meetings, I had a number of conversations about being "too SBL for AAR and too AAR for SBL" in the eyes of some of my colleagues. I chalk up my free agency to him. As I have understood his work, the critical interrogation of culture must confound canonical boundaries in all their forms, not submit to them.

As I take this moment to get my mind right for the semester, I am reminded of how his method of scholarship challenged the professional truisms against which I've also chaffed. I've been in the game long enough to have heard the following statements a few times:

- You can't be a (so-called) generalist and contribute to the field.

- Teaching isn't really scholarship.

- Essays are fine, but you can't make a career out of them in a book discipline.

If you know his work, then you're aware of just how arbitrary and false these ideas are. In this season of reflection I hope that we can focus on doing the work the best way we each know how and that we might explore the questions our particular efforts will bring to the broader conversation on our curious object of study, the human and all its names.

Richard Newton is Assistant Professor of Religious Studies at the University of Alabama. His research focuses on scriptures in social formation, the politics of identity, and the study of race and religion.

Acknowledgments

This originally appeared on the *Sowing Seeds* blog on January 2, 2018; see: https://sowing theseed.org/2018/01/02/on-j-z-smith-and-the-remarkable (accessed June 22, 2019).

References

Smith, Jonathan Z. (1982). *Imagining Religion: From Babylon to Jonestown*. Chicago, IL: University of Chicago Press.

——. (2009). "Religion and Bible," *Journal of Biblical Literature* 128/1: 5–27. https://doi. org/10.2307/25610162

——. (2018a). "The Dean's Craft of Teaching Seminar (2013)," in Willi Braun and Russell T. McCutcheon (eds.), *Reading J. Z. Smith: Interviews and Essay*, 85–108. New York: Oxford University Press.

——. (2018b). "The American Scholars of Religion Video Project: Interview with Jonathan Z. Smith [1999]," in Willi Braun & Russell T. McCutcheon (eds.), *Reading J. Z. Smith: Interviews and Essay*, 29–44. New York: Oxford University Press.

Chapter 19

"It Ain't Too High, and it Ain't Too Theoretical"

William D. O'Connor

> The human sciences try to increase surprise, unlike the natural sciences, which try to decrease it. They don't have much new data; they have to find new ways of looking at the familiar.
> —J. Z. Smith, University of Chicago lecture, March 4, 1997[1]

Each semester when my class on Shakespeare begins, the first thing I do is ask students to take out a sheet of paper and write down their answers to two questions: "Who was Shakespeare?" and "What is tragedy?" (or comedy, or a history play, or "romance"—the topic changes each term). On the last day of class, 16 weeks later, the topic for discussion is the revision of these 1-page papers which I will have asked them to prepare. We try to see what they have learned in the course of the semester and how their thinking has changed. This is an exercise (Smith 1988: 735) I learned from Jonathan Z. Smith, one of the most remarkable teachers—and human beings—I have ever encountered, and whose death is a deep loss for anyone who knew him, but also for the academic enterprise as a whole. Mr. Smith lived up to an ideal of scholarship few could hope to achieve, and possessed learning of a depth and breadth that is rarely seen today even in the most intelligent scholars. That these qualities were mixed with a sense of humor worthy of the Algonquin Round Table is another wonderful thing, in its strict sense—something to be wondered at—and another reason to lament his passing.

I'm not a historian of religion, to say the least. I'm a teacher rather than a scholar. I teach drama as an adjunct, mostly to students who are going to become actors, designers, directors, and so on. When I was a student I was obsessed with the ancient world, especially Greece. I took a course with Mr. Smith in graduate school and was so enchanted with his learning and his wit that I took every other course I could with him while in school, read everything by him I could get my hands on, and heard every public speech he gave, years after finishing. I am still working my way through the bibliographies he provided in class, some written on the board, as many former students have noted; others, long lists of books typed up, Xeroxed by Mr. Smith (at the local Office Depot, where I saw him standing at the copier more than once checking each copy), and passed out to us. He spoke of this insistence on doing things himself, not trusting his documents to either an assistant or a machine, in a long interview with Supriya Sinhababu in *The Chicago Maroon* (2008). I thought it was remarkable that a professor at the University of

Chicago would do this; yet I also knew it was perfectly natural. I was seeing in the flesh something Max Weber had written about the demands of scholarship: "One cannot with impunity try to transfer [small] task[s] entirely to mechanical assistants ..." (Weber 1958: 135). His standards for reading authors one will teach, and for reading journal articles which Mr. Smith described in his autobiographical essay "When the Chips Are Down" (Smith 2004a: 37, n. 27) are of a piece with his Xeroxing.[2] I could never live up to them, but merely knowing that they *ought to be* the standard, makes me a more responsible person and gives me a sense of appreciation for what humans are capable of. Keeping Mr. Smith's standard in mind has only done me good.

Mr. Smith's courses were lessons in intellectual maturation: one began by thinking one was going to get "the truth" about awfully important matters only to learn that Smith thought the search for origins in religion was fruitless, and that the important thing was what each retelling of a story could teach us about it, its teller, or society. He was a living example of how useful it could be to learn to think like Durkheim (see Smith 2004b and Smith 2005). There were nevertheless lots of demythologizing facts. He suggested that burial in the fetal position may not denote belief in life after death, but only make digging easier due to the need for a smaller hole. In the ancient Near East, where writing could take over two decades to learn, one only wrote things down which were economically justifiable. Thus over 90% of our records are business documents or legal decisions. In my notebook, I wrote "Writing brings its own sort of pragmatics—we know the names of flowers that have uses as medicine, but not those that smell good." He warned us that we'd have to learn to read Jacobean English subtly if we wanted to avoid misinterpreting the KJV. That creation *ex nihilo* is a later, Greek idea not found in the Hebrew Bible, where "'creation' is always out of *something*, a re-organization." One question to ask was, "What was the previous world like? How was it different from the one that gets created?" (Smith, January 14, 1997). To the question, why the Sabbath, the answer may not have been only "God rested," but also, "The Egyptians wouldn't let us, so we'll go them one better." Is Leviathan kosher? Some rabbis say yes, some say no. For the former, "when the Messiah comes, we'll all eat a piece of pickled Leviathan" (Smith February 25, 1997). Speaking of the controversy surrounding the politics of both Eliade and Joseph Campbell, Mr. Smith said that he tended not to judge the actions of intellectuals between 1930 and 1950 "since their choices were all pretty lousy" (Smith 1997: February 4). When we read *Enuma Elish* (Anonymous 1991: 228–277).[3] Mr. Smith said, "Marduk builds a frame and dumps dirt in it, like a sandbox." He is building a dam. He asked us what kind of dam. Silence. Then my friend Karla Heuer said, "A god dam?" And J. Z. cracked up and told her she would be getting an A for the quarter, which in fact she did earn.

He introduced me to the study of the history of Indo-European languages, and the work of Georges Dumezil, Walter Burkert ("the greatest living scholar of Greek stuff"; Smith, January 14, 1997), Carl Darling Buck, F. M. Cornford and the "Cambridge school," Eliade, and Cassirer's *Myth of the State*. The combination of big-picture, structuralist thinking, and tiny, particular cultural and textual detail, is what I take the classicist W. M. Calder III to have meant when he described Wilamowitz as always emphasizing the need to see both the forest and the trees (Calder 1998: 91). As someone who deals with dramatic literature from a historical perspective but also for the stage, what I learned from Mr. Smith about both context and close reading has been invaluable.

I happened to be among a group of students at the Billy Goat Tavern on lower Michigan Avenue with Mr. Smith and another professor, who had himself been Smith's student, shortly after the death of Princess Diana. Letting my youthful, vulgar Marxism show, I said I was surprised by all the weeping and gnashing of teeth at the pop-up shrines, by people who hadn't known her, and suggested that they had been sold a bill of goods. Smith and his colleague then had to remind me of Durkheim's "social fact" (I had read *Elementary Forms* with his colleague) and the discussion that followed had an immediate and permanent maturing effect on the way I think about social phenomena. (His essay on introducing Durkheim, above, and all his writings on pedagogy—which I gathered from the bound journals in the Regenstein Library and then photocopied[4]—have improved my own teaching as I've read, reread, and shared them over the years.)

Smith used to tell a story about lecturing at UCSB early in his career and strategically putting in jokes to make the content of the lectures memorable. He was later disappointed to discover that the jokes were all some students remembered, some even calling it a great night club act (repeated in Sinhabubu 2008). But of course, the jokes were not all we remembered. The points he was trying to imprint on us through the jokes continue to shape our own work as teachers.

For example, in my survey course on the history of theatre, I always keep in mind Mr. Smith's claim that each theory must be allowed to stand for students as if it were true, however briefly, and exercise what he calls its "monomaniacal imperialist power" upon them (Smith 1988: 737; also Smith 2005: 5). That is, they ought to be convinced that Adam Smith is right until Marx comes along, and Marx is then supplanted by Weber, etc. In that spirit I try, despite the rapid pace at which a survey course moves, to convince my students that Plato was right to condemn imitators, only to upend that with Aristotle's defense of theatre. I argue for the logic of neoclassicism and the importance of the Enlightenment, and then present the Romantics' critique on its own terms.

It was delightful to meet someone who seemed genuinely to know everything and yet was so down to earth and friendly. Years after class, running into him buying his cigarettes at Harper Market down the street from my apartment would make my day. I can still see him in his overcoat and the fishing hat he wore in the rain (the kind McLean Stevenson wore on *M*A*S*H*), with his famous cane. Seeing him in the Coop buying Leonard Barkan's *Unearthing the Past* made me begin reading Barkan myself, and gave me a sense of how widely outside his "field" he read. It was Mr. Smith's mention of John Livingstone Lowes's *Road to Xanadu* that sent me running for that book too. His knowledge of drama and of literary studies, was striking to me as a student of both. It was from him that I first heard Terence's "Homo sum, humani nihil a me alienum puto." I thought the line was great, a sort of motto for the Renaissance, or the academic outlook, something one should try to live up to. When I read the play from which it comes, *Heauton Timorumenos*, I was both crushed and tickled to learn that it is said by a nosy neighbor merely justifying his nosiness (Terence 2001: 186, line 77). That dual quality of profundity and lightheartedness seems in keeping with Mr. Smith's outlook.

I write this simply because there are many of us who are not scholars of religion whose lives (both intellectually and humanely) were changed for the better by Mr. Smith and his example and who have continued to tell stories about him, read his work and the work of others which he made us aware of decades after having studied with him, and despite knowing him only distantly, as members of his classes rather than his real graduate students. We, that is, my friends and classmates and I, are grateful to have learned from him and to have benefited from his example, and extend our sincere condolences to his family and friends. Mr. Smith once wrote that, "[a]s one who was not trained in History of Religions at Chicago, it has been a joy and privilege to become formally related to men I have long thought of as my teachers from a distance. Between us I hope for the continuing pleasure of agreement and disagreement as we go about our study of the excitement and adventure of being human. It is this, in the final analysis, that it's all about" (Smith 1969: 20). To compare small things with great, I can say that as one also not so trained, it has been a similar joy and privilege to have had Jonathan Z. Smith as a teacher, and to be able to continue to read and learn from his writings. I will always remain grateful for what he taught me about what it's all about.

William D. O'Connor is adjunct instructor of Theatre Studies at DePaul University, where he teaches courses on the history of world theater, and in the department of English at Columbia College, Chicago, where he teaches Shakespeare.

Acknowledgments

Regarding the title: in class at the University of Chicago in the 1990s, Smith once said, while praising an essay by Mary Louise Lord about the Homeric Hymn to Demeter that, "Until recently, this passed for high theory among classicists. But it ain't too high, and it ain't too theoretical." This article originally appeared on the *Bulletin for the Study of Religion* blog on February 6, 2018; see: http://bulletin.equinoxpub.com/2018/02/something-i-learned-from-j-z-smith-william-oconnor (accessed June 26, 2019). Thanks to Karla Heuer for permission to share her story.

Notes

1 From lecture notes recorded by the chapter author at Ancient Mediterranean Myth class, University of Chicago, winter quarter. Further citations below with 1997 dates are all from the same source.

2 In the Ancient Mediterranean Myth course I took with Mr. Smith, we were given a preview of this essay when, on the last day of class, he said, in effect, that he had talked about what he wanted to talk about for nine weeks, and now wanted to hear what questions we had. A classmate asked him how he came to know all that he did, and he told his "origin story," as later recounted in *Relating Religion*.

3   Translated as *The Epic of Creation* by Stephanie Dalley, this was one text assigned for the course, along with a Bible (NRSV), Norman O. Brown's translation of Hesiod's *Theogony*, Helene Foley's of *The Homeric Hymn to Demeter*, and Mr. Smith's Xerox copies. The syllabus was handwritten in Mr. Smith's distinctive printing, and then photocopied.

4   Christopher Lehrich edited and published a collection of the most important of these; see Smith (2013).

References

Calder III, William M. (1998). "'Tripe and Garbage': William Abbott Oldfather on the Limits of Research," in Gareth Schmeling and Jon D. Mikalson (eds.), *Qui Miscuit Utile Dulci: Festschrift Essays for Paul Lachlan MacKendrick*, 87–94. Wauconda, IL: Bolchazy-Carducci.

Anonymous (1991). *The Epic of Creation*, in Stephanie Dalley (ed. and trans.), *Myths from Mesopotamia*, 228–77. Oxford: Oxford University Press.

Sinhababu, Supriya (2008). "Full J. Z. Smith Interview," *The Chicago Maroon* (June 2); www.chicagomaroon.com/2008/06/02/full-j-z-smith-interview (accessed June 25, 2019).

Smith, Jonathan Z. (1969). "Coup d'Essai," *Criterion* 9: 19–20.

——. (1988). "'Narrative into Problems': The College Introductory Course and the Study of Religion," *Journal of the American Academy of Religion* 56/4: 727–39. https://doi.org/10.1093/jaarel/LVI.4.727

——. (2004a). "When the Chips Are Down," in *Relating Religion*, 1–60. Chicago, IL: University of Chicago Press.

——. (2004b). "God Save This Honorable Court: Religion and Civic Discourse," in *Relating Religion*, 375–90. Chicago, IL: University of Chicago Press.

——. (2005). "Introducing Durkheim," in Terry F. Godlove, Jr. (ed.), *Teaching Durkheim*, 3–11. Oxford: Oxford University Press. https://doi.org/10.1093/0195165276.003.0001

——. (2013). *On Teaching Religion*. Christopher I. Lehrich (ed.). Oxford: Oxford University Press.

Terence (2001). *The Self-Tormentor* in John Barsby (ed. and trans.), *Terence I: The Woman of Andros, The Self-Tormentor, The Eunuch*, 171–303. Cambridge, MA: Harvard University Press. https://doi.org/10.4159/DLCL.terence-self_tormentor.2001

Weber, Max (1958). "Science as a Vocation," in H. H. Gerth and C. Wright Mills (eds.), *From Max Weber: Essays in Sociology*, 129–56. New York: Oxford University Press.

Chapter 20

A Matter of Difference: On the Legacy of J. Z. Smith

Matt Sheedy

A few days before the death of J. Z. Smith, on December 30, 2017, I was thinking about writing a follow-up blog post (see Sheedy 2014) on the comparison between temperatures in parts of Canada and the U.S. with temperatures on Mars, which had resurfaced in the news media amidst a recent Arctic cold front.

Back in January 2014, I had been stuck by the ease with which media commentators had latched-on to this comparison and wrote about it on the *Bulletin for the Study of Religion* blog, using Smith as my theoretical touch-point. I began by drawing on Smith's essay, "In Comparison Magic Dwells," where he recalls J. G. Frazer's distinction between magic and science, noting how magic is classified as "a confusion of a subjective relationship with an objective one" (Smith 1982a: 21) Smith then uses this example to talk about a similar error commonly found in the human sciences (including the study of religion), writing: "[C]omparison has been chiefly an affair of the recollection of similarity. The chief explanation for the significance of comparison has been contiguity. The procedure is homeopathic. The theory is built on contagion. The issue of difference has been all but forgotten" (ibid.). With this idea in mind, I argued that drawing parallels between temperatures in parts of North America with temperatures on Mars was an example of comparison by contiguity, where apparent *similarities* were being used to *explain* complex phenomena, while ignoring important *differences.* The differences in this case were rather significant since comparable temperatures were only found on the surface of Mars in a few select areas, as measured by NASA's Curiosity Rover. Moreover, the surface temperature was markedly different than the air temperature, which, back in 2014, reached as low as minus 193°F.

Of course the Mars comparison does work as a playful analogy (though perhaps hyperbole is a better term). As someone who traveled to Winnipeg and Toronto over the 2017 holidays, two cities gripped in a polar vortex, I get it. The problem arises when analogies like this one slip into common usage as though they are describing something that is conceptually meaningful. This, to paraphrase Smith, is mistaking a map for the territory.

Some examples of this slippage can be seen with the recent spate of Mars analogies in Canadian media (e.g., Krishnan 2018; Hagey 2018). A *National Post* article dated December 27, 2017, provided a more nuanced use of the comparison, although the title, "Mars and the North Pole are Warmer than Winnipeg," reinforced the contiguity:

As Alberta was plunged into extreme cold warnings on Boxing Day, it was ironically the mountainous parts of the province that were its warmest. Banff and Jasper both escaped the "extreme cold" label by recording lows of only –19°C. This means that, for a few minutes, all of Alberta was about as cold as Mars' Gale Crater, the home of the Curiosity rover. Mars is subject to pretty violent temperatures shifts, and Curiosity regularly encounters temperatures below –80°C. But this week, the highest temperatures experienced by the rover were –23°C. A Calgary Boxing Day shopper, therefore, might have found themselves getting into a car that was literally colder than a Martian spacecraft. (Hopper 2017)

Despite the more nuanced description here this comparison doesn't do any conceptual work with these important distinctions, but simply falls back on this highly selective instance of similarity in order to claim a general correlation. One obvious problem here is that the comparison is being made to a planet that is inhospitable to human life and thus cannot be tested *as such*. This parallels a familiar problem in the study of religion, where terms like "numinous," "the sacred," and "religious experience" have been used as trans-historical and cross-cultural concepts, despite the fact that they lack any testable criteria.

For another thing, it has always been as cold as (the surface of) Mars somewhere on earth. We just never bothered to make the comparison until it began to effect large cities like Chicago in an age of social media, where the meme could easily spread. Perhaps part of the reason for this meme's return (at least in a Canadian context) is that it functions as a form of one-upmanship over those cites that can't seem to hack the cold weather. In this sense, claiming that one's city is as cold as Mars acts as a symbol of toughness and endurance (especially when Canadians compare themselves to the US), or, in a Canadian context, of authenticity, where cities like Winnipeg and Edmonton can feel superior when comparatively warmer places like Toronto or Vancouver complain about the cold weather (our minus mercury is bigger than yours, type thing). But I digress.

Something I've learned from J. Z. Smith is to pay close attention to the kind of work that comparison does in either reinforcing similarities that tell us very little, or, conversely, in drawing attention to important differences that can tell us a lot. The latter point is nicely illustrated in Smith's essay "A Matter of Class," when he writes: "Classification, by bringing disparate phenomena together in the space of a scholar's intellect, often produces surprise, the condition which calls forth efforts of explanation" (2004a: 175).

In calling forth efforts at *explanation*, the two or more things being compared are therefore less interesting for what they might share on the surface than for what new directions their differences may provoke, thus unsettling our normal ways of thinking. In one example, Smith illustrates this problem with the term "fundamentalism." Pointing out its coinage in the 1920s to describe a particular type of Protestant Christianity and its relation to biblical criticism, he observes that "fundamentalism," when used as a generic category, obscures the particularities of, for example, Islamic versus Christian variations–a distinction that can make all the difference in how we go about explaining things. As he writes in reference to certain "Islamic" varieties: "It would be better to classify these other 'fundamentalisms' as instances of 'nativism' or 'revitalization' movements, thus emphasizing, among other matters, their setting in colonial and postcolonial histories, a setting that is not present in Christian fundamentalism" (2004a: 175).

One passage from Smith's work that continues to stay with me, perhaps more than any other, is from his biographical essay "When the Chips Are Down," where he describes his "early interest in botany and fascination with taxonomy" (2004b: 19). I can still remember the light bulb that went off in my head as Smith prodded me to think about religion in relation to biological classification, and the idea that variation—whether we're talking about reptiles, mammals, Sikhs, Hindus, or Muslims—is all that we have. Noticing these variations, big or small, between seemingly similar groups, or by bringing together disparate examples to call forth a new type of explanation (see, e.g., Smith 1982b) showed me that the study of religion is a boundless field, limited only by our imagination.

Matt Sheedy is Visiting Assistant Professor in the Department of North American Studies at the University of Bonn, Germany, and a lecturer in the Department of Religion at the University of Manitoba. His research focuses on discourses on/about atheism, Islam, Christianity, and Indigenous traditions in popular and political culture in North America.

Acknowledgments

This originally appeared on the Bulletin for the Study of Religion blog on January 11, 2018; see: http://bulletin.equinoxpub.com/2018/01/something-i-learned-from-j-z-smith-matt-sheedy (accessed June 26, 2019).

References

Hagey, MacKay, Aaron (2018). "Report: Winnipeg Unable to Take Your Cold Weather Complaints Seriously," *The Beaverton*; www.thebeaverton.com/2018/01/report-winnipeg-unable-take-cold-weather-complaints-seriously (accessed May 28, 2019).

Hopper, Tristin (2017). "Mars and the North Pole are Warmer than Winnipeg: A Guide to How Damn Cold It Is," *The National Post*; https://nationalpost.com/news/canada/mars-and-the-north-pole-are-warmer-than-winnipeg-a-guide-to-how-damned-cold-it-is (accessed May 28, 2019).

Krishnan, Manisha (2018). "Canadians Are Obsessed With Cold Shaming Because It's All We Have," *Vice News*; www.vice.com/en_ca/article/gywj34/canadians-are-obsessed-with-cold-shaming-because-its-all-we-have?utm_campaign=Global&utm_source=vicefbca (accessed May 28, 2019).

Sheedy, Matt (2014). "It's Cold as *$#%! How Cold? Colder than Mars!" *Bulletin for the Study of Religion*; https://bulletin.equinoxpub.com/2014/01/its-cold-as-how-cold-colder-than-mars (accessed May 28, 2019).

——. (2018). "Something I Learned from J. Z. Smith," *Bulletin for the Study of Religion*; http://bulletin.equinoxpub.com/2018/01/something-i-learned-from-j-z-smith-matt-sheedy (accessed May 28, 2019).

Smith, Jonathan Z. (1982a). "In Comparison Magic Dwells," in *Imagining Religion: From Babylon to Jonestown*, 19–35 Chicago, IL: University of Chicago Press.

——. (1982b). "Fences and Neighbours: Some Contours of Early Judaism," in *Imagining Religion: From Babylon to Jonestown*, 1–18. Chicago, IL: University of Chicago Press.

——. (2004a). "A Matter of Class: Taxonomies of Religion," in *Relating Religion: Essays in the Study of Religion*, 160–178. Chicago, IL: University of Chicago Press.

——. (2004b). "When the Chips Are Down," in *Relating Religion: Essays in the Study of Religion*, 1–60. Chicago, IL: University of Chicago Press.

Chapter 21

On Articulate Choice

Vaia Touna

When I was asked to contribute to his blog post series on the work of Jonathan Z. Smith I realized, given the breadth of his work, how difficult it is for someone to choose just one thing that one learned from him and no less to talk about it in a brief blog post. But J. Z. Smith already provides the solution, and perhaps one of the things I learned from his work is the importance of *strategic choices*, of "less is better" when for example one is putting together a syllabus for one's own course (Smith 2013), when making comparisons (Smith 1982: 1990), or even when talking about the gains of a scholar's work.

I don't really remember when I first encountered J. Z. Smith's writings, it could be sometime during my master's, but I can vividly remember when I was suggested to read his book *Imagining Religion* (1982)—which I got a hold of in May of 2008—with the advice "do not get lost in the details of his descriptions but look for the moves he makes." At the time, given my training (specializing in classical Greek history, religion, literature, etc.), I'm not sure I understood what that even meant. How could I possibly pay attention to something other than his rich knowledge of the examples he was writing about, his insightful, rigorous, and erudite descriptions and analysis? In retrospect, though, that was the best advice I received, because I realized that it is exactly those moves that distinguish J. Z. Smith's work, at least for me, for it is not so much the importance of the example itself—as phrased by Smith "no datum possesses intrinsic interest" (1982: xi)—but rather the use in which he is putting it, in short, his work is an exercise in "articulate choice" (1982: xi). So with this idea of choice and J. Z. Smith's moves in mind, I would like to draw from two of his books *Imagining Religion* and *Drudgery Divine* and briefly talk about the thing I learned from his work. In fact it this idea of choice that has informed most of my thinking and actually helped me shape an approach that is stirred away from trying to better understand and describe the ancient Greco-Roman world.

Choice

As I already said, it is difficult to choose the one thing that I've learned from J. Z. Smith, or from my professors who, themselves influenced by him, guided me to his work. Nevertheless, choices are an important endeavor, as J. Z. Smith taught me in his chapter "The Bare Facts of Ritual" (Smith 1992: 53–65). Reading that chapter one learns a great deal about hunting and rituals but, as always is the case with J. Z. Smith, there's an implicit "more than" meets the eye, that is, "look out for his moves." Although the chapter appears to be about ritual and hunting, it is just as much about choice; how scholars make choices to compare things that seem incomparable, how they manage and control reality. A ritual, as J. Z. Smith writes, is "a controlled environment where the variables (i.e., the accidents) of ordinary life may be displaced precisely because they are felt to be so overwhelmingly present and powerful" (ibid.: 63) but isn't that also a scholarly endeavor where "contingency, variability, and accidentality are factored out" (ibid.: 65)? And, well, something to seriously think and reflect upon?

In his book *Drudgery Divine: On the Comparison of Early Christianities and the Religions of Late Antiquity*, one can easily be lost in the detailed and rich descriptions of both Early Christianities and the religions of Late Antiquity, but for me it became a book on what a scholar of religion should pay attention to, because in part it is a book about the divine drudgery of our work, of scholarly comparisons and what they entail. Although many things can be discussed from this book, there are two things I want to bring attention to in this post.

Unique

When it comes to comparison there is the problem with describing things or referring to things as being unique. Smith writes: "The 'unique' is an attribute that must be disposed of, especially when linked to some notion of incomparable value, if progress in thinking through the enterprise of comparison is to be made" (Smith 1990: 36).

Why I find the idea of uniqueness as something very important to guard myself against is because even though I haven't explicitly referred to something in my writing, prior to reading J. Z. Smith that is, as being unique, yet I think that I might have thought of my examples in those terms, as being special enough that needed my attention or given that many people have written about there must be something self-evidently important to them. The problem with something being considered unique and thus with some kind of, what J. Z. Smith describes as, "incomparable value," as I see it now, is that once you approach your data like that, you lose the opportunity to engage in discussions with other scholars who work in other data sets, for now you are confined and isolated to your scholarly endeavor, unable to make connections, to see similarities and differences operating elsewhere, and prevent yourself from gaining something of value from the insights of your colleagues who made progress in their work in other data sets. Although I'm not sure if that's what J. Z. Smith had in mind or counts as the kind of progress he wanted to see in the field, but once I dropped the whole idea of uniqueness I was able to make progress not only in the enterprise of comparison, that is in bringing together side by side things that seemed completely unrelated, but also in my work in general; for I was able to see the inter-connectedness of practices and ideas that at first might have seemed unrelated and incomparable. Of course that was the result also of the second thing from this book that I wish to talk about.

Tertium Quid

Once the data aren't considered to be "unique" anymore, and self-evidently of interest or of importance it follows that they have to be considered in relation to what J. Z. Smith describes as: the *tertium quid* or *τρίτον γένος* (as his translates it "a third something"; Smith 1990: 83), that is, they have to be thought of "with respect to" some theoretical question (and this is something that always operates at the back of my head, like the lyrics of a background song, every time I start a new project or every time I start writing something). For in regard to the enterprise of comparison J. Z. Smith writes:

> That is to say, the statement of comparison is never dyadic but always triadic; there is always an implicit 'more than', and there is always a 'with respect to'. In the case of an academic comparison, the 'with respect to' is most frequently the scholar's interest, be this expressed in a question, a theory, or a model. (Smith 1990: 51)

So, it is always with this 'with respect to' that I begin a project. In fact, as I'm starting now a new research project, I ask myself why do I want to put the happenings of an archaeological dig next to the happenings of a church? Sure both e.g.s are important for all sorts of reasons, but what is the theoretical question that I want to answer by looking at them, that is, what is the third something, the "with respect to" that I wish to draw my readers' attention to? It is a question that, as Smith writes, "is different from that to which it is being applied," in other words, although my project will be, on the one hand, about people connected in some way or another to archaeological digs (whether archaeologists or visitors) and, on the other hand, church goers, there will also be an implicit "more than." It will be about something that, quoting again J. Z. Smith, "is the scholar's intellectual purpose—whether explanatory or interpretative, whether generic or specific— which highlights that principled postulation of similarity which is the ground of the methodological comparison of difference being interesting" (Smith 1990: 53).

If I would want to summarize the things that I mentioned above in how J. Z. Smith has helped me in my work, in my approach to my data, in thinking that method is as important as theory and the kind of "articulate choice" that should inform my research as well as my teaching, then in the introduction of his *Imagining Religion* he very nicely states the conditions of this "articulate choice" and which I think worth quoting here in full:

> Implicit in this effort at articulate choice are three conditions. First, that the exemplum has been well and fully understood. This requires a mastery of both the relevant primary material and the history and tradition of its interpretation. Second, that the exemplum be displayed in the service of some important theory, some paradigm, some fundamental question, some central element in the academic imagination of religion. Third, that there be some method for explicitly relating the exemplum to the theory, paradigm or question and some method for evaluating each in terms of the other. (Smith 1982: xi)

Although, it might be appropriate to end this post with J. Z. Smith's own words, I'd like to end on a more personal note. I met J. Z. Smith (the person that is) in 2008 at the annual SBL conference held in November of that year in Boston, MA, back when I was a recently graduated master's student. I was among the lucky and very privileged ones—and now immensely grateful—to be invited to his Presidential Festschrift Dinner at Hamersley's Bistro. I travelled to Boston from Greece carrying one book with me, *Imagining Religion*, with the intention (and hope) that he would sign it. I remember spending most of that night at the dinner thinking that it was my last chance to get his signature but also terrified with the idea of bothering him with such, perhaps, a silly request, and I was even more terrified in the prospect of being denied. At the end of a lovely dinner—a dinner that was to become one of my most endearing memories of J. Z. Smith, of hearing stories of other scholars talking about him—when most of the guests had left, I gathered all my strength, and politely asked if it would be too much trouble for him to sign his book. With his unique, or better put individual and distinct, voice he said that he'd be happy to, and I was struck by how humbled he seemed and appreciative at my request, and signed: "With gratitude for meeting in Boston." The gratitude was certainly all mine for all the things I learned from his work both on how to go about my research but also how to approach my teaching (which I certainly didn't have the space to elaborate in this brief post but I hope readers can understand or at least be curious enough to find for themselves by looking into his work).

Vaia Touna is Assistant Professor in the Department of Religious Studies at the University of Alabama, Tuscaloosa; her research focuses on the sociology of religion, acts of identification and social formation, as well as methodological issues concerning the study of religion and the past in general.

Acknowledgments

This originally appeared on the *Bulletin for the Study of Religion* blog on January 30, 2018; see: http://bulletin.equinoxpub.com/2018/01/something-i-learned-from-j-z-smith-vaia-touna (accessed June 26, 2019). Many thanks to Matt Sheedy for inviting me to reflect upon the work of J. Z. Smith, and contribute to his blog post series on the blog for the *Bulletin for the Study of Religion*. I'm also immensely grateful to Willi Braun and Russell T. McCutcheon for introducing me to Jonathan Z. Smith's work, from which I greatly benefited.

References

Jonathan Z. Smith (1982). *Imagining Religion: From Babylon to Jonestown.* Chicago, IL: University of Chicago Press.

——. (1990). *Drudgery Divine: On the Comparison of Early Christianities and the Religions of Late Antiquity.* Chicago, IL: University of Chicago Press.

——. (2013). "The Introductory Course: Less Is Better," in Christopher I. Lehrich (ed.), *On Teaching Religion: Essays by Jonathan Z. Smith*, 11–19. New York: Oxford University Press. https://doi.org/10.1093/acprof:osobl/9780199944293.003.0002

Chapter 22

J. Z. Smith's Gift

Donald Bruce Woll

My wife has asked me for years why my experience of the Ph.D. process at the University of Chicago was so different from many other students she has met. My answer has always been the same: "Jonathan Z. Smith." Smith made the experience an adventure instead of an ordeal. In the almost fifty years since I met him in 1968 he has been one of my most important intellectual fathers.

The first lecture I heard when I came to Chicago in 1968, was the first, or one of the first, lectures Smith gave when he arrived that fall. I had never heard of him and chose the course because of the subject matter, Hellenistic Religions. My response to that lecture was instant and unreserved. I went up to him immediately afterward and asked if he would be my dissertation advisor. "Sure," he said.

He turned out to be just what I was looking for, namely, someone who came to the subject matter as a historian without *any* theological axe to grind, but passionately committed to what I have come to call the responsible exercise of cognitive power. He was also a historian not only equipped to talk about the factoids of history but to think *historically*, scrupulously, concretely, materially, as well as philosophically, and *imaginatively*, about the whole range of human experience, cutting across all of the disciplinary boundaries that had turned biblical studies into a patchwork of isolated silos of expertise.

A year after that first conversation, I went in to talk with him about selecting a dissertation topic. His response was clear and simple. The topic had to be something I was interested in, and I had to be able to handle the relevant materials. I felt something take hold inside, the beginnings of excitement. That moment set the tone for the rest of my program. Jonathan was a conscientious advisor from beginning to end. After I finished and left behind formal studies of religion I continued to read everything he published.

Looking back on that conversation about a dissertation topic in light of what I subsequently learned about how loaded the word "interest" is for Smith ("something in which one has a stake, ... which places one at risk, ... for which one is willing to pay some price") I know that was the moment he was inviting me into the *collaborative* adventure of thinking for myself, with him, about something that really mattered. That sense of collaboration was later confirmed when I read his extraordinary declaration that "the student of religion ... must be relentlessly self-conscious. Indeed," he went on "this self-consciousness must be "his primary expertise, his foremost object of study" (Smith 1982: xi).

I poured myself into the effort to interpret the Gospel of John as writing that was a product of its complex time and place in that world of Hellenistic Religions. My dissertation, the outcome of that work, was later published by Scholars Press as *Johannine Christianity in Conflict: Authority, Rank, and Succession in the First Farewell Discourse.*

Many years later, the week after the disastrous 2004 presidential election, an election in which *no mention was made of the torture chambers of Abu Ghraib in Iraq*, I was reading "When the Chips Are Down," the first chapter in Smith's just-published collection of articles, *Relating Religion.* One of the persistent pre-occupations he traces through this biobibliographical essay is "thinking" and its cognitive power. Near the end of the essay I read a sentence that stopped me in my tracks, excited all over again: "Religion is the relentlessly human activity of thinking through a 'situation'" (Smith 2004: 32). "That's it," I thought. "That *connection* between thinking and religion is the reason I have never stopped reading him."

I was thrilled with a notion of religion that was so precisely the opposite of the one being paraded at the time by the re-elected President's "faith-based" decision-making. I was also thrilled with the implication that seemed clear to me, even though I wasn't completely clear about what the sentence meant: *everything* Smith wrote about religion had some bearing, however minor, on *thinking*, its "liveliness," fascination, exhilaration, vigor, playfulness, imaginativeness, humor and potentially far-reaching consequences.

I began rereading Smith's writings about religion from the perspective of his commitment to thinking, or, as he also described it, cognitive power. For Smith, the scholar of religion in the academy acts as a representative of the academy's reason for being. It is precisely as such, as a representative of a collaborative enterprise, that the scholar's self-consciousness cannot be left outside the door of the study.

Smith's gift to his students is also a call to the responsible exercise of that shared gift of cognitive power. In what he called his second career he spelled out, in what amounted to a theory of the academy, what the responsible exercise of cognitive power entailed. Cognitive power, he insisted, included not only scrupulous, disciplined accountability to the data, but also the play of the imagination, which he defined, following Wallace Stevens, as the power of the mind over the possibility of things. In an article published in 2018 I argued that his career as a scholar of religion can only be understood from the perspective of his theory of the academy as exemplar for the exercise of democratic world-making cognitive power (Woll 2018).

We are living at a time when the need for us to *think/act together* about ourselves, our nation, and our world has rarely been more urgent. What I have learned from Smith is the "iron law" of democratic citizen responsibility, as co-representatives of the body politic. I will always be grateful to Smith for the gift of trusting me to join him in that ultimately *political* work.

Bruce Woll credits J. Z. Smith with making him into a philosopher and an anthropologist equipped to recognize that anything can be fraught, no matter how precious and rich it may seem; he retired in 2011 from a twenty-seven-year career in information technology and then returned to his central intellectual interest: a critique of parochial Modernity.

Acknowledgments

This originally appeared at the Bulletin for the Study of Religion blog on Feb 28, 2018; see: http://bulletin.equinoxpub.com/2018/02/something-i-learned-from-j-z-smith-bruce-woll (accessed June 26, 2019).

References

Smith, Jonathan Z. (1982). *Imagining Religion: From Babylon to Jonestown*. Chicago, IL: University of Chicago Press.
——. (2004). *Relating Religion: Essays in the Study of Religion*. Chicago, IL: University of Chicago Press.
Woll, Donald Bruce (2018). "Locating the Study of Religion in a Theory of the Academy: The Unexamined Relationship between Jonathan Z. Smith's Two Careers," *Method and Theory in the Study of Religion*; https://brill.com/view/journals/mtsr/aop/article-10.1163-15700682-12341445.xml (accessed March 16, 2019).

Chapter 23

Significant, Significance, Signifier

Ipsita Chatterjea

In what I freely acknowledge is a necessarily imperializing move, theology is *one* appropriate object of study for religious studies. From the perspective of the academic study of religion, *theology is a datum, the theologian is one native informant.* As I have argued ..., the study of religion is ill served by the "primordial" (itself, largely an interest of the "transcendent approach." We need to be far more attentive to the exegetical labors of religious folk, to their systematic projects of articulations and understanding.   —J. Z. Smith (2013: 74)

The elements of J. Z. Smith's work that we can take in, adapt, and apply to other case studies of "the labors, articulations, and understandings of religious folk" have been part of the common ground across critical scholars of religion within the AAR, SBL, SORAAAD, and NAASR and the community connected by the IAHR and those who happen to study religion globally for several decades. I want to talk about my experience of how he inhabited the role of "esteemed scholar of religion" and also how he surfaced in one of most idiotic moments at a professional meeting in which I have been involved, as both speak to part of his impact on the study of religion.

I should be clear, I have no reverence for J. Z. Smith.

I did not take "Bible in Western Civilization" as one my oldest friends did when we were at Chicago. I knew there was a lot of work involved, and that she enjoyed the class, Smith's lectures, and his wicked sense of humor, enormously. I recall seeing him on campus, we never interacted, but I knew he had, along with several others devoted himself to sustaining undergraduate education in the years just before and while the college almost tripled in size after I left. Looking at the adjunctification of higher education in the time since, J. Z. stood by undergraduate teaching when some of my former teachers abandoned it with ill-concealed glee. I had no intention of studying religion at the start of college, Smith was not a factor in my turn to the study of religion, that was driven entirely by the near total absence of any handling of this mode of human expression after 1800 within the political and intellectual histories of Europe—save for church histories that were of practically no use to me. Or, let me take a further step back. My turn to the study of religion began with a workshop on the history of political culture: papers by historian Mark Goldie on the Scottish Enlightenment prompted me to look at religion in addition to politics and introduced me to the crucial phrase, "the fallacy of premature secularization" (Goldie 2008).

I was encouraged by a Catholic theologian, Werner Jeanrond, who told me that I could continue to study religion as history after my first religion class, Religion as Intellectual History, taken so I could begin to parse a genre and complete a project. I read Smith during my "gap year" while auditing classes at the Divinity School and was particularly taken by "The Devil in Mr. Jones" and the rest of *Imagining Religion* (1983; N.B. I have lent and lost 3 copies of that book in the last 10 years) and *Map is not Territory*. There is also that I love essays as a genre, and J. Z. Smith's are wonderful examples. His anthropological readings of historical religious texts and events appealed to me in terms of the extensibility of his insights and a clearly implied frame for the analysis of religion. I had not realized he had specifically commented on our operating terrain (note the quote at the outset) until I reviewed *On Teaching Religion* years later.

I returned to the study of religion, post 9/11, deeply irritated with the public discourse led by religion professors who made thinly substantiated, dangerously over simplified claims about the event, religious violence, Islam, and American religion. I returned to the projects I had abandoned, the connections between religion, social orders, and social regulation to observe how humans assert themselves as they manipulate, regulate, and violence each other. J. Z.'s elaborations of the locative and the utopian (Smith 1978: 293) were among the conceptual links across my work in the study of religion, intellectual and political history, and sociology of deviance and criminology.

I do not recall the exact year, J. Z. responded to a Law, Religion and Culture panel he addressed the specifics of each of the papers in turn, without any "legend making incidents" or references to his own work. Before this, he lauded the program unit, the founders, and committee; among them at that time: Winnifred Sullivan, Robert Yelle, Natalie Dohrman, Greg Johnson, and Jason Bivins. He acknowledged that together they fought over years to establish and sustain the unit. He lauded them for moving discussions of religion, law, and culture in the United States past what he specifically characterized as a "field-limiting fixation on the First Amendment." He was genuinely pleased that Law, Religion, Culture had, and had for some time, attracted a wide variety of case studies connected by varied notions of law, religion, and culture in distinct and distant times and places. In his estimation, Law, Religion and Culture, was a flourishing hub of exacting scholarly activity and he was clearly happy to be able to observe the accomplishments of others to those assembled. Not a word about their fealty to carrying out his vision, or their implementation of "his agenda"—but he was absolutely elated that they had pursued their own. As he concluded, he mentioned in passing and with a bit of frustration, a spate of 10 Commandments cases in various U.S. states, he mentioned Judge Roy Moore in Alabama. He observed with resignation that it seemed just beyond public and legislative understanding that, "the 10 Commandments are not a thing ... to talk about the 10 Commandments ... which portion of the Hebrew Bible, which translation?" After the panel concluded, I made a point of seeking him out. He was approachable. "Dr. Smith, a Vanderbilt M.Div serving in the Tennessee legislature managed to stop a 10 Commandments bill in its tracks by talking about what religion scholars know about the 10

Commandments and that you have to ask 'which one?' and 'which translations?'"

I cannot recall J. Z.'s exact words, please note my bracket text is a translation of expression, he was genuinely surprised and unreservedly pleased, "[Holy Crap!] Someone used scholarship and made a difference?! [That's fantastic!]" I affirmed that the incident had happened earlier in the year and had made the local TV news in Nashville. We genially parted company.

His last years of active attendance at the Annual Meeting were disrupted by the AAR's unilateral decision to stop meeting jointly with the SBL, a decision that was reversed in late 2009 or early 2010. I know I wasn't alone in wanting to "go with Mom and not erratically behaving Dad" when what appeared to be a very final divorce, with baffling and ineffective visitation terms, was announced. I don't think many of us bought any of the rumored and not actually officially tendered rationales, among them that it would "mitigate Christocentrism." To be plain, analysts of religion within the AAR remained and remain vastly outnumbered by both (white Protestant) Christocentrism and those who Smith described as "transcendental" scholars. What it did was abruptly separate study of religion scholars in the AAR from the largest vibrant network of linguistically attentive critical theory wielding historians and archeologists whose perspectives on and practices for handling religious data were most akin to ours. We were separated from the milieu that, pre-dumping of "critical" from its mission statement, sustained and shaped J. Z. Smith as he shaped and sustained it as a member and one-time President.

The connection across qualitative scholars of religion globally, regardless of area of material specialization across generations of scholars have been through scholars like J. Z. Smith and Liz Clark and later Bruce Lincoln, Tomoko Masuzawa, Hans Kippenberg, Tom Tweed, and Ann Taves. This is not to suggest other scholars were or are not worthy of being shared as part of a wide-ranging analyses of religion spanning location and time, it is the case that they were not. As Rebecca Raphael has observed, the methods and theories of analysts of religion have been divided from the critical study of biblical literatures arbitrarily and with little utility. We do not have a wider array of contemporary common ground because the conversations have been broken up, or homogenized under threat, and for reasons that do not hold up. Our capacity to talk about theory, conceptualization, and method has been deliberately and chronically under-resourced and disrupted. Yet scholars of religion have never stopped trying to suss out religious utterances, affect, worldviews, and connections with other modes of human expression and behavior so we can better understand how religion functions in the world without presuming how we look at the world is normative and that everyone must handle religion, however formulated, as we do.

J. Z.'s impact, was made clear to me one very trying afternoon 8 years ago. The first SORAAAD meeting in 2011 was, to be plain, a brutal disaster for a few different reasons. It was salvaged with timely interventions by David Frankfurter (he gently shut down an unproductive "comment more than a question" and returned us to our task), Jens Kreinath (racked up two bystander interventions), and a spate of involuntary giggling by people who were not me. I am not even sure that the worst part of that afternoon was "Olav the interfaith dialog guy," (OTIDG) announcing to the room that, "you all are delusional if you do not understand you are theologians!"

OTIDG was one of a few interruptions over my allotted time to speak, the other two were study of religion scholars, who were, wait for it, white, male, cis, and hetero. From one, the red-faced angry pronouncement that, "Women and people of color are lowering the quality of scholarship at the AAR!" The other? An assertion and vehement reassertion that, "there was no tension between analytical work and theology." Assumed in the latter, working conditions in the U.S. were identical to those outside of the U.S. Implied, SORAAAD's premise (that of being a space for critical SBL and AAR scholars to work on method, theory, and research design separate from the demands of religious scholarship tasked with servicing specific religious communities and working subordinate to their hierarchies) was invalid.

Or, by the time OTIDG started up, I was already at my limits. I am not sure what heated follow-up remark of his to his to original declaration of our collective delusion prompted it, but my "conference face" failed and, I blurted out in half surprise "Thatamanil in that *JAAR* piece??!? (Thatamanil 2010, wherein it was asserted that all scholars of religion are inescapably in debt to Tillich.) Olav beamed, thinking himself triumphant, as if the assembled heathens' false god was finally smashed, said, "Yes! Exactly!"

Quiet giggling cut through the silence that followed. Floored and disgusted by the reaction and that we (the entire incorrigible lot of us) were unmoved by what he seemed to consider "Thatamanil's magisterial take down of J. Z.," OTIDG stalked off without another word.

I suspect OTIDG (Don't "@" me) thought "taking out" J. Z. would make the rest of us come to Jesus, or at least kneel penitently before a "homogenized white Protestant deferent, Interfaith dialoging" religious studies. OTIDG's pronouncements that afternoon, like Thatamanil's puzzling article were built on the problematic premise that J. Z. was a failed prophet or an apostate religious leader, and the rest of us as his "brainwashed" flock and that we shared a theological reverence for and dependence on origins, lineage, and celebrity religious leaders? I guess? We're not a new religious movement; we don't pay conference fees and membership dues to service theologians, note the candidate statements for the 2015 election for AAR Vice President (AAR, 2015).[1] Or, I don't. I do my work with the hope that, among other things, it is useful to the communities I study (and not their elite representatives at the AAR), that my research design choices do justice to the portion of the human legacy for which I have conscientiously sought evidence, and that the processes by which I conduct my work make sense to scholars outside of the study of religion. We're scholars who develop and deploy a body of knowledge and extensible, replicable, and falsifiable scholarly practices, like any other discipline in the critical humanities and social sciences. Save for structures we work in or are compelled to operate in for professional development, in our work we have not been subordinate to, interchangeable with, or indebted beyond a capacity to function independently of theology. However we are spoken of by those who want us deferent to their Christian beliefs, the work we do has existed, continues and will be taken up by others who stumble into our set of concerns as those appropriate for studying religion or derive them, along with the problems and blind alleys, on their own. To my knowledge Smith never directly responded to Thatamanil, but the essay quoted at the outset re-appeared just over a year later. I think it was response enough.

I do not revere J. Z. Smith. And this is a vital point as we work with his legacy. Within our own ranks? We don't need pre-digested interpretations bordering on would be pastoral guidance to deploy his insights. Indulge me as I repeat myself, from my first readings J. Z. Smith has been, for me, an anthropologically minded historian of the texts of antiquity and sometimes contemporary events, whose insights were useful directly and in their capacity for data-responsive adaptation. His conceptual work is useful and robust enough to take critique and have their limits identified (Gottschalk 2012). My ability to use the material insights of his work on Mediterranean Antiquity is limited, but his work provides functional examples (with no pretense of being exhaustive, much less eternal) for assessing how instances of social and political power and religious authority are normalized such that they can be productively compared in order to gain a better understanding of these dynamics function as a part of collective human behavior.

In the course of my work I can and have joined J. Z.'s insights into social scientific theories of human behavior (social theory) and critical theories. I find him useful. He was among the best historians deploying anthropology that I can recall—he happened to study religion. He has never been a substitute religious figure for me, my entrance to the field did not have its origins in my renouncing my religious background and I suspect this is the case for others. I care about the network of scholars that have devoted themselves to this work. I respect and sustain this community and our body of knowledge, but for me this has never been about fealty or regression (Riesebrodt 1993: 17; Smith 2013: 86) into the supposed thoughts (WWJZSD) of this scholar or that.

My sense of J. Z. through his writings, conversations with some of his graduate students, and very literally one encounter with him, was that he developed or clarified concepts derived from historically situated case studies for others to mess around with to serve as pivots so we can try to understand the stuff we call religious, or the people that identify as such. That freedom to create and discuss scholarship attentive to the data associated with the contextually situated particulars of "the exegetical labors of religious folk... to their systematic projects of articulations and understanding" so we can make a difference in public discourse, is at least some of what he wanted for his students, those of us (like me) who read him, and the community of people dedicated to expanding our understanding of religious activities, interpretations etc. Consider him license to assemble decentralized networks to pursue well anchored but free-ranging projects, to assemble and build or adapt the tools you need to do rigorous justice to those you study, and to find those who have gone without study to better analyze their complex and entirely human stories.

Please don't revere J. Z. Smith. Find him useful.

Ipsita Chatterjea is Co-Founder and Executive Director of the Study of Religion as an Analytical Discipline workshop (SORAAAD). Her research is focused on gender, race, and class as well as regulation and violence.

Acknowledgments

This originally appeared on the author's own blog on November 15, 2018; see https://ipsitachatterjea.com/2018/11/15/j-z-smith-1938-2017 (accessed June 22, 2019).

Note

1   Please note the text circulated as part of the ballot, via SurveyMonkey is no longer available, the more elaborate statements remain posted on the AAR website.

References

American Academy of Religion (2015). "Campaign Statements," www.aarweb.org/sites/default/files/pdfs/About/Elections/2015VPStatements.pdf (accessed January 24, 2019).

Goldie, Mark (2008). "Review of Tony Claydon, *Europe and the Making of England, 1660–1760*," *The Journal of Ecclesiastical History* 59: 577. https://doi.org/10.1017/S0022046908004314

Gottschalk, Peter (2012). *Religion, Science, and Empire: Classifying Hinduism and Islam in British India*. New York: Oxford University Press. https://doi.org/10.1093/acprof:oso/9780195393019.001.0001

Riesebrodt, Martin. (1993). *Pious Passion: The Emergence of Modern Fundamentalism in the United States and Iran*. Berkeley, CA: University of California Press.

Smith Jonathan Z. (1978) *Map is Not Territory: Studies in the History of Religions*. Chicago, IL: University of Chicago Press.

——. (1982) *Imagining Religion: From Babylon to Jonestown*. Chicago, IL: University of Chicago Press.

——. (2013). "Are Theological and Religious Studies Compatible?" in Christopher Lehrich (ed.), *On Teaching Religion*, 73–76. New York: Oxford University Press. https://doi.org/10.1093/acprof:osobl/9780199944293.003.0008

Thatamanil, John (2010). "Comparing Professors Smith and Tillich: A Response to Jonathan Z. Smith's 'Tillich('s) Remains'," *Journal of the American Academy of Religion*, 78/4: 1171–1181. https://doi.org/10.1093/jaarel/lfq088

Part III

Interviews

Chapter 24

Interviews

Mike Altman

As per the preface, the following transcripts are for the extended interviews carried out for a podcast on Smith produced by Mike Altman of the Department of Religious Studies at the University of Alabama, which was posted in the Spring of 2018; see: https://soundcloud.com/studyreligion/jonathan-z-smith-1938-2017 (accessed May 15, 2019).

Interview with Sam Gill

Mike Altman:	We had this idea to try to talk to some people who knew Jonathan earlier on or at different stages. We're going to put this together into a short podcast episode.
Sam Gill:	Sure. Yeah, that sounds great.
Mike Altman:	Yeah, to start with, so I get this on tape so I can use it, if I could just get you to say, my name is, and tell us your name, and however you want to identify yourself, affiliation, or whatever.
Sam Gill:	Okay, sure. My name is Sam Gill. I teach at the University of Colorado at Boulder.
Mike Altman:	So my first question is when did you first meet Jonathan Z. Smith, and what was he like when you first met him?
Sam Gill:	That's a great story. Actually, I'm glad you asked that one. I met him 50 years ago almost exactly right now. I was at the University of Chicago starting in the fall of 1967. I think it was probably Frank Reynolds that said, "Hey, you should go do some work with Jonathan Smith." I knew he had somewhat of a growing reputation at the time, but I didn't really know who he was.

So I made an appointment, found his office, and went to see him. When I did that, we had a very brief first encounter. I just very naively said, "I'm supposed to be here to do something with you." He said, "Well, why would I want to work with somebody like you?" I was shocked. I muttered around a little bit. He said, "Well, write me a paper and leave it by the end of the week, and I'll see." |

I did that. When I dropped the paper off, I made an appointment to see him the following week, and went in to see him then. It was a remarkable meeting. He sat on one side of the desk. I sat on the other. I could see that he, on the very first page of my paper, had just covered it with red ink. It was just amazing. He then started in, word-by-word, sentence-by-sentence, literally ripping the thing to pieces.

I remember particularly one word he stopped on, and the word was "infamous." I think that paper was on [Dwight Lyman] Moody or somebody, early twentieth century. He said, "This a word you should never, ever use." I just, frankly, didn't even know what the word meant. I thought it meant very famous, instead of negatively famous. He went on and on and on, and I just decided that I was done. I'd probably just need to leave and that was the end of my career in religion.

After a half hour or so of this, he said, "You know, this isn't really that bad of a paper." He handed it to me and said, "Rewrite it and get it back to me next week." I walked out of his office. As I was walking across campus, I suddenly realized that though I had, I don't know, at least one graduate degree, maybe two before that, this was actually my very, very first learning experience. It was the first time someone had taken me so seriously that they gave me their full attention and criticism.

So I really think that very first meeting with Jonathan was a major change in my whole life, the way I teach, the way I do research, and everything else. So that was a major, major event.

Mike Altman: That's excellent. I had to mute the microphone because I was laughing. There's that picture from that era that's in the Chicago Photo Archives. I think a lot of people have seen it of Smith with this suit on, leaning back on this couch with a cigarette in his hand. For I think a lot of folks my age, there's the Smith that we saw around the American Academy of Religion conference or whatever, and then there's that earlier one. I'm curious, as someone who knew that earlier Smith, what was he like then, and what do you think was different about that earlier part of his career versus what a lot of us saw as a much more avuncular Smith later on?

Sam Gill: Oh yes, yes. I think Smith, particularly in his early years, was ... I think he had a really strong reputation for being incisively critical, and almost overly harsh in his criticism. With that first experience I had with him, it was harsh criticism. But then I realized that that criticism came from his complete deep devotion to the subject, and his desire that it be really of value and not something that was just simply a light pastime. So things really made a difference to him I think. He expressed those sometimes in rather harsh terms. terms that I think some people found really quite difficult to take.

One story on that is ... I don't remember the nature of the meeting, but Walter Capps, who was at the University of California Santa Barbara at the time, hosted a meeting at ... well, it was a [S. C.] Johnson Wax family home somewhere. It was Wisconsin or someplace. It involved a whole lot of people from various fields in the study of religion. I was there and so was Jonathan. Near the end of that meeting, Jonathan sort of tore into the whole enterprise. Literally, almost brought Walter to a point of weeping. It was very, very harsh criticism. Yet, he did that because he really felt that things are important and things needed to change and things needed to be taken seriously. Frankly, that was what I always found so important about him.

Wendy Doniger came to visit at the University of Colorado. It was shortly after I got here, which was in 1983. She said she knew that I had worked with Jonathan. She said, "You know, I wanted to come to Colorado to meet you because I wanted to see how much you are like Jonathan," because I, at that time, had somewhat a reputation being similar to him, being rather harshly critical. So she wanted to see if I was patterned on the way Jonathan was at that time.

Now he was that way early on. I don't think that really ever went away, but then I think that got modulated as he got older. Certainly, it did also with me, to the point of finding humor more easy to modify that kind of criticism and be more open and connected with all kinds of people and things. I think that that did change a little bit over the years, but I think in terms of core values, Jonathan's always been extremely, incisively critical.

Mike Altman: When were you at Chicago? You said, I think is it '68?

Sam Gill: I was there. I started in the fall of '67 and I left there spring of '73 maybe.

Mike Altman: So panning back, what was it like at Chicago in that period? Did it feel like it was something special? 'Cause I mean looking back, it definitely was an incredible institutional space and moment, and the feel in that one University, and what was going on there. What did it feel like to be there then?

Sam Gill:	It did feel that way. Although frankly, I was a little isolated from that. I came to Chicago with an undergraduate degree in mathematics and a graduate degree in business. I already had a very successful career in business. I went to Chicago sort of on a lark just to regroup before I totally devoted myself to the study of ... to a business career.
	When I got to Chicago, it seemed like there was something really amazing and powerful happening. I wasn't necessarily very equipped to understand quite what that was because I didn't fit very well. As a matter of fact, I've never fit very well in the study of religion. But certainly, Chicago in those days was a place that was very exciting, a lot of things going along, a lot of people doing exciting work. You could tell that. You could feel it.
Mike Altman:	When you talk about Smith, the discussion of [Mircea] Eliade is always right behind that, I think, or connected to that. What did their relationships seem like to you while you were there and following?
Sam Gill:	Yes, Eliade was my teacher as well. I mean, I had classes from both of them. While, as it's widely known, Smith was very critical of Eliade, that wasn't necessarily reciprocated, because Eliade wasn't a critical kind of person. He sort of ingested everything, and it all came out in his pattern, so it didn't matter what you said about him. It all worked somehow. But Smith really felt that Eliade's approach to criticism, to the understanding of religion was not going to carry us forward. He then used Eliade, I think, frequently as a kind of foil to highlight his own approach and his own recommendations for the direction of the field.
	On a personal basis, however, I think they were really quite close friends. They spent a lot of time together. At least as Jonathan would often make reference to Eliade, it was always done in the most cordial, generous, friendly, open terms. From the perspective of the writings that Smith did about Eliade, it appears, I think, really quite different; I think that reflects accurately their personal relationship.
Mike Altman:	Having worked with Smith, what do you think from his work do you see that carries through into your work? Where do you see his influence on your work, first of all? Then what do you think his real influence overall in the field? I know that's a big question, but what do you think the most important of his influences on the field as a whole is?
Sam Gill:	That is a big question.

Mike Altman:	You can start with your work if that's easiest, probably smaller.
Sam Gill:	Yeah, my work is in fields completely different from Smith's. But for me as I look at how he influenced me and my career, he has been a fundamental and very foundational influence on almost everything that I have done. I see that largely in terms of the way he understands difference, and how that then shaped his understanding of comparison, and history, and creativity, and innovation, and a whole range of things. I actually think my entire career, including a book manuscript I'm reading this morning to send to press, is very deeply influenced by Smith's insights.

So that, in contrast to Eliade, who really wanted to see comparison as a way of finding uniformity in the whole world, which I think parallels late nineteenth century anthropological concerns ... How do we reconcile the enormous diversity in humankind? One way to do that is to find that ... well, it's really sort of all the same in some respects.

I think Smith then wanted to move past that early stage and say, "But what's really interesting, what's really fascinating are the differences. And one then needs to look at the differences, not simply to document them, but to allow those differences to give rise to new questions, new perspectives, new theories." I think that was one of the most important areas of development that he made for the whole field. It seems small in a certain respect, but then when you play that out, it really becomes ... It's a total ideological shift, I think, and a completely different way of looking at the world.

For me in my current work, my work is focused on the idea, let's not simply tolerate difference, but let's appreciate difference. To me, that's an issue that is fundamental to the future of the world. We do not appreciate difference right now. Yet, we need somehow to do that. The study of religion ought to contribute deeply to that. So, that's one area.

One other one, which I just really want to mention, is a really simple one as well, and that is check your sources. I think Smith's work began with his studies of [Sir James George] Frazer's book, *The Golden Bough*. As he told his students back in the early days, when he studied Frazer's *The Golden Bough* ... I mean, this is an enormous work, with thousands of documents contributing to it. Smith said that as he read what Frazer read, he would actually go talk to people that had also read the same works and discuss those. This gave him this enormous body of material to work with. But what was most important to Smith, particularly as he focused on *The Golden Bough* was: "How did Frazer use his sources?"

He felt that Frazer used them in a way that was almost always not accurate. So, much of Smith's work is simply saying, "I'm just going to check the sources of the people that I'm reading." In checking those sources, one discovers then, not the errors so much, as the story of the development of one's way of thinking, of a whole field of study, all those kinds of things.

My book *Storytracking* is really ... which it took me five years to research ... was really starting with an incident that Eliade had quoted, focused on Australian Aboriginal people, and spending years and years simply tracking down the source to the source to the source to the source, to try to get back to the original person. And that then revealed this entire story that was part of the development of the field. So check your sources. I've always taught my students that.

Mike Altman: That's great. I think immediately of the essay where Smith basically checks Eliade's sources and says, "No, these people didn't die because their Axis Mundi broke. It was this whole other thing about the patterns of their travel and of movement." Yeah, exactly.

Just I think to wrap this up, there's been a number of pieces that have come out from people about Smith recently and I'm just curious if there is either a story or just something about him that needs to be said that you don't think has been yet, that we should make sure people hear?

Sam Gill: I don't know ... The thing that I feel is that Smith was a pretty private person in many respects. So even those of us who knew him for 50 years, never knew him in an extremely personal way. Partly, that was because he didn't use email and it was difficult to have that ongoing conversation. I think his humor is really fundamental to who the man was. He loved to see the humorous aspect of things, and in a way that highlighted their depth, their humanity, their significance, their importance. I just feel like that's a rich part of Jonathan's heritage that we all need to appreciate and accept.

Sam Gill is Professor Emeritus University of Colorado at Boulder. J. Z Smith was his most important influence and mentor for nearly fifty years. He works on indigenous religions, dancing and religion, religion theory, and religion and technology.

Interview with Amir Hussain

Mike Altman:	We're trying to get a variety of different stories and whatever else we can from people—memories of J. Z. Smith, from folks that might have known him. I had never actually met him.
Amir Hussain:	Ah, that's such a shame, amazing guy.
Mike Altman:	Yeah, I know. I saw him once across a hotel lobby, that was the extent of it.
Amir Hussain:	So much of Jonathan, as I came to realize later was, the persona. I mean, that's a calculated look, you don't look that way by accident you know.
Mike Altman:	Why don't we start off with, for the purposes of our show and our recording, just to get you to say your name and your affiliation, where you are.
Amir Hussain:	Sure. So my name is Amir Hussain. I'm a professor of theological studies at Loyola Marymount University, which is the Jesuit university in Los Angeles.
Mike Altman:	I'm curious what's your connections or how did you know Professor Smith?
Amir Hussain:	I started my graduate work in the study of religion at the University of Toronto in 1989, doing a master's degree there. I was privileged to work with the other Professor Smith, Wilfred Cantwell Smith. Wilfred had retired from Harvard and come to Toronto. He wasn't technically on the faculty but he was there, and just someone working in Islamic studies. This extraordinary ability to work with Wilfred was amazing. So I did my master's, started my Ph.D. and, in 1992, the University of Toronto held a conference to honor Wilfred Cantwell Smith, and they brought in a number of key speakers, including Jonathan ... I say Jonathan Zed Smith, as a Canadian. I still use the zed, not zee. So Jonathan Smith was there, and that was my first meeting with him.
	I had read in a method and theory class ... I don't know why it would have been assigned, but the assigned article from *History of Religions* was Smith's "When the Bough Breaks." He started out doing his work on James Frazer's multi-volume *The Golden Bough* series. I'd read that piece as a grad student and was excited to meet this person, because that's one of those really lovely moments as a grad student where you actually sometimes get to meet these people that you've been reading. You only know of them as these mythical characters in books and articles. And even then— this is over 25 years ago—Jonathan had this reputation as

the great historian of religion in North America. His reputation certainly preceded him. And he comes to the conference and I thought this is going to be interesting, because at that time I didn't know his work really well. I'd read a couple little things, but they were very different in orientation from Wilfred Smith's kind of work.

But Jonathan gave this lovely talk that was later printed in *Method and Theory in the Study of Religion*. That journal printed all the keynote talks that were there. Jonathan Smith's talk was looking at the fact that when he first started teaching at Dartmouth, he used Wilfred's *The Meaning and End of Religion*, so it was a really interesting connection, for here's this guy who you wouldn't think has a lot in common with this other guy other than the last name, but yet they have a really interesting connection here. There's Jonathan speaking and as I said earlier, the persona's just fascinating, because you look at this guy and he's got the hat, he's got the long hair that comes out in a pyramid shape, he's got the beard, he's got the walking stick. He looks striking there. Gives his talk and it was just this amazing kind of talk.

But at the end Don Wiebe—who was one of our teachers at the University of Toronto, the great method and theory scholar—sort of gets on Jonathan for something or other. I can't remember what it was but the phrase logical positivism came out. And he kept poking at Jonathan, talking about him being a logical positivist, and Smith finally just sort of loses it up at the podium. I'm going to try to do his voice but you can't do his voice, but it really was that, "Jesus, Don, you're like a pig on a truffle hunt. I'm a logical positivist. Fine. Here I stand a logical positivist." But just that, "Jesus, Don, you're like a pig on a truffle hunt." It was just amazing to me as an off-the-cuff remark to come up with that analogy was just astounding. Then, it was really lovely because at the end of the conference—it was like a 2, 3 day conference—they brought Jonathan up at the end, when they were doing the thank yous, and Don actually presented him with a chocolate truffle, which was just this priceless moment there.

I was able to talk with him for a little bit. It was one of those really nice ... as you only get to do in top graduate programs, where you have these conferences where people come for a couple of days where you can actually mingle and talk with them and I talked for just a few minutes with Jonathan. It was my first interaction with him and I said how much I appreciated what he had to say and included the regard that he held my mentor, Wilfred Cantwell Smith, in. And Jonathan was really lovely about saying, "Well, of course, how could you not come, how could you not honor this person given his contributions." That was my first encounter with him and that was in like April, May, it was the end of the semester 1992.

That fall I went to my first AAR, that was in San Francisco. We were all grad students. It was me, Willi Braun, Russell McCutcheon, Bill Arnal, you look back and think, those are some really important people that I get to hang out with. We went to San Francisco. I was able to see Professor Smith again. I was able to connect with him over the course of 25 years at AAR meetings, but then also with colleagues. So I taught for eight years at Cal State Northridge from '97 to 2005, and I taught from 2005 since here at Loyola Marymount University. Any decent religious studies department is going to have folks who've come out of the Chicago Ph.D. program, hopefully including some folks that have been trained by Jonathan. So at Cal State Northridge, there was a woman, Linda Lam-Easton, who did East Asian Confucian things. She'd worked with Jonathan. Here at LMU, my colleague Jim Fredericks who retired a couple of years ago, he did a Ph.D. on Japanese Buddhism working with Joe Kitagawa but also with Jonathan. It was great to get those kinds of stories from them, the connections at AAR meetings and that kind of thing. And of course, reading his material.

Mike Altman: Yeah, the truffle statement is so great because I think it's ... you said it's an interesting analogy, and he really has ... all of his stuff, there's these interesting analogies.

Amir Hussain: Absolutely.

Mike Altman: These things that you don't see coming. I was talking about the walnut and the praline the other day. And it's like there's always something that it starts with, right? I think that that's such a great example that even in the writing where it seems thought about and planned out, that even off the cuff, there's an unexpected—

Amir Hussain: Exactly. It was off the cuff, and then that was ... the writing was amazing because this, as you know, I'd asked him at that point ... This was long before the *MTSR* special edition came out with the papers. I'd asked him for a copy of his paper, and he said, well, I can't give you a copy. I can't print, because it's literally, like he had this notebook and it was literally handwritten. I think okay, that's amazing. Here's this guy who's like in hand, longhand, writing out his talk.

Mike Altman: To close this out, because I don't want to keep you too long, there's been a lot of stuff written recently about Smith, such as that series they're doing at the *Bulletin for Study of Religion*'s blog. So what's the thing that, to your mind, hasn't been said so far that needs to be said about Smith?

Amir Hussain: How do you capture his work, his influence? But then also the fact that this was a person—and a really interesting person. I think more people down the road will talk about his legacy for example. And that's something I think to be determined later. So for example, Wilfred Cantwell Smith died in 2000, it was just last year that a book came out from SUNY Press called *The Legacy of Wilfred Cantwell Smith* ... People talk about him being great for the twentieth century. But what about the twenty-first century? I'm assuming those are the kinds of things you're going to see 10, 15, 20 years from now, concerning Jonathan. That people are still going to be reading him. It's not like okay, he's done. That's it. There's nothing there. No, you keep going back. You keep mining the material. I think those kinds of things.

No one person can capture someone as amazing and complicated and fully human as Jonathan, so you would need 15 different people writing six pages each to get some sense of who this person was.

Mike Altman: Yeah, I think that's right. I think that's kind of what we're trying to do here. To get a bunch of people to talk about him.

Amir Hussain: I think what you guys are doing here is really important because there's literally generations of us in the plural who knew Jonathan, who worked with him, and met him, who read him, and I think being able to get those kinds of stories down ... like I said, for a first encounter with someone that, "Jesus, Don, you're like a pig on a truffle hunt." I mean that's just this amazing, amazing kind of moment that I still remember over 25 years ago.

Mike Altman: Yeah. I think there's been a lot of people, my generation—I got my Ph.D. in 2013—who grew up with him ... I read "Religion, Religions, Religious" as an undergrad and now teach it. So for me it's been interesting as a younger scholar to get to sit down with people who have those first hand encounters.

Amir Hussain: Yeah. Jonathan was sui generis. There's not another one like him.

Amir Hussain is a Professor in the Department of Theological Studies at Loyola Marymount University in Los Angeles, where he teaches courses on Islam and world religions.

Interview with Donald Wiebe

Mike Altman:	The main reason I wanted to talk to you is Amir Husain, who is one of the people I talked to, told this story about you and Smith that I just wanted to get your side of. I don't know if you remember this, but there was some event for W. C. Smith at Toronto, and Amir was there, and J. Z. Smith was giving a paper. And apparently you were giving him a hard time about being a positivist. Do you remember this?
Donald Wiebe:	Giving him a hard time about being a positivist?
Mike Altman:	Yeah.
Donald Wiebe:	Actually it was the other way around. I was giving him a tough time in a positivist fashion, as he saw it, for his crypto-theology.
Mike Altman:	And so apparently he, as Amir told it, you're going after him and he turned to you and said, "Jesus, Don. You're on me like a pig after truffles!" Was that it?
Donald Wiebe:	Yes. He put it this way: "Don, you're like a pig after truffles." The conference itself had been set up to honor Wilfred Cantwell Smith. The Director of the Centre for the Study of Religion in Toronto was Neil McMullin, who had studied with Smith at Harvard. And of course I'm a fellow Canadian with Wilfred, and we had our differences, but Neil and I had about $10,000 left Center's budget before they closed it down and we decided to honor Wilfred by way of a mini-conference focused on his work. Jonathan Z. was one of the big speakers for this event.
	As Jonathan was delivering his paper, I felt that he was far too close to Wilfred's way of thinking. So I said something to this effect: "Jonathan, why is this not just another kind of theology?" At which point he said, "Good God," or, "Jesus Wiebe," "you're like a pig after truffles." This conversation added a little color to the conference. But that was not my only "encounter" with Jonathan but was typical of those that followed.
Mike Altman:	Do you remember any of these other experiences?
Donald Wiebe:	Well, there was an early one in about 1983 or '84, where I had been asked by one of Jonathan's students to participate on a panel on ritual at a regional AAR meeting at, I think, Sarah Lawrence College. I told her I knew about as much about ritual as I could put on the back of a postage stamp. "That doesn't matter," she said, "it's the discussion and debate that's valuable."
	Well, it was embarrassing. It was a plenary session and I knew very little about religious ritual, and what little I

knew about ritual was from my reading in ethology—not religious studies. I was particularly interested in the work of people like Konrad Lorenz and other animal behaviorists. And so I made some comments about ritual-like behavior in animals. Jonathan said something to the chair about them having overheard some animals on their way to breakfast that morning in vigorous debate about some ritual behavior or other.

Not sure how I could respond to what I took as polite mockery, I finally relayed a bit of information I had learned about killdeers as a schoolkid— that they will feign a broken wing if you get too close to their ground nests, lead you away from the nest and then fly away. So I told a story about a killdeer I came across on my way to breakfast that morning having lied to me by feigning an injury and then flew away. This was my first encounter with Jonathan and I was grateful for his positive response to my "encounter" with the killdeer. That experience, I think, was the beginning of my friendship with Jonathan.

Mike Altman: You were heavily involved in NAASR, and you ended up bringing Jonathan in, who was president for a couple of years, right? How did you get him interested and involved in NAASR?

Donald Wiebe: Well, you know, this started quite early. I think it was Ivan Strenski and I who had asked Hans Penner and Jonathan Z. Smith to help us form a kind of group within AAR itself that would look at religion from a scientific point of view. They emphatically said, "It can't be done." We had a pleasant conversation and we left it that. Then, several years later Tom Lawson, Luther Martin, and I—at the International Association for the History of Religions meeting in Sydney Australia—tried this again; now, however, working outside the framework of the AAR.

And I think it was probably that earlier conversation with Hans Penner and Jonathan that kind of gave us the courage to go back to him and ask him to get involved. I can't remember the details about that, though. Luther Martin might have more of a memory on that score than I do. In any event Jonathan became involved. Oh! I do remember how it happened. Jack Neusner was at the IAHR congress in Australia as well, and we got him involved first.

And then Jack, without our knowledge, bought several memberships in NAASR, one for himself and one for Jonathan Zed Smith, or Zee Smith, among others. And so Jonathan became a member of the NAASR just at its very

	birth. But Jonathan didn't much appreciate the way it happened; or thought it was rather odd that Jack would sign him up without his permission. So, as I've been told the story, Jonathan signed Jack up to a Marxist society or association in the United States as a return gift. So that's the connection. It actually happened because of Jack Neusner.
Mike Altman:	I had to mute the microphone, because I was laughing in the middle of that. That's great.
	There's been a lot written lately by former students of Smith's and I was just curious if there was anything you think that needs to be said about his life, or his work, that hasn't been said or written out yet?
Donald Wiebe:	I don't know that I can add anything new here. Jonathan, in my experience, was one of the most relaxed scholars in religious studies that I ever encountered. He was not uptight about "religious studies." He wasn't uptight about criticism. In my experience, I don't think there was anybody in the field, then or now, who was sharper on his feet than Jonathan.
	I mean, he was just … For all his criticism, which could be very cutting and deep, it was never a personal attack on anyone. It was just a matter of discussing and debating the issues. And on that score I remember a more recent experience with Jonathan in which I had pressed him, Burton Mack, and a few others on what in the world they meant by the notion of redescription; the task of redescription.
	I said, "Does it mean you describe it again? You describe it in a different way? Or is there a theoretical element here?" And we didn't get anywhere. That was in a NAASR session. Shortly thereafter, Jonathan was on a panel on redescription in an AAR session. I was sitting in about the third row with Luther Martin and before the session started Jonathan pointed his finger at me to draw me up to the dais.
	So I went up there with some trepidation, and he very quietly said, "Don't raise the redescription issue here." And the way he did it, it was both a "lecture"—don't be like a pig after truffles—and, I think, an acknowledgement that there was a problem with the terminology. I loved my encounters with Jonathan.
Mike Altman:	That's great. Thanks, Don. I really appreciate you doing this. When I heard Amir's version of the story I just needed to get your side. So that's helpful. And there's something remarkable about Amir mixing it up, and getting it backwards. About the positivism being backwards.
Donald Wiebe:	I was the "positivist," not Jonathan.

Donald Wiebe, Professor of Philosophy of Religion at Trinity College, University of Toronto, has spent much of his academic career arguing for a clear demarcation between Theology and Religion. In 1995, with Luther H. Martin and E. Thomas Lawson, he founded the North America Association for the Study of Religion.

Interview with Carole Myscofski

Mike Altman:	There's all these pieces being written right now on Jonathan Z. Smith life and his work, and so we're just trying to find those who might have some stories that people don't know or haven't heard ...
Carole Myscofski:	I have so few enchanting stories about Jonathan ... What I remember is mostly meeting with him, telling him everything I was doing and he would say "Yeah" and elaborate on different directions I might take. Then I would leave and not remember anything we'd done. He was really, as you must know, an incredibly charismatic man.
	I began taking classes with him when I was a sophomore in college and stayed with him all the way through grad school. So I have been trying to think of the things that he used to do in class. He had several small but fascinating habits. For example, he would sit on the back of his chair and rock backwards and we would all wait thinking that he was about to crash over. He did it repeatedly in class. This was in college. He never fell over but he kept our rapt attention on his situation.
Mike Altman:	Do you think that was intentional?
Carole Myscofski:	I've never quite figured out. I don't think so.
Mike Altman:	Like if they are thinking about the fall, they'll listen more ...
Carole Myscofski:	I don't think anyone would put himself in danger like that.
Mike Altman:	Before we go any further, so I have it for our purposes, can I just get you to say "My name is" and then just say who you are and where are all your affiliations, just so we have that on tape.
Carole Myscofski:	Yeah, my name is Carole Myscofski. I teach at Illinois Wesleyan University. I'm the McFee Professor of Religion here and I'm also the director of Women's and Gender Studies.
Mike Altman:	Thank you. And if you're telling a story and you don't hear me doing a lot of "Uh huh" and "yes" or laughing it's because we're going to cut all these together. So I'm trying to keep me out of it as much as possible.
Carole Myscofski:	Well, he also had another fascinating habit with his cigarettes. When a student asked him a question, he would have a very elaborate ritual of opening his cigarette box, taking a cigarette out, tapping it against the box. So it would take

about five minutes to get around to answering the question, but he also used to, you know he smoked in class, and he brought his own ashtray. A little, tiny pocket ashtray with a little cover and this is another thing that students were fascinated by. We talked about it later. He would let the ash burn for a very long time, until we were convinced it must fall off (and he meant it now), but it would never do it. And then he'd casually pull out his pocket ashtray and flick it in, put away his pocket ashtray and continue.

He smoked even when students asked him why he did it. He would, with a wave, just dismiss the question. He also dismissed the question of what religion he was and whether he was religious. I remember in class he said, "That's of no interest to me."

And one more anecdote from college days. There was one particular class I was in. He had missed a number of classes without telling us ahead of time. So we met in the classroom, waited and realized he was not there, and a couple of the students were really furious that he kept missing classes. I'm sure he was giving talks and lectures but we were cheerfully unaware of that sort of thing. So with one of the students leading us, we figured out how much we were paying him per class and therefore how much we were losing per class when he was absent. Now this was back in the days when a year at the University of Chicago was less than $5000. It's a very long time ago.

So, what more can I tell you?

Mike Altman:	You met him as a college sophomore. So when was that?
Carole Myscofski:	1972
Mike Altman:	You know there's that picture, I don't know if you've seen it, that floats around the internet of him in this suit with a cigarette. Do you know the one that I'm talking about? Do you know this image?
Carole Myscofski:	The one with the cane or the one where he's leaning back in the chair?
Mike Altman:	Leaning back in the chair. It's from somewhere around, in my mind, it's gotta be from this period that your describing, right?
Carole Myscofski:	Yes that's exactly it. That's the way I remember him. I'm always surprised to see him with gray hair and the cane because I remember him as having, he always had the long hair, but dark hair. Even then, I think he was in his thirties when I met him, it was already touched with gray. So I had a class with him my sophomore year and then I was in the History and Philosophy of Religion program as an

undergraduate and it was just closing because all of the faculty were leaving and he was sort of the last man standing. And he agreed to take me on as a student. So I took classes, at least one independent study, with him every year and then, every class I could get into of his. So I took Religion and the Humanities, I took his Ways of Understanding Religion, Texts and Contexts and then when I started running out of undergrad religion classes I took classes in the Divinity School with him too. And then, I did my Master's and Ph.D. in the Divinity School.

Mike Altman: So for me, I'm 33, been out of grad school since I got my Ph.D. in 2013. So, in my mind there's a Jonathan Z. Smith that I know. I never actually met him. I saw him across the hotel lobby one time. It seems has a kind of avuncular feel to him in a way but you, it seems like, know a very different era and so I'm curious what can you tell the folks like me, who in many ways grew up with a Jonathan Z. Smith that had kind of already won the war in so many ways.

Carole Myscofski: Oh, yeah.

Mike Altman: I think a lot of us would like to know what was that Smith that's in that picture, with that suit, what was he like? Who was he?

Carole Myscofski: He was a dynamo. It's stunning for me to go back ... In preparation for this ... I've kept one notebook from undergraduate classes with him and he was like a tidal wave in the classroom. He was so full of energy and information. His erudition was astonishing when I look back at that. So he was sort of an overwhelming presence but one also got the sense, even as a naïve undergraduate, that he was creating a new field in a way. We were all aware of Eliade. That he was the next Eliade, that's a very strange thing to say, but he was someone who was as knowledgeable, as widely read, and as innovative, more innovative in some ways. So it was like, I would say, like catching a will-o'-the wisp but he was much more solid than that.

You know, I've followed in my head these independent studies with him while he was Assistant Professor, then Associate Professor, while he was Master of the Humanities and Dean of the College, so I kept seeing him during our independent studies together. And he really never changed. He never took his prestigious positions or his accolades as an opportunity to change relations with students. He loved teaching and I think, from all of the things that I have recorded about him and the few notes from him, from various points when I was in college and graduate school and then later, that he cared about his students tremendously. He was also aware that there were a lot of demands on his time, so he was modest about his own accomplishments and he was generous in some ways, but not given to waste his time, I suppose I'd say.

Mike Altman: You mentioned Eliade. Even when I was first introduced to his work, it was in the context of Eliade, who was right there with him, and I'm curious what, from your observation, your experience, what was the nature of that relationship that I think both happened on the pages of chapters and journals but also happened in private spaces too. What did you see about their relationship between the two of them?

Carole Myscofski: Well, you used the term avuncular earlier, and I think that is part of what I would have said at the time. Jonathan viewed him as a wonderful colleague, a kind man, sort of an elder in the field, even while he was, of course, very carefully critiquing and pulling apart Eliade's methods and his evidence in a very serious way, but the personal relationship seemed very positive.

Mike Altman: Yeah, that's what I've gathered from other people too.

Broadening out a little bit, what was Chicago and the Divinity School like in the '70s? It seems, from an outside perspective, a kind of fascinating place but did it feel that way at the time? Did it feel like something field-changing was being built here? How did it feel in that moment?

Carole Myscofski: It's hard for a person right in the moment to realize that that's what's going on, but it was very exciting. I was, as I said, in the college and the study of religions was in the New Collegiate Division, so it was an experimental program in an experimental division. I mean, Chuck Long was there at the same time and being part of it opened doors for me in all sorts of directions. When I look back to see who I worked with, I also worked with Joseph Kitagawa. I took several classes with him and, of course, Martin Marty too; being part of that was really very exciting.

So being in a place where methods were changing and where methodology was coming to the forefront, was really very exciting. When I look back at the notes that I took, I see Jonathan Smith doing critical methods in his undergraduate classes. In every single class, he did the broadest studies you can imagine. The most in-depth background work. The most scrupulous care being taken with the approach to the study of each idea. So, we spent days in the approach to the study before ever getting to a theorist or a text.

Mike Altman:	In some ways, that's what we try to do here [at the University of Alabama] but he was doing it forty years ago and paving the way so that folks like us could do it in our classrooms, which is just kind of remarkable. I have one last question: What's the thing that hasn't been said so far, that you think needs to be said about Smith?
Carole Myscofski:	I think ... when I thought about my relationship with him, what I recall is his incredible generosity as a teacher. He made himself available to me when I was a college sophomore. He was not off putting. He was kind and welcoming and supportive all the way through my career at the University of Chicago. He helped me get into classes. He helped me write proposals and then enroll in the Divinity School. He helped me construct and change fields while I was there. I started off in Greek studies which is why I worked with him and then shifted to colonial Brazilian studies and he stayed with me right through it and helped me work out what I needed to know to move. He also wrote me a really touching note after I left. I had sent him a copy, a bound copy, of my dissertation in the year after I left and he sent a note back to me saying thanks and that he hoped I would someday understand that this was one of the best moments for a teacher, when a student goes out into the world and I still have that. It's really very touching.
	That was his view of his students. That he would help them and support them to move on.
Mike Altman:	That's awesome. Thank you so much. This has been so great. This is stuff that, again, no one else can say ...
Carole Myscofski:	I hope I helped in some way ... I really liked the guy.

Carole A. Myscofski is McFee Professor of Religion and Director of the Women's and Gender Studies Program at Illinois Wesleyan University. She began working with J. Z. Smith in her third year in The College and completed her dissertation in the Divinity School under his guidance.

Interview with Christopher Lehrich

Mike Altman:	So, before we get started, could you, just so I have it on tape to use in the podcast, say, "my name is," and who you are, however you want to identify yourself, just in a sentence for me.
Christopher Lehrich:	Yeah, my name is Christopher Lehrich, and I'm a scholar of religion, interested in magic, early modern history, and comparison, and I was Jonathan Smith's student, graduate student at the University of Chicago.

Mike Altman: Yeah, so we'll start there. When did you first meet Jonathan Z. Smith?

Christopher Lehrich: Well, I met him very briefly when I was a college student, which would be sometime around 1990, I guess. But then, I only met him extensively in about 1994 or '95, something like that, and then I was his Ph.D. student through 2000.

Mike Altman: So, I've been talking to his various students of his throughout his career, in fact, earlier today I was talking to someone who knew him in the '70s, when he was just getting started. What was he like when you first met him in the '90s and into being graduates? What was your first impression of him?

Christopher Lehrich: Well, he was very intense. I mean, I think probably everybody who spent any significant time with Jonathan had the experience of discovering that, on the one hand, he could be an extraordinarily attentive listener, and listened very closely, and on the other hand, if he wasn't in that mood, he would just talk, and you just sort of sat there, like a lump, and listened. And he would just talk on, and on, and on, and then he would kind of pause, and you'd say a couple of things, and that would start him off again, and then he would talk. Just how he was.

Mike Altman: So, can you tell us the story of how you went from his student, then you took him as an undergraduate, and then as an advisor, to putting some of his essays together in *Teaching Religion* ...? How did you go from Ph.D. advisee to editor of this book?

Christopher Lehrich: First of all, I was never his student in college; I met him, once or twice, and he was a pretty recognizable figure around campus, and I heard about him once or twice, but I was never his student until grad school. So then, after I finished my degree, I went and taught general education, essentially, at Boston University. I did that for, I don't know, six or seven years, and then I finally got into the situation of teaching Religious Studies. And what I found was that, if you've ever taught college writing in a small seminar kind of setting, it's very intense, and very focused, and if you take it seriously, you end up learning a lot about how to teach, so I worked at it, I published on teaching writing, and so forth. I was very serious about it. And then, finally I got into the Religion department, and I discovered that the teaching of religion was appallingly primitive. People were giving lecture courses on things like, "Religions of the East," as though that was a sensible category, and this is 2010. I just thought, "what the heck is going on here?" I then sort of asked around, and some people kind of said, "yeah, well, these are these old courses, but you know, the kids, whatever." It was quite clear to me that most people didn't really care, and then those who did care really just weren't very competent, they didn't really have any sense of what they were doing as teachers, in any kind of focused sense. People would say, "well, you know, sure, we do these vague things at the beginning, but you know, when people are serious, then, we're planning for them to be graduate students," and all of this struck me as deeply wrong, and wrongheaded. And I could remember reading the odd article by Jonathan about teaching religion—there was a famous article in the *Journal of the American Academy of Religion* (*JAAR*) for example—and I thought, this is very odd, and I started looking for these articles, and I discovered that there were a lot of them. And most of them had appeared in relatively obscure journals for a number of reasons.

So most people hadn't seen them, people in religious studies. They knew of Jonathan as the guy that wrote *Imagining Religion* and so on, but they didn't really know anything about this whole other dimension of his work. And as I read more and more, I thought it was interesting, and stimulating, and challenging, and some of it was much wilder than I had expected. Until I read the pieces, it had never occurred to me that he was opposed fundamentally to the notion of a college major. With hindsight, it's obvious, but at the time I didn't realize this. He's really leveling very strong challenges, and I thought, this is good stuff. So I wrote him a letter, and I suggested to him that I edit the book—you know, he was ill off and on for 35 years or something—so I said, look, there's a lot of labor that goes into editing something, and I'll be happy to do it. And he said that he was interested in doing it, but that he had already proposed that book to University of Chicago Press, and they had said that they absolutely had no interest in the book. So he didn't think that it was very saleable, so I said, well, that's fine, we'll try selling it to a different press, which was another piece of labor that he didn't feel like doing. So I sort of took it up, Oxford University Press was very excited about it, and from there, it was just the usual editing work, but it was just a matter of stumbling on this trove of material that nobody seemed to know about, that struck me as eminently important and relevant, and, like much of his work, didn't really seem to have penetrated the consciousness of the discipline.

Mike Altman:

My question, coming out of that is, sort of, is what do you think his impact was on teaching in the field? I mean it's kind of hard to measure that, there's no citations of what one does in the classroom, but do you think what you gathered up was evidence of a long standing influence, or do you think it was a chance to increase an influence that he'd been underappreciated up until that point?

Christopher Lehrich:

Well, if I'm entirely honest with you, I think that the great tragedy, in a sense, of Jonathan's career, whether it's the analytical work on religion and ritual and so forth, or the material on teaching, or whatever, is that there's an awful lot of talk, and an awful lot of citation, but I don't think there's very much influence at all. I was at the North American Association for the Study of Religion (NAASR) meeting, I don't know, four or five years ago, when this book, *Teaching Religion*, came out, and there were a lot of people there, scholars of all ages, who had theoretical, J. Z. Smith, whatever kind of credentials, and they started this whole conversation about how his dictum, that's "there is no data for religion," was just obviously stupid and idiotic. And I think the same thing is true with teaching. You saw that there was that kind of response/review essay thing in *JAAR*, which was quite negative. I think fundamentally, people don't want to be influenced by J. Z. Smith, they want *to say* they're influenced by J. Z. Smith, but they don't really want that. They don't want religion to be a construct, they want it really to refer to something, but they want to pretend that they think in a very sophisticated way.

The same goes for the teaching, they want to think vaguely, "oh, I'm thinking these interesting ideas, and challenging, and whatever." But in the end, people want to just teach Judaism, Christianity, Islam: "that's going be a good course, you know, the kids will love that." They want to start off with, "well, first, you have to get the facts, you have to get the information, later on, we'll deal with theory and stuff like that," setting aside entirely the fact that without any kind of theory, or framework, or whatever, those facts mean nothing. You can't do anything with them. Nobody really wants to take on what Jonathan proposed, pretty much across his career. So, yeah, the book came out, and I think there were various accolades, but my sense is that the people who are really influenced in a concrete, practical, actually-doing-something-in-the-classroom kind of way, are people who already knew about a few of those articles, and were influenced by them, and were delighted to get some more. I would be surprised to learn that there are a lot of—maybe graduate students—but I'd be surprised to learn there's a lot of people, let's say 40 and older, teaching in the profession for whom this book has changed anything.

Mike Altman: I think you're right about ... I always joke about the sort of, hat tip to Smith and others, like, we have to admit, yes, yes, yes, and then move on and do whatever we wanted to do from the beginning.

Christopher Lehrich: It's a kind of ritual, in fact, I suppose he would have said it was apotropaic, right? He's going to ward off the evils of being Protestant, triumphalist, you know, or whatever it is, and then go right ahead and do what we always did. I think these days, in my experience, the Protestant triumphalists tend to be rather quiet about what they think, and they've been replaced by kind of, it's a mode of philosemitism I suppose, a kind of, "we are good historians, and we are good J. Z. Smith students because we're defending Judaism from its Protestant detractors," but frankly, nobody with a brain could read *Imaging Religion* and not see that he was already criticizing Jack Neusner and others for doing that back in the late '70s. So, yeah, anyway ...

Mike Altman: No, I think you're right, I think you're right. Just transitioning a bit, what was it like ... so he was your advisor, right? For your dissertation ...?

Christopher Lehrich: Right.

Mike Altman: What was he like as a dissertation advisor?

Christopher Lehrich: Well, again, I mean, fascinating, and infuriating, as you'd expect. I don't know if you ever met Jonathan, but I think anybody who spent much time with him would sort of expect an answer like, "fascinating and infuriating." On the one hand, when I would talk to him, and spend time talking about how the dissertation was progressing, or whatever, I would just sit there in his office, he'd be there chain smoking, and I'd be there for like an hour and a half, or two hours, and it would be extremely stimulating, there'd be lots of interesting stuff. He'd read everything, I could sort of toss out ideas, or things I'd been reading, notions, whatever, and he always had something to say that was interesting and helpful. And he could be very pragmatically helpful, because let's face it, he almost exclusively taught college students, and you learn a certain kind of pragmatism from that, which can be very handy when you're dealing with someone who is stuck somewhere in the midst of the dissertation, mounds of paper and files. But that said, I mean, it was a project to get into his office. I mean, he had a note on his door, there was like a schedule sign-up thing for office hours, and then there was a note next to it that said, "this is for undergraduates, or college students, only. Graduate students, leave a phone message," or "drop something under my door," I forget what it was. But of course, as anybody who's known Jonathan knows, he doesn't answer the telephone, he never did. So, I mean that was essentially a very indirect way of saying, "graduate students, go away." And that's fine, I guess, if you've made that choice, but it's rather difficult when one is actually his dissertation student, right? So there were times when I had to get a form filed, signed, or whatever, and it would take, like a week, just hunting him down. I had friends that had entered graduate school with me, and lived relatively near where he lives, and I remember calling up one of my friends and saying, "look, I've got to get this form signed in the next few days. Listen, if you see him, wherever you are, if you see him, call me, and I'm going to come over, and just corner him so that he can't get away, because otherwise, the form will never get signed." So he could be infuriating, but I think it was kind of, he liked the intellectual challenge of things, and he liked the teaching, and we always got along extremely well.

But he took his dislike, which I'm sure most of us share, of the kind of bureaucratic stuff that goes into advising a graduate student or whatever, he took that dislike to such an extreme that it was a burden, frankly, for me.

Mike Altman: Yeah, that's interesting, because I talked to Carole Myscofsky who was his graduate student in the '70s, and she made a similar point about ... I'm sure there was less bureaucratic burden then, but as she put it, he was very careful with his time ...

Christopher Lehrich: Back then, of course, he would have spent much more time on campus, and could not have avoided things as drastically as he could get away with later on. So I think that being careful with his time probably does reflect her experience, and by the time I was at the tail-end of his teaching career, yeah, it was much more extreme than that.

Mike Altman: Is there any single story you feel that needs to be told? There's been a lot that's been said about him ... I'm actually part of an upcoming *MTSR* issue about his work. So is there a story, or just something that you think needs to be said that hasn't been said yet...?

Christopher Lehrich: What sort of story do you have in mind?

Mike Altman: I have nothing in mind; I'm just curious. This has been my go-to sort of question: what's the thing that hasn't been said, or hasn't been told that needs to be...?

Christopher Lehrich: Well ... I mean ... This is about Jonathan as a person, you mean ... He ... One of the things that I never made sense of with Jonathan, was that, and I have a theory, which I'll end with, but on the one hand, as I've said, and as Carole says this was true throughout his career, he was careful with this time, whatever, eventually he became kind of like a hermit, right? He didn't answer the phone ever. I would leave what I needed to—even when we were working on the book, for something, it's like, "Jonathan, I do need your input on this ...," and I would end up leaving message after message after message on his answering machine, and eventually his wife would sort of say, "Look, I'm passing on the messages, okay? It doesn't help to just leave more messages," and he just wouldn't call back.

He really was kind of a hermit, and at the same time, when you did catch up with him, then it didn't really matter whether he was a good friend, or your teacher, or if you were just somebody who bumped into him at AAR, he could be quite generous with his time, and he would talk, and he would sit with people, and be the life of the party in many respects. So, these two sides of him kind of seem to clash in my head. I remember one time the AAR was in Chicago and I came down from Boston, and he had—I guess he'd sort of forgotten to do some kind of registration or something, and so he ended up staying not at the hotel that everybody else was at, but at this second rate place just next to it, because he didn't want to go back and forth every day from the South Side. So I cornered him and said, "let's get together," and he invited me up to his room, and we ended up sitting there, talking for about three hours or something, and he gave no indication that he wanted me to go or something, and I was very attentive to that. He was having a wonderful time, and telling me all these horrible, gossipy stories about people who he hadn't been the most fond of, and you sort of think, "if you enjoy this sort of thing so much, why do you hide from people?" And my theory in the end, is that he was very bad at saying no, and when people would ask him to do something, and people were always asking him to do this or that, to contribute to an article, whatever, he'd say, "yeah, yeah, yeah, sure, I'll be happy to. Just send me a letter," or, "give me a phone call," whatever. Then he would never actually respond to that.

So his way of saying no was, "oh, sure, sure, sure, just send me a letter." Which was quite awkward, but I don't know, there's something funny about that, that I never quite put my finger on.

Mike Altman:	Yeah, it's just interesting though, as he went through a time where, I think, scholars in particular became more connected, and it became harder and harder for people to say no, you know, "send me a letter," seems like a really useful strategy.
Christopher Lehrich:	He never used email or anything like that, but I mean, let's face it, even back 100 years ago, it was pretty standard that people would say, "oh, I'm going to put together a volume about such and such," and then they'd write to all their friends and say, "hey, I'm putting together this volume, will you contribute," and people would say, "ugh, all right, sure," and they'd write, "oh, sure, I'll be happy to," but on the inside, they're thinking, "oh, God, that's another article to write." This is kind of the way, now it's done by email, whatever. And Jonathan would always say yes to that sort of thing, but in the end, he actually didn't really contribute the articles that much. And in the middle of his career, when he's always teaching things, I mean, those were public lectures, like, he went around delivering lectures, he must have been invited constantly to do these things. So, I feel like if somebody, I doubt anybody's ever been able to put together much of a biography of him, but I feel like somewhere in that period that he was going around, he must have decided, "you know what? That's it, I'm done." Same thing with this intense dislike of all kinds of bureaucratic whatever. I mean, the guy was Dean at the College at Chicago for, I don't know, six or eight years I think, maybe even longer. You don't survive that if you can't function with bureaucracy, and yet ...

In the end, the moment that stays with me most from working together on *Teaching Religion* is when we were about halfway through, and I'd just sent him the first complete rough draft, and we spoke at AAR, I think in San Francisco. He seemed kind of uncertain, and said he was worried that the whole thing was going to be totally out-of-date, because he hadn't been keeping up with the pedagogical literature, he hadn't revised the pieces, all that. I said I thought the book *should* be out-of-date, but unfortunately it wasn't, which I meant as sort of a bad-tempered joke, but he took it very seriously and started asking me all these questions, and he seemed kind of depressed, because nothing had changed. Same with the paper and panel topics at AAR, they didn't seem to have changed much in a generation, and he seemed to me very frustrated about that. Pretty soon he reverted to type and was telling funny stories, but that one moment really sticks with me.

Christopher Lehrich trained under J. Z. Smith at the University of Chicago; he was the editor for Smith's collection of pedagogy articles, *On Teaching Religion* (2012), and the author of a forthcoming volume on Smith's work for the Key Thinkers in the Study of Religion series.

Interview with Eugene Gallagher

Mike Altman:	First thing, could you just say my name is and just tell us who you are and identify yourself for us?
Eugene Gallagher:	My name is Eugene Gallagher, I used to teach at Connecticut College in New London, Connecticut and I retired from there in 2015, and now I teach part-time at the College of Charleston.
Mike Altman:	So how did you know Jonathan Z. Smith? When did you first meet him?
Eugene Gallagher:	I entered the University of Chicago Divinity School in History of Religions in 1972 as part of a fairly large class of 10 or 12 people. At that point, there was no common MA, we were just admitted right into HR. The first course I took was called Texts and Contexts in the History of Religions with Jonathan Smith. I had seen that he was teaching things I'd be interested in but I'd never met him or really heard much about him by the time I got there. It was quite a revelation when I entered that classroom and met him for the first time and began to work with him as a teacher.
Mike Altman:	Now, you've done some interesting work yourself, bridging both between New Testament stuff and new religious movements. What was Jonathan's influence on the study? When you ask people of my generation his work on Jonestown seems like one of the things that everyone's read, for some reason. In fact, one of my favorites, I think, is his less frequently cited chapter in Susan Mizruch's *Religion and Cultural Studies*, on UFO abductions: "Close Encounters of Diverse Kinds." But I'm curious how do you think Jonathan's work shaped this subfield of New Religious Movements?
Eugene Gallagher:	The one thing that struck me from the beginning was that he truly was a comparativist, but a comparativist in a very different mode than say Eliade, Kitagawa, and Wach—whose books that they had us read the summer before we arrived for our first classwork. I had gone to Chicago mainly to study the ancient world with him. Judaism, Christianity, other Greco-Roman religions was going to be my focus but when I saw Smith just cut through wide swaths of material and put them in interesting juxtapositions, it fascinated me. So even though I stuck with work in Hellenistic

religions as my focus throughout my time at Chicago, when I got to be a teacher and I learned that students and parents and alumni and trustees weren't as interested in the second and third century as I was. I started to pay more attention to what was going on at the time.

This was the late '70s, early '80s and it was a heyday of a bunch of different new religious movements, and the Moonies were quite notorious then, also the Children of God, which became the Family later on. I started to poke around in that and the thing that fascinated me most was that they were all producing large theological texts often in the forms of commentaries on or actually additions to the Bible. It brought together the two halves of my head that I had been training at Chicago in the history of religions field.

Mike Altman: Is Smith an important figure in that subfield or...

Eugene Gallagher: I don't think he's important enough! I think that the sub-shield is still dominated by the sociology of religion approach. There's a lot of participant observation and there's not as much attention to careful comparison, let alone global careful comparison as there should be in the subfield. So I think he hasn't really had sufficient impact there as he's had let's say in the study of Hellenistic religions including early Christianity. I wish he had more impact.

Mike Altman: You came to Chicago in 1972, you said, one of our audiences for this interview is, I think, a lot of people of my generation who are relatively new in the field and we look back at what was happening in Chicago in the '70s. It seems like a ... I don't know, Gilded Age might not be the right word, but there just seems to be a lot happening and it just seemed like a crazy place to be in a good way. I'm curious, did it feel that way? What was Chicago like in the history of religions in the '70s?

Eugene Gallagher: Yeah, when I arrived, I was, I think, the only person in my incoming history of religions class who hadn't been taught by a person with a Chicago degree. I was something of an outsider to the whole thing but the ferment was palpable almost every day. I think one of the things that contributed to that was not only Smith's leadership but the fact that he drew in a pretty large class of 10 or 12 Ph.D. students in that one year. As a result, there were a lot of colleagues to work with in the student body. Of course, we worked across the years with other students but our class was a real bulge in that sense. There were more in our class than there were the year before and than there would be in the next couple of years.

So I had a really rich array of fellow students to work with Smith. One of the things he did was he took us all out of that Text and Context class and had a special seminar for us I think every couple of weeks at least during the first quarter there. We get a sense of being part of a cohort and I think that was really important for us.

Mike Altman: Was he your advisor?

Eugene Gallagher: He was my advisor, yeah.

Mike Altman: What was he like as an advisor?

Eugene Gallagher: At times he was elusive, midway during my time there he became Dean of the College, which made him a little bit harder to find and harder to schedule an appointment with. But it also made the conversations more interesting as he would go off on tangents about the shape of undergraduate education and other topics like that. One of the things about him as an advisor is when you had his attention, you had all of his attention. I don't think I've ever had anything read as carefully as he read the successive drafts of my dissertation. Those were the days when you could get a job without being finished, so I went back to Chicago at one point to review my dissertation with him. And I remember meeting with him after he introduced a speaker and then cut out through the side door so that we could go over the final parts of my dissertation to get it ready for acceptance during that summer. He was a very, very careful reader and a very insightful reader. I think that's maybe one of his major strengths as a teacher as well.

Mike Altman: That's actually been a theme that everyone I've talked to has gone back to: how thoroughly he read their work which has been interesting.

Eugene Gallagher: Yeah, it wasn't always easy to get his attention but when you had it you really had something.

Mike Altman: That exactly sums up what I've been hearing. There's the Smith that I think a lot of us know, as the gray-haired avuncular Smith with a cane, and then there's the Smith of the '70s that was your advisor. I'm curious about these Smiths. Did you notice him change? Was he different over time? Because I guess, in my mind, I keep hearing these stories about what he was like then and it's just been interesting to see that there was this almost earlier Smith that seems quite different than how those of us who saw him across hotel lobbies in the 2000s imagined him.

Eugene Gallagher: Yeah, he lost a little bit of physical vigor as time went on. I think one of the more fascinating things to me as I go back to that class on Texts and Context is that I eventually ended up reading most of that class in the form of essays over the next decade or so. You could really see him working out his take on various things in that classroom and then eventually you would see them in print, and that was a fascinating process. I wish I could go back now to that class and see what essentially amounted to 75-minute oral drafts of articles that would appear in the various collections later on. Some of the characteristics that you see in the later Smith, if you can really make such a distinction, I think were there at the beginning.

I remember walking into that Text and Context course and he was in the process of covering the blackboard with bibliography, using chalk on the board. Eventually, a lot of this stuff came in mimeo form but he would always have this comprehensive bibliography for whatever the class-work of the day was going to be. That was both impressive and very daunting. I think that self-presentation as a guy who knew lots of stuff could organize it, analyze it, and interpret it very effectively was there from the beginning. I think he was still an Associate Professor when I started at Chicago. I remember writing a letter for his promotion.

Mike Altman: Is there any particular story that sums up your, you know, you think of him that comes to mind that you could share with us?

Eugene Gallagher: Yeah, I was thinking about that. I remember him saying to a group of us at one point that on occasion he would ask his wife, Elaine, to get his oldest suit ready for class because he was going to take a dive off the stage that day. It made me think of how his individual class sessions were extraordinarily carefully composed. He wasn't just winging it, he knew exactly what he wanted to accomplish from one minute to the next and that really stuck with me. He went in with a plan, he had it timed out, he knew what the beginning, middle and end were going to be, and he just made sure that it all happened. So that was real generative insight for me as a teacher to see how carefully he took it. He remains the best lecturer I've ever seen in a classroom. He was not so hot as a discussion leader because I think everyone was too afraid to speak up. I lay that on the students rather than him.

Mike Altman: He seemed to have a remarkable way of threading, teaching and research together. Is there something you saw in the way he did that? I think, for so many professors, one gets in the way of the other. But there's a way that he..., this is the way you told the story about the lectures being drafts of the essays. How was he able to weave research and teaching together so well?

Eugene Gallagher:
Well, I think one thing for him is he had the great benefit of being at the University of Chicago and not teaching courses that were assigned to him. I think he embraced this idea of teaching the introductory course in History of Religions for Masters level students, that he was always able to follow his intellectual interest and work them into class. I think that for folks who don't have quite the freedom and the latitude that he had at Chicago, it still remains a challenge. How can you weave into class what you're working on? I think that's one of the important lessons I took from him. He makes a big deal, as you know, in his writing about teaching, that nothing is necessary and that everything is to be chosen as an example of something else. That's liberating; that means if you are teaching intro to religion, it can take multiple forms that are legitimate and defensible. Therefore, you have the opportunity to work into a course like that something that you're working on. I was always happy when I was teaching a 3/3 or a 3/2 load when I could get a couple courses that would directly hit something I was working on, however briefly. I think that's a difference between people who are primarily or entirely teachers of undergraduates and folks who get to teach graduate students, as he did.

Mike Altman:
Alright, last question: there's been a lot of written, a lot of pieces written since his passing, I'm just curious if there's anything that hasn't been said about him, about his work, about his life, that you think needs to be said?

Eugene Gallagher:
Well, I was thinking, as I was getting ready for this ... one of the things that I'd want to highlight about him is his work as a teacher. I think that lots of people have what I call a shadow audience for their teaching; they're teaching through their students to their colleagues in the guild or maybe when they're starting to their dissertation director. I find him an extremely helpful, congenial, stimulating shadow audience for my teaching. Not that I'm teaching to him but I find that sidling up next to him and thinking about what I'm doing in my courses, as I imagine that he might think about it has been very powerful and sustaining for me over now some 40 years of teaching.

I'm extremely grateful for that and I think that he might not get the credit he deserves as a careful, intentional, and creative teacher.

Eugene V. Gallagher is the Rosemary Park Professor Emeritus of Religious Studies at Connecticut College. He received his Ph.D. from the University of Chicago for a dissertation written under J. Z. Smith.

Interview with Ron Cameron

Mike Altman:	Can you tell us who you are, for the recording?
Ron Cameron:	My name is Ron Cameron. I'm a Professor of Religion at Wesleyan University in Middletown, Connecticut.
Mike Altman:	Excellent, thanks. So, I'm curious, when did you first meet Jonathan Z. Smith and what was that like?
Ron Cameron:	Well, I remember it well. At the AAR and SBL annual meetings one was always seeing him, of course, and he's famous so you know who he is. But I actually first met him in the spring, probably March or April, of 1986. I was on my first sabbatical at Claremont, California, using the office of Burton Mack, a very close, dear friend and longtime colleague and coworker with Jonathan. Burton Mack's an emeritus Professor of Religion at Claremont.

So he had a bunch of students and also me over to his house one evening and Jonathan was there, because he'd been giving a lecture in, maybe, Santa Barbara, and so we all spent a mesmerizing evening with Jonathan for several hours that evening. And that was very nice.

Then I started talking with him seriously at the AAR/SBL annual meetings, starting in November of '89, which would have been, I think, in Anaheim, California. I had asked him for a meeting. We spent several hours in fact over a very long Tuesday morning breakfast and I had written him a letter asking for clarification about part of his argument in his important book on ritual, *To Take Place*, and he immediately wrote back after Thanksgiving.

And we started talking seriously and, in fact, met at every SBL/AAR annual meeting since '89 until the last one he went to, which was something like 2011 or so. If I have the year right, that would have been in San Francisco.

Then he was progressively getting more ill and wasn't able to walk and move and so he didn't go, I believe, to any AAR meeting after that, including the next one in Chicago, which is his home town.

So we had a 15, 17, 18-year serious conversation and it was very, very gratifying.

Mike Altman:	Now, you've worked with him on this, some of this work, on Christian origins. Can you talk about how his work expands on so many different topic areas, for example, what were you all working on in this Christian origins project?

Ron Cameron:	I had asked him after the San Francisco AAR/SBL meeting in '92. I met with him over some lunch and we'd made a proposal, Merrill Miller, my colleague and I, to do a Consultation and then subsequent SBL Seminar called Ancient Myths and Modern Theories of Christian Origins. And we asked Jonathan if he would participate and join in, that we needed him, that Mack needed him. And Jonathan thought for a good long while in his vintage way, you can see him, sort of looking down and thinking. And then he said, "What do you want me to do?"

So then he was a very active participant. Burton Mack and Merrill and Jonathan and I were the four conveners of the Consultation for three years and then the six-year Seminar that followed, on how do we describe the beginnings of Christianity as religion. And so we've subsequently published three fat volumes of papers and commentary and introduction and conclusion. Jonathan has a small, important piece in volume one in 2004 and then he's got an important statement in our 2011 book, *Redescribing Paul and the Corinthians*, an essay that's also reprinted in his *Relating Religion* entitled "Re: Corinthians." And then of course, in the latest volume, *Redescribing the Gospel of Mark*, Jonathan has two very long essays.

So he was extremely important in helping us theorize and problematize what we wanted to do in biblical studies as a subset of religious studies, not just the typical, you know, biblical studies, what Jonathan would call paraphrasing, the same old gospel paradigm. So that was very gratifying.

So we talked and wrote letters and called each other and all, though he doesn't like the phone. But it was very nice. So he was invaluable and is a much beloved, dear friend whom I, of course, miss very, very much.

Mike Altman:	To continue with that, he was the SBL president and I think, for me, I've always kind of just worked sort of within Religious Studies ...
Ron Cameron:	Of course.
Mike Altman:	... and used his theoretical work only there. So how did he influence ... how did he change biblical studies? He was never an AAR president but he was an SBL president. So what was that influence like?
Ron Cameron:	He was one of the two finalists for the AAR president one year and the AAR people voted Catherine Albanese in instead. But he was never the AAR president, which surprised me of course. But he was an SBL president relatively

late in his public career when he was still able to get to the meetings and walk and all.

Well he's helped a number of us, anyway, try to think about biblical studies as a subset of religious studies. Of explanation and of comparison. In Jonathan's vocabulary, his methodological vocabulary of redescription and comparison and with the rectification of categories of scholarship. He's helped us try to do that invaluably.

Early on he had a paper that's published in *Relating Religion*, a paper that was called "Bible and Religion" that he delivered at the Boston meetings, maybe around '99. He addressed that to the SBL. And then when he became the SBL president, roughly a decade later, naturally he gave his address there called "Religion and Bible." And, of course, it was a challenging essay to the Society of Biblical Literature to try to get them to think more broadly about what constitutes authoritative writing or scripture or bible.

I'm not certain that what he would like to see happen in terms of graduate students going on to study bible and religion the way he describes it, I'm not certain that's going to happen for a variety of reasons, including scholars are going to have to work cooperatively in widespread areas beyond just their philological areas of expertise as the SBL is typically constituted.

But his influence is, of course, immense to many of us and not just methodologically, but in terms of trying to think theoretically about what it is that we're trying to do and why.

He's also, of course, a hell of a guy as we all know and just a pleasure to be with and listen to, enjoy his company and his ability to think on his feet, which was astonishingly impressive. His sense of humor, his telling observations, his deep humanity. He's interested in religion in part because he thought that religion could, in fact, be understood as an intellectual activity that made sense even if part of it was thought to be bizarre and curious. But as you know, he was interested in the gap between the ordinary and what's thought to be unusual.

So we tried to pay attention to what he would call discrepancy and diversity, difference and gap. Rather than just having the way we looked at biblical texts, say, be sort of transparent upon reality, we tried to see the difference between what people were doing and what they said they were doing.

So that's part of what he's helped us do and we're still, the redescribing project, we are still trying to extend the work as best we can.

Mike Altman: Is there, with all the time you've spent with him, is there a story that comes to mind that you think needs to be told?

Ron Cameron: Yeah, but there are a number of stories because he was a great storyteller and he and I would often just schmooze. And we'd talk. I would take him out for lunch, sometimes breakfast and dinner. I'd scout out places in the cities we were in where he could have good vegetarian food and the like.

And generally we would just schmooze and every now and then I might ask him a specific sort of scholarly question that I needed his help with. But generally, we were just talking.

But I'll say two little stories about Mircea Eliade. Eliade, of course, was his longtime colleague whom he loved dearly, though disagreed with enormously, as is well known. But Jonathan told me some time ago, I believe it's in the mid-'60s, maybe '66, '67, sometime around then, that he and Elaine, his wife, were driving cross country to go to Santa Barbara where he was to teach for a year or two. So they're driving from presumably Chicago across country and they're going through Wyoming, the state I was born in. And so they stopped to get some gas and use the facilities. Jonathan would have another cigarette. And so there he is at a gas station in Wyoming on the interstate and he said, a guy coming out of the men's room. And the guy was still zipping up his fly, but under his arm as he was walking out zipping up his fly, under his arm was a copy of Eliade's book, *The Sacred and the Profane*. And Jonathan told me, quote, "He's everywhere. Eliade's everywhere!"

And then one more Eliade anecdote. This was when Jonathan was lecturing in Jerusalem in the lectures that were related to his *To Take Place* volume. So that would have been, presumably, in the late '80s or perhaps the early to mid '90s. And so he said that they were given, of course, a special tour of the Western Wall with heavy security and, of course, Mayor Teddy Kollek of Jerusalem. And they're walking along there upped with security because it's a dangerous place. And, of course, Jonathan with the cane is walking more slowly with Elaine his wife, so they're bringing up the rear. But they're up on top of the wall where otherwise you wouldn't be. And so they're walking and all of a sudden he hears a kid say, "Halt." And so he stops and he said, quote, "Don't fuck with a kid with an Uzi." So Jonathan stops and then the kid says, "Who are you?" And Jonathan says, "We're scholars." And he says, "What are you here for?" Jonathan says, "A conference." The kid asks, "What's it about?" Smith says, "Sacred space." And then the kid says, and I quote, "Oh, Eliade."

So Jonathan took enormous pleasure in those two anecdotes about the sacred and the profane. Eliade is everywhere, even when Jonathan is doing a critique of space rather than place and, of course, the critique of Eliade's reading of the Australian Aborigines in the first chapter of *To Take Place*.

So those are two of my favorite little anecdotes, but there were others. I'll say one more, if I may. It was on the same trip, he told me, when he was driving out with Elaine to go to UC Santa Barbara and they stopped at the Grand Canyon, which is lovely. And they were, in fact, not at the south side, but on the north side which is more rugged. And he said he and his wife, I swear to God he told me, he walked down the trail, all the way down to the bottom where the river is, which I find amazing. But he said, quote, "I used to be spry." And he did, apparently, used to be spry. But, of course, when I knew him the general problem with the back was so painful that it got so he couldn't even walk one block, much less down 1.8 billion years to the bottom of the Grand Canyon.

So he was a great storyteller and those are three of my favorites.

Mike Altman: Those are great. I had to mute the microphone so I didn't laugh in the middle of the first one. "Eliade's everywhere!"

Ron Cameron: He's everywhere! He's everywhere! He's in toilets in the men's room, he's at the top of the Wailing Wall, the Western Wall. He's everywhere.

Mike Altman: I have one last question till we wrap this up. What do you think needs to be said about his life, his work, that hasn't been said yet, that you would maybe just like to add?

Ron Cameron: That's a good question. I'm not certain. I have been asked, or invited, to give a paper on Jonathan's work at the SBL meeting in Denver this fall and I've been re-reading all of his essays. Or I'm in the process of re-reading all of his essays. So I'm taking assiduous notes and trying to think about exactly what to say. But I actually...I was going to say that I actually am not certain what should be said, but I will say one thing or two things.

One of them is: I would say that Smith's imaginative discourse makes thinking about religion possible. And the second thing I would say is that I think that what he was doing could be called an anthropology of the Enlightenment. He doesn't, of course, go outside. He never liked to travel much. But the anthropology of the Enlightenment is what he's doing with all the history and the footnotes, trying to see how it is that we got to understand what it is that we know and where we might go from there.

And that's really his agenda. So if one could really come to grips with Jonathan's emphasis, not just on theory but emphasis on intellectual sense-making. His intellectual anthropology. That's at the heart of what he's about. And so I'm trying to see if I can get at that as best as possible in his honor and in his memory, because he's so special. He is, in fact, to use a word otherwise he would not use, he, in fact, is unique and sui generis. He's not just individual. He's Jonathan Z. Smith and we'll probably never see another one like him again in our lifetime.

Mike Altman: I really like that idea of the anthropology and Enlightenment, because I'm working on a project now on the history of conscience in America and questions of religious, freedom of conscience, religious liberty, all this and where it comes from, what it does ...

Ron Cameron: Yeah, me too.

Mike Altman: And Russell sent me, because he's teaching our senior seminar right now on Smith's work ...

Ron Cameron: Good, good.

Mike Altman: ... and he sent me a quote from the book of Smith's interviews that he just edited with Willi Braun. It was Smith talking about the way that we made this deal back during the Enlightenment, that we would separate church and state so that people could do whatever they wanted in private but we'd still have toleration in public. And now, the descendants of the people who we made that deal want to call it off. And it was this moment when I realized that's at the bottom of all of his work. So much of it, like you said, is about the Enlightenment and about tracing out that deal in lots of places.

Ron Cameron: That's right. No, that's exactly right. That's *exactly* right. And the deal or the wager that the Enlightenment made and that Jonathan exemplifies, yeah it looks like right now people are trying to call it off. And that's a great loss.

Mike Altman: This has been really good. We could do this forever, but I need to cut this. So I'm going to hit this stop button ...

Ron Cameron is Professor of Religion in the Department of Religion at Wesleyan University, Middletown, Connecticut. He is the author or editor of a number of essays on the Gospel of Thomas and book-length studies of the New Testament and Christian beginnings.

Michael J. Altman is Associate Professor in the Department of Religious Studies at the University of Alabama. His research and teaching use examples of religion in America to explore larger questions about how people and groups use "religion" to separate "us" from "them."

Part IV

Afterword

Chapter 25

Clues to a Great Mystery

Emily D. Crews

A few years into my Ph.D. at the University of Chicago Divinity School, I became an editorial assistant at *History of Religions*. The journal—one of the Div School's two print publications devoted to original work in Religious Studies—was founded in 1961 by renowned historians of religions, Mircea Eliade, Joseph Kitagawa, and Charles H. Long, and was later edited by some of their most well-known colleagues and students. Among those was Jonathan Z. Smith, who was an editor for over a decade and the contributor of a number of its most widely read essays (e.g., Smith 1972, 1973). During my tenure as an editorial assistant I often encountered traces of Smith's presence, though he had long since left both the journal and the Divinity School by the time of my arrival. This was never more the case than on the frigid winter day that my colleague, Andrew Durdin, and I undertook a massive clean out of the office that housed both *History of Religions* and *The Journal of Religion*. Over the years it had collected a thick sediment of dust, documents, and meaning, and we were curious about what lay underneath (and also hopeful that a good scrubbing might help our poor allergies). In the course of our excavations we came across boxes upon boxes of papers produced and stored over the decades, including many written by or related to Smith. There were letters and reviews, each filled with his characteristic wit and critical acumen; copies of meeting agendas or official memoranda with doodles and notes scribbled in the margins; and responses to queries from editorial assistants and fellow editors, many of which included some bit of rare trivia that he seemed to think the reader absolutely must know. Most treasured among our discoveries were several annotated original manuscripts of essays Smith published in *History of Religions*, including "I Am a Parrot (Red)," which was later included in *Map Is Not Territory* (1978). The red strokes of his editing pen seemed to us latter day, digitally minded beings as signs from an arcane language, filled with secret possibility (instead, upon closer reflection, simply an indication that a paragraph break was needed), and the simple fact that we held the first iteration of what would become a revered text felt significant, in spite of our own pretensions to more skeptical leanings.

Indeed, Drew and I treated each of our Smith-related finds as if they were clues to a great mystery. And perhaps they were, if the mystery was something like, "What is the study of religion, how is it done, and why does it matter?" Smith's reflections on the quality of a submission or his suggestions for authors—even the pithy asides jotted on stray pieces of paper—felt like pieces in a puzzle of method and meaning. It is clear from the essays and reflections collected in this volume that we were not alone in casting Smith as a guide to understanding our field. He has served as the interlocutor and critic to whose writings so many of us have turned as we have established ourselves and our ideas. He has been the voice in the head of more than one generation of scholars, reminding us of what is at stake in the intellectual riddles we attempt to solve (and in the ones we choose to leave undone). I cannot claim that the ephemera Drew and I exhumed or the experiences of the contributors to this volume solved the mystery of Religious Studies. But as I reflect on them alongside the greater corpus of Smith's work and on what they might tell us about the field in which we position ourselves, I am left with a few conclusions.

First is that Religious Studies can be a space for play.[1] From clever language and inside jokes to puns constructed around obscure data, Smith's work tells us that the things we study and the ways that we study them offer the opportunity for whimsy and humor. Joking and play, as Lehrich is quoted in Grieve's articles, were not beneath Smith's dignity, nor should they be beneath the dignity of our field. Rather, they are a great leveler, a way of seeing the joy and absurdity in any aspect of any life in any place or time. Nothing is without humor, not even those things we might call "sacred," and no one—scholar, priest, acolyte, or god—is without recourse or vulnerability to it. Such an approach has been central to my teaching, especially in my introductory classes, where laughter has destabilized the sometimes unproductive hierarchy of teacher over students and has helped to create a sense of intimacy and irreverence that forms the foundation of my ideal pedagogical environment.

Second is that the field remains a space in which normative claims of all sorts can (and do) masquerade as neutral and natural, and that insufficient attention to such claims impoverishes the work we do. In the editorial comments on authors' submissions and notes to fellow editors that we unearthed, as in the larger body of his published work, Smith offers repeated concern and critique of such phenomena, even (and perhaps especially) those that the authors seemed unaware were operating in their work. Whether interrogating categories, connections, or the privileging of certain languages or sets of data over others, Smith's scholarship encourages us to ask ourselves, "Why?" and "For what purpose?" I have returned, again and again, to these same questions, both for myself in my writing and with my students, arguing that they are at the center of our work as scholars of a thing we might call "religion."

The final conclusion that I have come to in reflecting on each of the small pieces of Smith—the essays published here, the unearthed archive from *History of Religions*, and the work he wrote and published throughout his career—is that the endeavor to solve the mystery of the field is a fool's errand, but a necessary one. For Religious Studies, like "religion," is not any one thing. It has no inherent definition or contours, but is defined and shaped by those who make use of it, and each definition offered is equally true or troublesome. Even as well-respected and oft-quoted as he may be, the same must be said of Smith's. To paraphrase one of his most beloved pieces, what we study (or read or write or discuss) when we study (or read or write or discuss) Smith is one mode of constructing and approaching an object of inquiry, one in which some scholars "find themselves and in which they choose to dwell" (Smith 1978: 290). Ironically (and rather beautifully, given his love of narrative and play), his work on the category of religion has made it possible for us to read him simply as one voice among many. If it is a voice we choose to heed, we must take seriously the notion that it is our responsibility to know what it is we mean when we say we study "religion," that we are scholars in some grand project called "Religious Studies." If religion "is a term created by scholars for [our] intellectual purposes and therefore is [ours] to define," so too is the field that we have constructed around it (Smith 1998: 283). Of all the things that I have learned from Smith (and from my doctoral advisor, Bruce Lincoln, my co-editor Russell McCutcheon, and other critical scholars like them), this perhaps has been the most challenging and the most vital to my thinking and teaching. Every student who leaves my class has been asked (or forced, some might say) to contend with their own definition of religion, *why* they have chosen it, and what the consequences are of that choice, as I continue to contend with my own.

It is left to readers of this volume to decide whether the contributors have accurately represented Smith's approach to the academic study of religion and, if so, whether it is one that is useful to them. Speaking for myself, Smith has been and will remain a crucial interlocutor, as I hope he will also be for future generations of scholars, even those who enter the field after he passed from this life. The ways in which his thoughts have shaped my research and my teaching (and in particular my Introduction to the Study of Religion classes at the University of Alabama) are numerous and profound, even well beyond those I've shared above.[2] It is thus my great honor and pleasure to have been part of collecting together the reflections of others who have been equally influenced by his scholarship, even if I know that Smith himself would have told me that doing so was a poor use of my time. "Go to the library," he would likely say, were he alive to offer his opinion. "Go to the library and read something." And so I shall, but not without first saying: thank you for reading, and most especially thank you to Professor Smith, whenever and wherever he might be.

Emily D. Crews is a Ph.D. candidate in History of Religions at the University of Chicago Divinity School. Her work focuses on the formation of gendered and embodied subjects in African and African immigrant religions.

Notes

1   That one of Smith's early students, Sam Gill (also included in this volume), ended the *Guide to the Study of Religion* with an essay simply entitled "Play" may be significant here (Gill 2000).

2   For further and more detailed reflection on Smith's impact on my work, see Crews (2019).

References

Crews, Emily D. (2019). "Always Know What You're Asking When You Ask It: Questions, Answers, and the Enduring Legacy of Jonathan Z. Smith," *Method and Theory in the Study of Religion* 31: 14–22. https://doi.org/10.1163/15700682-12341455

Gill, Sam (2000). "Play," in Willi Braun and Russell T. McCutcheon (eds.), *Guide to the Study of Religion*, 451–464. London: Cassell.

Smith, Jonathan Z. (1972). "I Am a Parrot (Red)," *History of Religions* 11/4: 391–413. https://doi.org/10.1086/462661

——. (1973). "When the Bough Breaks," *History of Religions* 12/4: 342–371. https://doi.org/10.1086/462686

——. (1978). *Map is not Territory: Studies in the History of Religions.* Chicago, IL: University of Chicago Press.

——. (1998). "Religion, Religions, Religious," in Mark C. Taylor (ed.), *Critical Terms for Religious Studies*, 269–284. Chicago, IL: University of Chicago Press.

Part V

Appendix

Chapter 26

Academic Freedom and Academic Responsibility

Jonathan Z. Smith

At a very basic, shared human level, no one of us likes being misrepresented.

It is the troublesome prefix, "mis-," that gives rise to the ubiquitous, but largely uninteresting duality, insider/outsider, expressed in a variety of contrastive synonyms that we have heard this morning ... even if we dignify them with technical sounding terms such as "emic" and "etic." Such dualities are uninteresting—though scarcely disinterested—because they have yielded little theoretical or methodological fruit. At best, such dichotomous taxa, especially when only one member of the pair is granted a positive valence, yield counsels of prudence, "choose the good," not procedures. (Although, if pressed, I would suggest the counsel, "shun the dual.") After all, as we have come to learn in the case of dichotomies native to our field of study, sacred/profane, pure/impure, such terms are both oppositional and ceaselessly relative. The dualism always requires a third term, a "with respect to" to make the system both intelligible and interesting. A is pure with respect to B, but simultaneously impure with respect to C ... and so on. Each segment may be oppositional, but the system as a whole is relativistic and relational.

There are, thus, no insiders/outsiders *tout court*. Inside/outside are matters of degree, not of kind. We find ourselves in a nexus of relations in which we are simultaneously relatively more or less inside or outside with respect to this or that element or aspect of a situation which itself condenses a system of complex relations.

One consequence of focusing on the initial prefix "mis-" in misrepresentation is the danger that we lose sight of the more significant second prefix, "re-." "Re-" reminds us that, whether it be intercultural or intracultural discourse, we are distanced from presence. We describe, we discuss, we compare, we interpret re-presentations of cultural representations without overcoming that distance, whether the latter be characterized as spatial or temporal, linguistic or iconic, familiar or unfamiliar. (One might argue, in the latter case, for a double activity, an attempt at reducing difference through processes of familiarization; an attempt at increasing difference through processes of defamiliarization.) Shifting terms, whether in interlinguistic or intralinguistic situations, we all engage ceaselessly in translation, with the consequence that we never speak directly, that our speech is mediated by translation and constrained by that mediation. (As, for example, right now, as I am speaking.)

One implication of both of these observations of relevance to our topic is that we are required to reject the ascription of "authenticity," as inhering to either insider or outsider, substituting instead notions of varying degrees of adequacy or of sorts of competence.

Both the "insider" and the "outsider" (each relative, shifting positions with respect to this or that re-presenting), re-represent and translate "their" traditions both to their peers (however conceived) and to others (however defined). It is this on-going activity that allows a tradition to be traditional, to endure, and to be compelling.

Both the "insider" and the "outsider" negotiate difference and, therefore, both encounter resistance from the object of attention, whether of opacity, of distance, or of change. For some, in some circumstances, their rhetoric will be in a reproductive mode which claims advantage in reducing difference. For some, in some circumstances, their rhetoric will be in a transformative mode which claims advantage in exploiting difference. But, these modes describe strategies, not states of being. (It is rather like the difference between a lexical dictionary which seeks to report the common usage meaning of a word [either statistically or historically], and a specialized dictionary which seeks to rectify common usage. [Think how differently words such as "myth" or "cult" are represented in each]. But both sorts of dictionaries stand within the tradition of their linguistic community.)

Concurrent with the strategic choice of a reproductive or transformative mode is an equally strategic choice as to the degrees of disclosure, the extent to which one finds relative cognitive or pedagogical advantage in particular situations in highlighting difference and distance, in situating oneself as "near" or as "far," in emphasizing consensus or tension, in foregrounding or backgrounding one's constructive and reconstructive labors.

Regardless of the strategic choices made, the language of "pristine" and of "authentic" should give us pause—for they set aside the question of work. Nothing that is touched remains untouched—though we should take some version of the Hippocratic Oath to "do no harm." Regardless of the rhetoric adopted, we cannot deny that we have worked, that we have shared in a transgenerational (and often, transcultural) network of colleagues, whether near or afar, who have labored at making intelligible, making plausible, making relevant, making interesting that particular set of representation that some of us would name "religion."

* * *

If I may be permitted an addendum, speaking as an educator. I am troubled that the way our conveners framed our topic might lead to the thought that "academic freedom" was in some way to be contrasted with "academic responsibility." In fact, the latter is the precondition of the former. Academic freedom, despite some departmental fantasies, is not autonomy. It is a claim that, rather than the state, rather than civil or ecclesiastical authorities, it is the educational institution as a corporate body that will police itself. Academic freedom is not so much an individual right as it is a collective, reflective responsibility.

J. Z. Smith, who passed away in late 2017, was retired from a long teaching career at the University of Chicago. Known for his careful attention to the methods scholars use when studying religion, Smith worked with a wide variety of ancient and contemporary textual and ethnographic examples, becoming one of the most influential scholars of religion in the last fifty years.

Acknowledgments

This chapter was originally a brief response presented by Smith on November 22, 2004, at the San Antonio annual meeting of the American Academy of Religion, as part of a panel entitled "Academic Freedom and Academic Responsibility in the Study of Religion"—a panel that preceded the AAR's Board of Directors coming up with its own statement on academic freedom, via a resolution adopted in November of 2006 (see the February 2016 amendment of this 2006 document at: www.aarweb.org/node/188 [accessed August 30, 2019]). Apart from Smith, the panel (presided over by William K. Mahony) included: Laurie L. Patton, John Voll, Francis X. Clooney, and Karen McCarthy Brown. A typescript copy of the response was sent to one of the editors as part of a January 15, 2005, letter from Smith; this previously unpublished paper is printed here with the kind permission of his widow, Elaine Smith—who, in a role of proofreader that was not unfamiliar to her, caught a typo or two in the manuscript from which we worked to produce this text. It is included in this volume, after the preceding commentaries on his work and memories of his person, to draw specific attention to Smith's own thoughts on the inevitable role played by mediation and translation in any act of re-presentation.

Index

In recognition of the role that J. Z. Smith played in the modern field, readers will find only one main entry in the index, followed by a series of detailed sub-entries to assist them with identifying those places in the preceding chapters where themes and topics of relevance to his work are discussed.